Stage Fright in the Actor

Stage Fright in the Actor explores the phenomena of stage fright—a universal experience that ranges in intensity from a relatively easy-to-conceal sense of anxiety to an overwhelming feeling of terror—from the actor's perspective, unearthing its social, cultural, and personal roots.

Drawing on her experience as both an actor trainer and a licensed psychotherapist, Linda Brennan recounts the testimonies of professional actors to paint a clear picture of the artistic, behavioral, cognitive, physiological, and psychological characteristics of stage fright. This book encourages the reader to reflect on their own experiences while guided by the stories of fellow actors. Their personal accounts, combined with clinical research and practical exercises, will help readers to identify, manage, and even conquer this "demon in the wings."

Stage Fright in the Actor is an essential tool for actors and acting students. Its insight into the many manifestations of stage fright also renders it as valuable reading for acting/performing arts teachers and directors, as well as anyone who fears stepping "onstage."

Linda Brennan, PhD, is on the faculty of the American Academy of Dramatic Arts (Voice and Speech Department Chair, Director) in Los Angeles. She is also a psychotherapist in private practice specializing in anxiety disorders.

Stage Fright in the Actor

Linda Brennan

Routledge
Taylor & Francis Group

LONDON AND NEW YORK

First published 2020
by Routledge
2 Park Square, Milton Park, Abingdon, Oxon OX14 4RN

and by Routledge
52 Vanderbilt Avenue, New York, NY 10017

Routledge is an imprint of the Taylor & Francis Group, an informa business

© 2020 Linda Brennan

British Library Cataloguing-in-Publication Data
A catalogue record for this book is available from the British Library

Library of Congress Cataloging-in-Publication Data
Names: Brennan, Linda, 1961– author.
Title: Stage fright in the actor / Linda Brennan.
Description: Abingdon, Oxon; New York, NY: Routledge, 2020. |
Includes bibliographical references and index.
Identifiers: LCCN 2019058588 (print) | LCCN 2019058589 (ebook) |
ISBN 9781138680678 (hardcover) | ISBN 9781138680685 (paperback) |
ISBN 9781315564050 (ebook)
Subjects: LCSH: Stage fright. | Acting–Psychological aspects.
Classification: LCC PN2071.P78 B76 2020 (print) |
LCC PN2071.P78 (ebook) | DDC 792.02/8019–dc23
LC record available at https://lccn.loc.gov/2019058588
LC ebook record available at https://lccn.loc.gov/2019058589

ISBN: 978-1-138-68067-8 (hbk)
ISBN: 978-1-138-68068-5 (pbk)
ISBN: 978-1-315-56405-0 (ebk)

Typeset in Bembo Std
by Newgen Publishing UK

Contents

Acknowledgments

I would like to dedicate this study to actors with stage fright. Trust your gifts and share them with others. Follow your path. Have courage. I wish to wholeheartedly acknowledge the participants for generously sharing their experiences and insights with me. Without them, the study that is the basis of *Stage Fright in the Actor* would not have been possible.

I want to thank my colleagues at the American Academy of Dramatic Arts: Brenda Beck, Judith Bohannon, Joe Garcia, Theresa Hayes, Karen Hensel, Betty Karlen, Chip Killingsworth, Mark Knowles, Tim Landfield, Ben Martin, Jamie Nichols, and Perry Hart, to name a few. These exceptional individuals humble me daily with their love, kindness, talent, dedication, and passion for the arts, education, and for life. I am truly blessed to know you. And to all my students, thank you for being my teachers, my guides, and my daily inspiration.

Thank you to my family, especially to my mother, Ruth Brennan, who has always been there for me and whose strong work ethic taught me to get the job done. Thank you to Louis Felder, who helped me to appreciate love and the humor in life. Thank you to my father, Edward Brennan, who put me on the actor's path. Thank you to my wonderful friends, especially Carey Deadman, Monique Jansma, David Nichols, and Phillip Spencer, who provided invaluable support throughout this process. Thank you to Leni Belshay, who served as an anchor and a touchstone. Thank you to Rocco Dal Vera, my guide, mentor, and friend.

Finally, I wish to express my gratitude to Dr. Stanley Pavey for remaining a steady influence throughout this process. He does not know it, but he played the role of "Clarence" perfectly. And he did not miss a cue.

Disclaimer

This book was written to shed light on a subject that is seldom discussed: stage fright in the actor. Some individuals may experience mild forms of stage fright, while others may experience forms that are severe and debilitating. Some may use this book to understand stage fright more deeply, and some may see it as a type of self-help. In either case, it is hoped that this book helps the reader to understand stage fright in the actor with more depth.

The statements here are not intended to diagnose, treat, or cure any mental health condition. This book is intended to provide insight into the condition and to inform the reader about what research exists. Although it was the intention of the author to conduct a review of published research, it is possible that important insights may have been missed.

Most actors have experienced stage fright at some point and to some degree. It is hoped that by facing it, this fear may be converted into courage and that investigating its aspects will help to manage the discomfort it causes. If reading about or recounting stage fright experiences initiates greater anxiety, please see a practitioner or counselor to address your discomfort.

Definition of terms

Actor. An actor is defined as "a person who acts in stage plays, motion pictures, and television broadcasts" (Webster's, 1989, p. 15). The term stems from the ancient Greek word, *hypokrites,* meaning "one who interprets" (Onions, 1996, p. 456). An actor is a "stage player, doer, speaker, or prosecutor." Rooted in the Latin word, *agere,* meaning, "to do" (Onions, 1996, p. 10), the term historically has been applied to any person who acts, regardless of sex.

Until the 17th century, men traditionally played female roles. In Western theater, women were forbidden to act by custom, law, and social censure (Brockett, 1977). When women began to appear onstage, the term *actress* was used to apply to them (Howe, 1992). Some contend that the term actress is sexist, diminutive, and politically incorrect. However, others take pride in the term, noting that women historically faced formidable hardship in breaking barriers that kept them from the stage. This perspective holds that the use of the term honors this historical achievement, retains the feminine, and does not negate femininity by taking on a male term in the name of equality.

Today, females who act can be referred to by either term. The term actress is still used to describe female actors in the theater and in awards presentations such as the Tonys and the Oscars. However, to avoid gender stereotypes, and while noting the differences in perspective regarding the terms actor and actress, *Stage Fright in the Actor* will use the historical and nongender-specific term actor to define those who interpret characters in dramatic performances.

Stage fright. The term stage fright is not tightly defined in the literature. In the context of this book, Gabbard's (1983) definition of stage fright presents a clear picture:

> A universal experience of performers and others who stand before an audience; but it varies widely in degree, from a transient and well-concealed sense of anxiety as the performer steps before the footlights to a devastating autonomic response that actually prevents the performance from taking place, however well it may have been rehearsed. Stage fright generally connotes that feeling of stark terror in the heart of the performer during moments before his entrance and during the first few minutes of performance. Although the anxiety usually dissipates after several minutes,

the symptoms may persist throughout the performance and even extend beyond the final curtain.

(p. 423)

Essence. Essence refers to elements of a thing that are inherent or funda-mental. It is rooted in the Latin word, *esse,* meaning, "be" (Onions, 1996, p. 295). Greek philosophers considered essence (i.e., "the being or power of a thing") as a quality combined with substance and used the word *ouisa* to describe this unity (Runes, 2010, p. 97). Later philosophers made a separation between idea and substance. The essence of a thing describes those universal characteristics without which the object would not be itself. Even things that do not exist have an essence. Seeking essences is a philosophical maneuver, as it aims to reveal universal understanding (Giorgi, 2009). Simply stated, essence "is what it is."

Preface

Stage fright is a common and difficult experience for actors. It is a specific type of fear that occurs in variety of situations related to acting, including auditions, rehearsals, interactions with directors and other actors, and performance itself. It will touch performers as well as individuals at some time in their lives (Reichenberg & Seligman, 2016). This universal experience ranges in intensity from a well-concealed sense of anxiety to a feeling of sheer terror that feels like impending death (Berry & Edelstein, 2009). In *The New Yorker* magazine, John Lahr chronicles a disastrous stage fright episode in which the actor Stephen Fry became actively suicidal during the run of a play, fled to another country to hide, and vowed to never act again (Lahr, 2006).

Stage fright presents a considerable dilemma. It diminishes or even extinguishes the expression of talent and creativity. Specifically, stage fright negatively influences an actor's performance goals in several ways, by causing bodily tension that interferes with the free physical expression of the character. This causes a negative and painful backlash in the actor, which ranges from mild frustration to feelings of humiliating defeat. Furthermore, the apprehension and tension inherent in stage fright often obstructs the actor's truthful emotional connection to—and expression of—the emotional truth of the character being portrayed. The frightened actor is often preoccupied and is therefore emotionally distant or even cut off from the dramatic situation. Stage fright robs the actor—and the audience—of what could be.

As an actor, I experienced stage fright. Because stage fright is not acknowledged as a common occurrence, I concluded that my anxiety must have been a personal issue, or at the very least a necessary part of performance. Like most actors, I handled my own stage fright silently, with "white knuckles." The show did go on, but often with a degree of anxiety. As a theater educator in an acting conservatory and as a professional coach, I have worked with hundreds of actors over the years, much of that time spent at the American Academy of Dramatic Arts in Los Angeles. I have seen stage fright manifest in the classroom, in rehearsal, and in performance. Despite the revelations of many famous actors, most actors routinely feel that they are alone in their suffering. Later, as a psychotherapist, I discovered that stage fright is a common experience. However, a complete understanding was elusive. As an actor, teacher, and therapist, stage fright has been an ever-present issue. My interest in the topic of stage fright stems from a desire to integrate my experiences in the fields of theater education and psychology with a topic that would inform and be of service to each one.

The research for *Stage Fright in the Actor* began during my doctoral studies in psychology. Originally called *Demon in the Wings*, it was my attempt to understand this condition more completely. However, as my research began, I was surprised and confused by the lack of attention this "actor's anxiety" has received. Stage fright in the actor has been almost completely ignored in clinical and popular writings (Hays, 2017). The existing writing and research (i.e., "the literature") on stage fright primarily focuses on its occurrence in musicians, dancers, singers, public speakers, and athletes. There is little mention of stage fright (i.e., *performance anxiety*) in the actor. In fact, Alice Brandfonbrener (founder of the *Performing Arts Medicine Association*) called actors "The Forgotten Patients" in 1992, and there seems to have been little added to the subject since that time (Battaglini & Martin, 2019).

This is puzzling, as actors receive more interest from the public than almost any other social group (Nettle, 2005). Yet, the "exceedingly limited" research of performing artists stands in sharp contrast to the enormous public interest performers generate (Kogan, 2002, p. 1), especially the actor. If you ask just about anyone to name the leading actors in the field, it is highly likely that they will be able to list notable and favorite performers. It is less likely that the average person would be able to name the top violinist, premiere ballet dancer, or top goalkeeper in their respective fields. Yet, the research on other performers far outweighs research on actors, and actors with stage fright. Why is this? This question deserves investigation. If we look to research for support and direction in understanding this emotional and psychological event, we find that the lack of research on actors leaves us with even more questions. Additionally, although stage fright in the actor has been described objectively by a very few psychologists and theorists, research based on accounts from the actors themselves seem to be missing in current inquiry.

The purpose of the research that is the basis of this book is to provide a subjective account of stage fright by and for actors. Although many books on stage fright offer helpful insights about this painful state in musicians, dancers, and athletes, we must ask ourselves how actors' needs may be given more room in the conversation. In *depth psychology*—the approach to human psychological life as codified by Sigmund Freud, Carl Jung, Heinz Kohut, and others—we attempt to understand the unconscious, the psyche, and the internal states of a psychological event to reveal the meaning of a symptom as the beginning of its eradication and cure. Symptom reduction alone, without illuminating the symptom's message, often leads to the condition returning again and again (Nagel, 2017). From this perspective, when facing all forms of psychological and emotional distress, our understanding of the meaning and message of a symptom begins with compassionate and empathic *listening*. When the message is delivered—and heard—the symptom can be named, faced, addressed, and perhaps no longer needed. In *Stage Fright in the Actor*, it is hoped that we can hear the meaning and the message of stage fright—from actors themselves— so that its limiting and at times harmful presence may be transformed into a benign and perhaps even helpful aspect of the actor's journey.

The research that is the foundation of this book is based on *phenomen-ology*, which is a prevalent research philosophy and method deemed appro-priate to study underinvestigated populations (Kvale & Brinkmann, 2009).Van Manen (1990) states that phenomenological research "borrows other people's experiences and their reflections on their experiences in order to be better able to come to an understanding of the deeper meaning or significance of an aspect of human experience in the context of the whole human experience" (p. 62). It seeks to investigate the subjective perspective of a person's encounter with an event or occurrence and to illuminate the feelings, thoughts, associ-ations and memories (i.e., the *lived experience*) of the event (van Manen, 1990). This methodology uses "in-depth" interviews to investigate how a certain life event is experienced and to augment understanding of the event.The resulting investigation reveals the *essence* of stage fright from the actor's perspective.The description of the essence allows the actor's experience to be heard, and in this book, aims to assist the reader in hearing the message and meaning of stage fright in their own experience.

By noting how stage fright was presented in the psychological literature (i.e., within the context of the actor's personality, of the actor's motivations to act, and of the consequences of stage fright), the interview questions were created to provide a context that would reveal the stage fright experience with as much detail as possible. This was undertaken by asking selected actors questions about their stage fright experiences framed within (1) the draw to acting and the acting experience and (2) the nature of stage fright in their lives. Once the responses were transcribed, the individual interviews were analyzed using the phenomenological method. This yielded specific aspects of the stage fright experience known as the *essential themes*, which, taken together, comprise the *essential descriptions*.The contents of these individual descriptions were then combined to yield an *essential composite description*, which conveys the aggregate narrative of the experience of stage fright in the actor. The descriptions are written in the first person, monologue style, to present a sense of the person who offered his or her experience. These are followed by a presentation of the *nonessential themes* that did not meet the criteria for incorporation into the descriptions. However, their inclusion is intended to deepen the reader's understanding of the types of nuance and detail present in the responses.

The actors in the study, Alex, Bill, Elizabeth, Jake, Jimmy, Kathryn, Marty, and Peter, are a group of accomplished and professional actors who have had stage fright experiences before live theater audiences and who were willing to describe their experiences it in detail during in-depth interviews.The names used are pseudonyms that the actors chose to protect their identity and con-fidentiality. The criteria for participation in the study included those actors who had completed a professional training program consisting of conservatory studies, held an MFA in Acting, or had at least 15 years of professional experience as a stage actor before participating in the study. The benefits of possessing a honed craft and technique of acting as well as ongoing experience acting in the theater helped to ensure that the anxiety that they described was not due to a lack of experience or technique. Their descriptions bring the actor's experience to light by giving the reader a clear and specific account of the manifestations of their stage fright. It is hoped that the data from these interviews will help the reader identify and understand this common condition in the actor.

How to use this book

In this book, we will be addressing the fact of stage fright, its objective components, and how it may appear on and offstage in the actor. We will also be reviewing the subjective components of stage fright: how it emerges and how actors experience it. Although this book may be helpful to teachers, directors, and others interested in stage fright, this book is addressed to actors.

The beginning chapters will conclude with questions that are intended to orient you—the actor—to the presence of stage fright in your life. Chapter 6 will include interviews from professional actors regarding their experience of stage fright. Chapter 7 will invite you to reveal your own experience and to investigate and amplify each aspect of your stage fright, guided by the experiences of your fellow actors. After reading a section, you will see questions that appear next to the bullet points. The questions in this book are intended to be a guide for you. Feel free to answer all of the questions, or simply the ones that resonate with you or your experience.

The purpose is to join the actors interviewed for this book by delivering an account of your own stage fright. You will begin to give your stage fright a voice and to hear its meaning and message for you as you gain greater insight and understanding about its presence in your life. It is recommended that you respond as candidly as you can, in as much detail as possible to the questions in the book. Allow memories, images, songs, lines of dialogue, impressions, and so on to come up to be seen, heard, and recorded.

In answering the questions, you may write your responses using any format you wish. If you feel inclined, draw or paint images that represent your answers. Your answers are not "onstage," are not being exposed to the critics for judgment, and are serving to reveal stage fright in *your* life. Your courageous and honest responses are not only contributing to revealing stage fright for yourself, but for your fellow actors and the world at large.

You may wish to gather:

- a blank journal or paper
- black, blue, and colored pencils/pens for writing and drawing
- paints/pastels/pastels for painting
- magazines
- a recording device

Steps for reviewing each question/theme:

- find a comfortable space free from distractions
- take a few moments to relax
- enter a reflective frame of mind
- read each question at the end of the chapter(s)
- answer each question as completely and honestly as possible
- read each theme
- answer the question related to each theme as completely and honestly as possible
- notice any thoughts that come up about the theme
- notice any emotions that come up about the theme
- notice any sensations in your body regarding the answers to the questions, the themes, or any of your responses
- ask yourself how the question/theme resonates with you
- allow any associations, memories, thoughts, lines of dialogue, and so on to emerge
- write them down in any form you wish *until you have nothing more to say*

I've always experienced stage fright.

—Peter

My stage fright has happened ever since I was very little. It is blankness. I feel like I'm running. I have shortness of breath. Stage Fright is chasing me. I feel like I'm gonna be found out.

—Alex

It seems to come out of nowhere, which is what makes it so frightening, because I never knew when it's gonna happen.

—Elizabeth

Waking up in the morning with a knot in my stomach and then waiting and waiting and waiting. I do everything in order to make this growing, growing fear go away.

—Jimmy

Stage fright made me feel like I was untalented and in the wrong profession and should be selling insurance like my father suggested.

—Marty

Stage fright is protection. Absolutely. Self-preservation. To keep you from going up there and being eaten alive by that monster we call the audience.

—Bill

It's huge. It's trying to destroy me. Definitely. It's trying to annihilate me.

—Jimmy

Well, the audience is a firing squad that can kill you. Stage fright is feeling like you're frozen in time, waiting for them lift you on their shoulders, and carry you out of the room.

—Kathryn

Stage fright prevents you from being the best that you can be. Stage fright wants you to think about your inadequacies, and wants you to be filled with self-doubt, and wants you to fail.

—Jake

To this day, I still have the classic dream. I am onstage and I've forgotten my lines. I don't know where I am. I have no conception of what the show is, or what character I am. It's the absolute lack of knowledge, the blackness, and the dark...the black thing.

—Peter

What happens is you begin to doubt yourself. You begin to feel you don't have talent. You begin to feel that you shouldn't be an actor. You begin to feel that you can't make it. You're a failure.

—Marty

The fear is failure. I mean, what can I do? Look at the audience and say, "Sorry, you can go home now." You know? I mean failure. Failure.

—Elizabeth

Stage fright is a horrible experience. It is constricting. It feels like certain and impending death. Truly like you are going to die.

—Jake

1 The presence of stage fright

The truth above the roar: questions about stage fright

It's one of the darkest, blackest fears for any performer. It's so dark, it's so black, do not say the name. You can mention that you have stage fright, but we're not getting into it. It's too overwhelming. It's too powerful.

—Peter

The actors interviewed for this book—Alex, Bill, Elizabeth, Jake, Jimmy, Katherine, Marty, and Peter—are professional actors. Their experiences span decades of work in the professional theater. Some of them have acquired considerable fame and notoriety, while some are "working actors." These names are pseudonyms that they chose to protect their confidentiality. They have dedicated their lives to acting and they reveal here that they have never really talked about their stage fright in depth. Have you ever talked about it, openly? Why do you have stage fright? What does it mean? What if stage fright prevents you from doing your best work in class or onstage? What if you believe that your teachers, directors, and fellow actors think you are not as talented as you know you are? What if your performance could have been more effective if it weren't for this horrible fear? What if your fear is perceived at an audition and it influences your being cast for a role? What if a director finds out that you throw up before performances or you have to have a few drinks before you go on? What if a producer finds your opening night rituals bizarre and odd? It might seem better if people don't know. The fear of being "found out" keeps many actors silent about this painful condition. Our actors divulge what stage fright is like for them. Having the courage to acknowledge, name, and face it is what this book is about. The actors interviewed here have been asked these questions. You will be asked these and other questions as well. Their answers along with your own self-discovery will hopefully shed some light on this condition in you, or an actor you know.

A conspiracy of silence

The truth is that nobody talks about this. Actors may say they have stage fright, but it's as if everyone has agreed to not dive into what it means, or what it feels like, or what it is.

—Jake

Almost—if not every—actor has experienced some form of stage fright (Goodman & Kaufman, 2014). It can occur in childhood, during training, at any time during one's career, and at any level of experience or expertise. Its arrival can be expected or unexpected. Whether it appears as a single case of "the butterflies," a debilitating physical and emotional collapse, or something in between, stage fright is a frequent—if unwelcome—visitor. It has been called "the commonest disease of the acting profession" (Moss, 1991). It is generally associated with the feelings of sheer terror and dread that register as physical, emotional, psychological, and artistic anguish. When stage fright strikes, it affects auditions, rehearsals, performances, and the actor's self-confidence. The general population dreads performing in front of others more than anything else, including sickness and financial disaster. This fear is thought to be worse than the fear of death (Berry & Edelstein, 2009). Actors with stage fright share this belief. It would seem that a fear as intense as this—a fear that directly attacks the actor's artistry, craft, and self-worth—would be a common topic of conversation. But it is not. Most actors do not discuss their stage fright (Nordin-Bates, 2012). Alex, our first interviewee, says that she has never discussed her stage fright because, "No one's ever asked me." The other actors interviewed for this book also reveal that they have never really talked about their stage fright. This silence leaves many actors feeling that they are alone in their suffering. It is a dark secret that is rarely—if ever—discussed openly by actors, instructors, or directors. Gabbard (1979) calls this "a conspiracy of silence." But why is this?

The show must go on!

I have a responsibility to the people who came to see either me or the world that the ensemble is creating. And I have a duty. And no matter how frightened I am, no matter what's going on with me, I have to go out there.

—Alex

Silence concerning stage fright may be influenced by the fact that actors feel duty-bound by the adage, "The show must go on." This well-known theatrical phrase, which is rumored to have been coined in the circus around the late 1800s, means that a performance must take place despite any accidents, emergencies—or fears. This code also contributes to the silence concerning stage fright. There is a sense of momentum that occurs in rehearsal, at call-time, and when the stage manager calls, "Places!" The immediate nature of live theater performance does not allow for edits, stops, or repeats, and the "curtain" represents the beginning of an event that *must* occur. Like the rising and setting of the sun, "the show must go on" (Nordin-Bates, 2012). Therefore, any mishaps that occur will be corrected—and fears will not be acknowledged—and the curtain *will* rise. This ethic contributes to the climate in which stage fright is not openly addressed. Unless the circumstances are dire, not being ready to go onstage is considered a transgression, much like abandoning a loved one. The great acting teacher Stella Adler (Adler, 2000) held that the theater is like a church, and that the actor's time onstage is like that of a ritual. This attitude makes missing a performance—for any reason—a kind of sin. This inevitability seems instilled in actors from their earliest theatrical experiences. Actors will perform despite illness or injury or even physical threat, as in London during bombings in World War II. In New York, immediately after the 9/11 attacks on the World Trade Center, actors performed on Broadway to exhibit their resilience and defiance to terror. These actions reflect an ethic of duty felt by most actors. From technical difficulties to falling sets, actors will reflexively continue performances even when their "world" is crumbling. Actors routinely manage internal as well as external catastrophe and "go on with the show." Jimmy tells us, "There is no not going out there … no matter how bad my stage fright gets … even when my doctor said my heart can't take the stress, there is just no not doing the job."

We're gonna go through it together: the ensemble

Yes, it's a conspiracy. We're in this together. We are comrades … we are in this together, like soldiers … you are not in this alone … it's us.

—Kathryn

In addition to individual fortitude, casts often band together to save a production. Actors share deep feelings of camaraderie and a common purpose that form the basis of the ethics of the profession. The theater feels like home, and other actors like chosen family or a "tribe" (Robb, Due, & Venning, 2016). Coming together in the face of mishaps—like an ideal family—is an unspoken value held by a cast of actors. This loyalty extends to the paying audience. One of our interviewees, Marty, recalls a production where an actor fell ill—too ill to continue—and an actor cast in a smaller role continued his part—script in hand—while the stage manager went on in the smaller role:

So, two actors were on-book, but there was no question of stopping the show. We were all nervous as hell, but we just figured out what to do and did it. "Just do it. Make it work." That's how I came up in the ranks. We band together and make it work.

Furthermore, actors often frame the performance experience as "going out there" as if to "do battle." Actors will aim to "knock 'em dead!" After a good show, an actor might say, "I killed 'em!" or "I slayed 'em!" A good show is a "smash hit." The unspoken assumption is that actors will endure and overcome their stress and fear with sometimes violent endurance. The most visible participant in a show—the actor—will make sure that it will go on.

And then I don't feel so bad: some ways of coping

I know actors who meditate in the dark for half an hour. I knew an actor who had to jump rope for 20 minutes before every performance.

—Elizabeth

With this kind of determination routinely in place, it is no wonder that stage fright is banished from significance with a curtain about to go up. And, when the curtain is about to rise, there is no escape. Actors routinely "suck it up," cope, and go on despite mild to severe stage fright.

Historically, the theater has been thought be a dangerous place. Backstage life often includes practicing rituals, honoring superstitions, and using lucky charms to calm precurtain nerves and keep bad luck at bay. Actors say, "Break a leg," instead of "Good luck!" This is rooted in the idea that theater ghosts who like to cause mischief will be confused by this phrase and the actor's wish for something bad to happen will yield a good result instead. Whistling in the theater is considered unlucky, as it was used in the past as a signal to change scenery. When done incorrectly, a whistle could initiate disaster. Saying the name, "Macbeth" supposedly opens up the dark forces of actual spells Shakespeare used in writing the incantations of the witches. The pattern on a peacock feather resembles an "evil eye," which summons misfortune in the theater. Wearing blue is considered an unlucky color to wear onstage. A stage should never be left dark and a "ghost light" should always illuminate it to keep lonely theater spirits from entering the stage and causing mishaps (Robinson, 2019). In this spectral climate, actors' internal fears are often ignored. As well as these traditional rituals mentioned here, actors create their own habits to ward off their fears. Alex uses preshow rituals for good luck and to combat her stage fright. These include a set vocal warm up, "… and I must get every section in or I feel jinxed." One actor has a cracked hand mirror that she takes to every audition and performance. "I know it's supposed to be bad luck, but when I look in that mirror three times and I say my character's name, I feel a little better. Now I must do this, or I can't go on!" Another actor goes to the bathroom alone—to get the nerves out alone.

> I'm always in the bathroom when they call "Five minutes." I have to say my prayers and look in the mirror and tell myself I can do it. I could do it in the dressing room, but I'd be too embarrassed.

Not even a nod: state of research on stage fright

> *I think it's really cool that someone cares enough to do something like this, where my opinions and the opinions of other actors really matter. It's nice to know someone wants to know more about this.*
>
> —Bill

The "conspiracy of silence" that actors keep seems to be reflected in research. The study of stage fright in acting is one of the most overlooked performance domains in research (Goodman & Kaufman, 2014). Although attention has been paid to public speakers and other types of performers, surprisingly there is little mention of stage fright in the actor in the popular or psychological literature (Robb, Due, & Venning, 2016). Although there has been some research on stage fright conducted on musicians (Kenny, 2005b, 2006, 2011; McGinnis & Milling, 2005; Osborne, Kenny, & Holsomback, 2005; Fehm & Schmidt, 2006; Langendörfer, Hodapp, Kreutz, & Bongard, 2006; Taborsky, 2007), singers (Kokotsaki & Davidson, 2003; Kenny, Davis, & Oates, 2004), dancers (Sandgren, 2003), and student speakers (Jangir & Govinda, 2018), there has been little mention of stage fright in the actor in the psychological literature (Nettle, 2005; Grand, 2008; Southcott & Simmonds, 2012; Hays, 2017). This gap in research has been widely noted, yet the gap remains (Nagel, 1993; Hays, 2017; Battaglini & Martin, 2019). Treatment studies of actors with stage fright are next to non-existent (Clason, Johansson, & Mortberg, 2015). A review of *Medical Problems of Performing Artists* shows that only one of 164 studies of performance anxiety on performers was related to actors (Anderson, 2011). This silence does not reflect lack of need. A 2015 study showed that over 25 percent of actors responded that they coped with debilitating stage fright (Maxwell, Seton, & Szabo, 2015). This number has been quoted to be as high as 50 percent (Trueman, 2012). It seems, then, that along with actors' suffering, there is little attention paid to actors or actors with stage fright in the literature. Later, we will look at the roots of this ambivalence toward actors that seems to be reflected there.

Reviewing the situation: stage fright or performance anxiety

I think they're confusing stage fright with just nerves. Like anybody who goes up in front of an audience should have nerves or you're not human.

—Alex

Are *stage fright* and *performance anxiety* equivalent terms? This question has still not been adequately answered (Hays, 2017). However, the distinction between fear and anxiety has been well documented in the literature (May, 1977). *Fear* is the emotional response to a real or perceived specific threat, where *anxiety* is anticipation of a future and perhaps undifferentiated threat (APA, 2013). From this perspective, we could say that an actor may feel fear if a critic is in the house and may feel anxiety that they may not perform well. However, the use of the terms when applied to performance is inconsistent in existing research, so there is not yet a conclusive answer. Some make no differentiation between them and use the terms interchangeably (Salmon, 1990; Arial, Danuser, Gomez, Hildebrandt, & Studer, 2011; Sonnenmoser, 2006; Scott, 2007; Zakaria, Musib, & Shariff, 2013; Nagel, 2017). Others make a distinction between the terms. For example, some use the term *stage fright* with reference strictly to the actual performance situation. Powell (2004) describes *stage fright* as a subtype of *debilitating performance anxiety,* which occurs in diverse types of stages, theaters, or public arenas. Conversely, Nagel (2017) states that the term *stage fright* is a misnomer because there is no literal fear of the stage but fear of performing. Still others use the singular terms *stage fright* or *performance anxiety* to describe a range of manifestations of the condition. For example, Berry and Edelstein (2009) and Steptoe and Fidler (1987) use the term *stage fright* to describe mild to severe forms of the condition.

Others also use the term in the same way (Jackson & Latane, 1981; Cahn, 1983; Ayres, 1986). The term *performance anxiety* has been used to describe varieties of the condition ranging from helpful and facilitative to destructive and debilitative forms (Mor, Day, Flett, & Hewitt, 1995). Kenny and Ackermann (2007) state that *performance anxiety* occurs on a continuum of severity from everyday stress inherent in performing occupations to the more incapacitating symptoms of *stage fright*. The term *stage fright* has been used to describe only a debilitating form of the condition (Southcott & Simmonds, 2012; Goodman & Kaufman, 2014). Hays (2008) describes *stage fright* as "the debilitative end point of performance anxiety among performers" (p. 104). There is discrepancy in the use of terms, as there has not been enough rigorous, detailed, and differentiating research on this condition (Kenny, 2005a; Fehm & Schmidt, 2006; Helding, 2016). Current conceptualizations of performance anxiety await further investigation (Kenny & Holmes, 2015; Hays, 2017). At this time, the term *stage fright* is best applied to the actor because it is more evocative and less technical. It has historical standing and is more likely to be identified with and used by actors.

Side by side: stage fright in different types of performers

> *The purpose of acting. Well, you could say, the showman unto himself. To entertain. To enlighten. To communicate something that's difficult to communicate in life.*
>
> —Marty

All categories of performers—musicians, dancers, stand-up comedians, mimes, performance artists, to name a few—are as vulnerable to stage fright as are actors (Southcott & Simmonds, 2012). It seems to be an inherent part of appearing before audiences. However, some maintain that stage fright is different in diverse types of performers. Hays (2017) studied performance anxiety in musicians, dancers, and actors. Although her comments on actors were limited due to lack of research, she notes that various genres and types of performance within each group require specific performance demands and may differentiate types of stress in these diverse performance domains. For example, there have been attempts to define and separate performance anxiety in musicians from that in other performers, including actors. The term *music performance anxiety* (MPA) is the term now used to describe performance anxiety in musicians rather than the terms *performance anxiety* or *stage fright* (Helding, 2016). Nagel (1993) states that although performance anxiety touches many individuals in addition to musicians, musicians are unique in that (1) a majority of musicians begin training in childhood, creating "monumental" (p. 493) implications for personality development and later adjustment; and (2) musicians routinely face uncertain opportunities for employment. These factors may be applied to actors. However, distinct developmental differences between various types of performers have yet to be clearly identified or defined. Hayes (2017) points out that the lack of research on actors and the differences in their training means that these conclusions cannot yet be made.

True as it can be: the actor's instrument

We have to be superhuman in some way, don't we? A good actor has to be specific and aware and perceptive about the world. Art reflects the life, doesn't it? We're showing a mirror to the world. That's huge.

—Jimmy

Aaron (1986) specifically separates stage fright in the actor from other performing artists. He contends that the actor's "radical transformation of the self onto another character" (p. x) creates a different psychological intensity than that of other performers, and it has a direct relationship to the emergence of stage fright. Actors engage in a kind of "play" (p. 38), where childlike feelings are activated and attributed to the director. These make the actor more vulnerable to the perceived threats of the stage. Aaron also argues that actors do not have psychological safety nets such as musical scores, limits on movement and timing, and the sustaining presence of the conductor enjoyed by dancers and musicians. Most actors would feel that their performance requirements—and therefore fears—are quite different from those of musicians. Actors must "play" their emotions. Their "instrument" is the whole of their being: their psychological, physical, and emotional selves. Their craft requires that they attain dramatic truth at all of these levels. Therefore, fear not only influences the player, but in the case of the actor the instrument is influenced as well. Hays' (2017) contention that actors differ from other performers along with the fact that of the three performing arts domains—music, dance, and acting—only musicians and dancers have had significant research—means that understanding stage fright in the actor still is unclear. This may account for the lack of differentiation of terms and lack of researched interventions (Helding, 2016).

Magic to do: actors and society

We help the audience to rehearse for the big moments that are coming. But at the same time, we are helping them to remember things they have already experienced: love, death, fear, and joy. So, we are allowing the audience to feel through us, sometimes things that they don't allow themselves to feel.

—Kathryn

Kathryn believes actors help audiences to live out their lives by viewing theater performances. Actors have served society in profound ways for thousands of years. In ancient Rome, the theater affirmed the existing political and cosmic order by forging a bond between the emperor and the people and was a major vehicle for the education of citizens (French, 1998). Today, our culture is similarly bound by the shared experience of viewing and relating to acting performances, which have become our societal focal points to which we relate. Almost everyone has an emotional reaction to a popular character or performance that brings joy or interest to our lives. Furthermore, although acting may be associated with entertainment, acting fulfills an important psychological service to society (Dal Vera, 2001). Long before Freud championed *catharsis* in his consulting room, Aristotle contended that this aim of tragedy is to incite "terror and pity" in the audience so that this purging of the soul may be experienced (Freud, 1952, p. 460). The "father of psychotherapy," Freud, reiterates Aristotle's view of the healing nature of emotional release, and he posits that cathartic effects may be greatest when viewing drama (Neuringer, 1992, p. 142). Aristotle believed that when we encounter our repressed and unexpressed emotions, we may become reconciled to our fate (Fergusson, 1961). Dal Vera (2001) states:

> Just as real warriors perform anguishing tasks for society, actors similarly serve as courageous "soldiers of the psyche" when they express the shadow side of the psyche truthfully in performance. This courageous act allows the audience—and society—to process darker aspects of the human experience and come to terms with them.
>
> (p. 2)

By accepting Dal Vera's notion, understanding stage fright becomes a function of assisting actors who serve as our societal channels of expression of the full range of the human experience. Bates (1991) suggests that because actors spend a significant part of their lives portraying the human condition, investigating the experiences of actors may be a parallel for understanding wider human functioning. Beyond entertainment then, the actor's role in the world may be thought of as an aid in processing our collective dreams and nightmares. This happens through the act of embodying characters in the place where our shared, societal consciousness comes to life: the performance space. By addressing stage fright, actors may be helped in assisting society.

When I'm calling you: the acting vocation

There really was no other choice for me, and I knew it as a kid. I am an actor. There really was no other option. I feel it is what I was born to do.

—Bill

The *Dictionary of American Slang* (2018) defines actor as "a noun: show-off. 'He's got nothing going for him; he's just an actor'." Most actors would argue this definition. In addition to feeling bound by loyalty to the show, to their fellow actors, and to the audience, actors seem to feel committed to acting as a *vocation*. A vocation is a "strong impulse or inclination to follow a particular career … a call" (Webster's, 1989, p. 1559). Actors routinely feel that they were "born to act" and they are driven by passion for their craft. Being an actor feels intrinsic to the actor's sense of self and sense of being. It is this that has become so much a part of the self that it is inherent to one's identity (Nordin-Bates, 2012). Later, we will hear that all our actors feel this way. As we shall see, for thousands of years actors have dedicated themselves to their craft, above and beyond ordinary commitment and stage fright. Perhaps answering the call to acting includes addressing stage fright. Actors routinely feel duty to others, yet addressing stage fright may be seen as a duty to the actor. Like any vocation or "calling," the path is at times filled with obstacles, and facing this one is part of that call.

That ain't it kid: consequences of stage fright

> *It's never your best performance when you're afraid. Because, you're self-conscious, you're not in the moment. You are the farthest thing from being in the now of now. You are not in the world of the character. You are not at that audition. You are not on that stage. You are somewhere else.*
>
> —Jake

Performers must address fundamental issues across various performance domains. These are: a high standard of excellence, the role of emotion, memorization, the role of the audience, consequences of performance, and performance stress (Hays, 2017). Actors perform in front of audiences and the fear of their disdain is a central feature of stage fright. Whether the audience is a crowd, a director, peers, an administrator, or a teacher, being viewed is a necessary part of acting. Jake lets us know that the overall outcome of stage fright is an inhibited performance that has artistic and professional repercussions. The physical symptoms of stage fright (i.e., increased heart rate, changes in breathing, muscle tension, etc.) cause physical restrictions like constrained vocalization and impaired movements and coordination. The emotional symptoms (i.e., fear, sadness, anger) interfere with emotion that the actor is attempting to generate, which influences the actor's emotional expression and artistry. Stage fright is almost always accompanied with negative thoughts (i.e., "I'm a failure"). These preoccupy the actor, causing the inability to make decisions, to focus, and to problem solve onstage. This impaired focus detracts from effective memorization of lines, remembering blocking, and connecting to the character. Negative thoughts prevent a true communion with the character. This preoccupation influences "being in the moment." It causes the actor to anticipate, to watch, and to struggle. Actors may fight this downward spiral in less than productive ways. For example, an actor might chase perfection to ward off stage fright, but these inhibitions are worsened by fear of criticism—and inner criticism. These consequences accumulate and they are fueled by the central feelings of self-doubt and the battle against feelings of potential failure. A fearful actor is often physically and emotionally armored, preventing their performance from being what it could have been.

You are not alone: talking about stage fright

> *That self-doubt demon. And it's there in all of us, whether we're actors or lawyers, parents … all of us humans.*
>
> —Jake

Jake also lets us know that all actors—and all of us—struggle with this "demon." Stage fright "is not a neurosis that occurs only in certain people with predisposing personality organizations" or in those individuals with particular intrapsychic conflicts (Gabbard, 1979, p. 386). It occurs when *anyone* places himself or herself in front of an audience. It can occur in a variety of settings and will touch most people at some time in their lives (Gabbard, 1983; Seligman, 1998; Naistadt, 2004). Acting is not restricted to the stage or screen. In a sense, we are all actors. We play various roles in life using our lines, props, and sets (Bates, 1991; Barton, 1993). Actors playing their roles are therefore metaphors for the roles we play in life. We are parents, children, friends, siblings, workers, and heroes: "In many ways, life itself is a performance and playing one's part is made difficult by the experience of unwanted emotions, thoughts, and behaviors" (Kenny, 2006, p. 1). It follows, then, that what afflicts actors afflicts us all. Stage fright then can be a metaphor for the fear of taking part in the center stage of one's own life (Kenny, 2005a). We face each day, in the wings, preparing for the next scene in the play of our lives. Therefore, by addressing actors' fears, we may be assisted with voicing and managing our own. As we address stage fright openly by naming it, talking about it, and breaking the silence obscuring it, like in all forms of distress, we are starting to heal it.

Putting it together: taking stock of the problem of stage fright

> And acting goes back to the beginning of time. It's an ancient art form that we need ... that society needs. It's part of the fabric of being human.
>
> —Jake

We have discussed the silence surrounding stage fright and the fact of its existence. We have seen that research on stage fright in actors is limited compared to other performers. Bringing fear into conscious thought gives it less power over us, and we can continue to diminish its power if we keep looking, delving, and talking about it. Later, we will look at how stage fright specifically affects our actors. But for now, let's acknowledge that *recognizing* stage fright and *accepting* its presence is a significant step to take. In the next chapter, we will review historical attitudes toward actors and the acting profession that have had a significant influence on how actors have been viewed in the helping professions and by society in general. These societal prejudices have caused anxiety in many actors and have fed the stage fright demon. Before we move on, please look at the following questions and try to answer them as truthfully as possible. Your answers are not being exposed to the critics for judgment but instead are serving to reveal the presence of stage fright in your life.

To the actor:

- What do you think about the topic of stage fright?
- Do you have stage fright?
- How often do you have stage fright?
- Have you ever talked about it, openly?

- When was your first experience with stage fright?
- What was the performance? Role?
- What were the circumstances?
- Did you feel prepared for the role?
- Did you ever continue a performance despite an injury?
- Describe your own *the show must go on* story.
- What habits or rituals do you have to help you get onstage when anxious?
- How do you cope with stage fright?
- Do you use alcohol or drugs to cope?
- How do you feel about the lack of research on stage fright in actors?
- How has stage fright influenced your performances?
- Have you considered quitting acting because of stage fright?
- Have you quit acting because of stage fright?

2   No dogs or actors allowed

Life upon the wicked stage: ambivalence toward actors

> *Acting was definitely the thing I wanted to do. But I didn't want to tell people that I wanted to become an actor because I thought they'd go, "Ah, he wants to be center of attention. He wants to be cool. He wants to be different. He wants adulation."*
>
> —Jimmy

Think about it. You announce to family and friends that you wish to be lawyer, an accountant, a classical musician, or an actor. It's highly likely the lawyer or accountant will get the most accepting response. Acting is one of the most creative art forms, and as we know, actors provide a great service to society. However, actors often face discouragement from others when they choose acting as a career (Goldstein & Winner, 2009; Thomson & Jaque, 2012). This often stems from loved ones who are concerned that the acting profession is uncertain and financially unstable. Actors are sometimes "shamed" for being in an unstable career (Percival, 2019). There are long-standing negative preconceptions about actors (Robb, Due, & Venning, 2016). These include that actors are unstable, neurotic, and untrustworthy. Actors may internalize these negative societal presumptions about what it means to be an actor, which may diminish their self-concept. One of our actors, Jimmy, came from a "business family." When he stated he wanted to be an actor, his father said he should be "realistic" and "grow up." As he began his career, his father's apprehension seemed to worsen his stage fright. This concern is not only a modern-day reaction. Traditionally, society has had an ambivalent response toward actors (Hammond & Edelman, 1991b). Actors are historically admired yet disliked, celebrated yet defamed, and acclaimed yet dismissed (Bates, 1987; Novick, 1998; Duncan, 2000). This ambivalence may be reflected in the lack of research conducted on actors. The understanding of, empathizing with, and management of stage fright in the actor may be compromised by some of these assumptions or by the influence of preconceived ideas about the actor's personality and process. It is important to acknowledge the history of this ambivalence to understand the context in which actors are seen and understood. By understanding the cause of some of these societal perceptions that influence how actors are seen, stage fright in the actor may be considered in a balanced light.

A touch of star quality: idealized actors

> *Actors had an exalted place in the society in which they performed the works of the great playwrights to an audience and, as Aristotle would say, enlightened and changed them through catharsis so that their soul was in harmony.*
>
> —Jake

Actors have been called "the divine among mortals" (Payne, 2006, p. 101). They become the glamorous focal point for dreams and seem to fill the role that gods once occupied. Jake notes that actors have been exalted and idealized throughout history. In Ancient Greece, actors were a privileged class, had their own union—the Artists of Dionysus—and were excused from military duty (May, 1987). They were thought to have achieved the best that life can offer. In Ancient Rome, some actors acquired great wealth and status (French, 1998). Today, actors shape public policy, are elected to high governmental office, are knighted, and marry into royalty. Their personal struggles, tastes, and opinions are the focus of TV, magazine, and internet content. They are hunted, and when captured, they are photographed by *paparazzi*. Their images are everywhere: on billboards, on newspaper front pages, and on subway stops. These images command a high price. The public imbues *stars* with a luminescence and actors who have reached these heights become our societal gods. At the highest levels of fame, actors are revered as *icons*. This traditionally religious term, used to describe a holy figure worthy of worship, has come to be identified with being a *superstar*, a famous figure who is the focus of *fanaticism* (Braudy, 1997). Long after their deaths, actor-icons are venerated and attain a type of everlasting life, much like our long-ago saints. This potential for exaltation is part of the landscape of being an actor.

Tale as old as time: devalued actors

> *Actors wore earrings because of their kinship to gypsies ... those hedonistic, bohemian, actor-types. That way people could separate them. 'Cause the common man wouldn't wear them. That has been propagated throughout the centuries, and now we're kind of stuck with it.*
>
> —Bill

There is no guarantee of attaining fame or remaining famous. Idols may fall off the pedestal. This shift from an idealized state can be seen in the fact that those actors who have not achieved fame and fortune are often devalued by society (Reciniello, 1991). A recent study on actors' sense of well-being reported that they felt devalued by others (Robb, Due, & Venning, 2016). This also has historical precedent. In first-century Rome, actors suffered legal and social prejudices, despite their popularity. Branded as *infamia* (Tenny, 1931, p. 16) or "infamous persons" (French, 1998, p. 294), they were prohibited from marrying a freeborn person. French (1998) notes that any child born of an actor—then legally considered a prostitute—or through an actors' lineage, was declared illegitimate and would therefore never enjoy a citizen's rights. This classification remained even if actors left the profession, as their natures were thought to be inherently inferior. Early church groups prohibited actors' baptism unless they renounced acting, as they were considered shameless and opposed to God's plan. During the rite, the actor would renounce the "pomps of Satan" (p. 301), thereby cleansing the soul of the actor's sin. Centuries later, in 1372, the British parliament passed an act that punished the activities of actors (Bates, 1987). In the Puritan United States, theater was considered morally unacceptable and was forbidden (Brockett, 1977). The assassination of President Lincoln by an actor, John Wilkes Booth, further entrenched distrust of actors, who were regularly denied charity and often were refused a proper burial (The Actors Fund, 2019). The latter 19th century continued this prejudice. Within the theater, playwrights such as Shaw and Coward struggled with the dilemma of how to produce plays without actors (Reciniello, 1991). Even into the 20th century, the phrase, "no dogs or actors allowed" maintained its legendary status. It described the policy of U.S. hotels to ban actors, as they were considered deceitful. Legend has it that an actor who saw this sign lamented that the dog got top billing (Cullen, Hackman, & McNeilly, 2007).

A question of misunderstood: dual assumptions

Actors will often tell you it's as if you announce to the world you want to be an actor and immediately, they roll boulders down the hill at you.

—Kathryn

Most actors live somewhere between these extremes, yet ambivalence about acting remains. Bates (1987) suggests that these historical discriminations are rooted in the distrust of acting, because actors pretend to be someone they are not. This may be due to misunderstanding the actor's art. Novick (1998) states that the actor's great struggle is gaining respect in a society that holds him or her in ill repute. Hammond and Edelman (1991a) state that unfortunately, "psychology has done little to alter or indeed to investigate seriously, the actor stereotype" (p. 123). Actors' association with pathology is firmly rooted. Being "neurotic" has been accepted as the norm within the arts (Hays, 2017). Even within acting, actors are sometimes told that pain and suffering are part of their talent. An actor often is expected to be unstable, and at times this instability is cultivated. One acting teacher made mention of a student actor who was moody, depressed, and unpredictable. When met with the notion that these may be signs of stage fright and should be addressed, the response was, "But they're an actor! Their pain is what makes their work so good!" Some acting techniques even value activating past trauma as a means of developing a character (Seton, 2006). On the other hand, might actors be engaging in aspects of higher-level functioning? Some believe that the creative impulse is a hallmark of healthy expression of the self (Kohut, 1966; Lee & Martin, 1991; Nordin-Bates, 2012). Actors feel this way and are passionate about their craft. They are engaged in their work, feel a heightened sense of empathy, are self-aware, and have a powerful sense of identity (Robb, Due, & Venning, 2016). These aspects stand in contrast to the idea that as a group, actors are lacking in psychological well-being. This conflict speaks to age-old attitudes concerning actors specifically as well as artists in general. These have shifted depending on the mores in effect at any given time. It is important, therefore, to locate where perceptions about artists began in order to understand its disposition toward actors and toward actors with stage fright.

We're the loonies: creativity and madness

If we go back to the Greeks and even before them into ritual, it was the shaman and the medicine man and then eventually the actor's responsibility to explain the supernatural forces in the universe to the tribe. That's a great responsibility for a performer.

—Jake

The nature of creativity has been the subject of debate for thousands of years (Prentky, 2001). Although no universal definition of creativity exists, it is generally associated with play, originality, and producing something new (Lauronen, Veijola, Isohanni, Jones, Neiminen, & Isohanni, 2004). It is a common assumption in Western society that profound creativity has a close connection to psychopathology (Lauronen et al., 2004; Chessick, 2005; Koh, 2006). One of the earliest references to this connection dates back to Aristotle's *Problemata,* where he notes the relationship between the artist and the melancholic temperament (Prentky, 2001, p. 96). Also central to ancient Greek thought concerning the artist is the concept of the *demon,* a semi-deity who presided over philosophers, poets, artists, and actors. The demon was endowed with powers to shape artists' destinies positively or negatively (Becker, 2001). In the first clinical history of genius (i.e., creativity), *Du Demon de Socrate,* Lelut (1836), cited Prentky, 2001) states that Socrates' inclination to be inspired by his conscience (i.e., the voice of a supernatural agent, or this *demon*), confirmed his madness (Becker, 2001; Prentky, 2001). The wider association between the artist, melancholy, and madness can be traced to this point (Becker, 2001). Prentky (2001) describes early studies that associate genius with the same maladaptive gene pool as criminals and lunatics, supporting the "degeneracy theory" of creativity (p. 96). The first systematic study relating genius (i.e., creativity) to insanity was published by Lombroso in 1864. Later, in *The Man of Genius,* Lombroso (1891) suggested that genius was associated with psychosis and that both have genetic ties that run in families. In *Heredity Genius,* Galton (1892, cited Lauronen et al., 2004) also hypothesized that creativity was inherited. Studies such as these constitute the foundation of the earliest psychological literature on the subject. This redefinition of genius linked madness to creativity (Becker, 2001).

You twinkle above us: creativity and the divine

> *I really feel connected to the holy origins of theater. Particularly if you're in a good play, a play that makes the audience weep. They are so ready for the transformation. That moment of transformation is holy.*
>
> —Kathryn

The assumption that creativity is connected to psychopathology has not been present throughout history. Although various interpretations of the concept of the demon associate creativity with madness, Socrates conceived the demon as a positive and benevolent agent. Its visitation was a godly gift. Plato accepted this notion, and endorsed the doctrine of *enthousiasmos*, or "divine madness" (Koh, 2006, p. 214). The early Greek actors wore *masks* that they believed were occupied by a whole and distinct personality, often a deity or demon (Bates, 1991). This personality overcame the actor wearing the mask, or the *persona* (Jung, 1989, p. 397). The actor became possessed by the entity who then allowed the actor to speak the essence and truth of the character within the mask. The entity needed the actor's presence in order to be seen, heard, and understood (Bates, 1987, 1991). Perhaps this mingling with the divine is the root of the combined awe and dread that actors elicit from audiences. Acting talent was not believed to be a skill of the individual actor, but actors engaging in the creative process were instead considered servants and messengers of the gods. Inspiration was a desired virtue. Furthermore, although Aristotle believed that extraordinary talent and creativity were characterized by a melancholic temperament, it was understood that *homo melancholicus* could be either sane or insane, that is, "divinely distinguished or mad" (Prentky, 2001, p. 96). Creative expression was clearly distinguished from clinical insanity (Becker, 2001). Sanity was associated with spontaneity, creativity and the numinous. Insanity was associated with depression, anxiety, and degeneracy.

I hope I get it: the role of the artist

> *We've always been looked on as the fly-by-night devil-may-care Puck entities that people think we are. And it's just something that's been handed down through the centuries.*
>
> —Bill

The Romantic movement of the late 18th to mid-19th centuries saw an important change in the dominant conception of artists (Becker, 2001; Lauronen et al., 2004). In this period, status was attained primarily by birth and wealth. While creativity was associated with divinity and high status in prior periods, the Romantics were generally deprived of status and strived to separate themselves from the ordinary by replacing creativity as a superior criterion for attaining prominence. Therefore, they began to embrace the ancient notion of the *demon*, that is, that "possession" or madness was necessary for the creative process (Becker, 2001, p. 48). However, as had happened in the past, they did not separate inspiration from insanity. Suffering, eccentricity, mania, and an air of the mystique allowed them to be seen as separate and exceptional, and confirmed their position as *genius*. Their embrace of the irrational distanced them from the capacities that safeguarded sanity. It also distanced them from the prevailing appreciation of the objective, the logical, and the explainable. This left them defenseless against the label of madness. The assumption spread to other creative individuals (Becker, 2001; Lauronen et al., 2004) forming a pervasive train of logic that precluded the expectation of health and sanity in creative individuals and setting the stage for bias against actors. Moreover, "the expectation of madness continues to be part of a professional ideology of what it means to be truly creative" (Becker, 2001, p. 45). In our modern world, accountants, engineers, and scientists are expected to display qualities of stability, objectivity, and reason. However, the artist is expected to display intuition, sensitivity, and emotional expressiveness, those qualities our society deigns "mad." Artists may invite it, as they may believe it is what is necessary to be called a creative individual, therefore taking part in a self-fulfilling prophecy, or what Becker (2001) calls, a "role expectation" (p. 52).

You could drive a person crazy: a psychoanalytic theory about actors

I know my husband divorced me because I was an actress. He'd read an "important" article about how we were crazy, and he got scared. He didn't want to deal with the awful things I supposedly was.

—Kathryn

The early 20th century saw the establishment of *psychoanalysis,* which articulated the original attempts to understand ourselves—and stage fright. Artists and actors embraced the "irrational" role which contributed to how they were viewed. Several early psychoanalytic theorists have hypotheses regarding the roots of stage fright, which are framed within theories of the actor's personality. Otto Fenichel (1946) has been noted to have authored the seminal paper on the subject. He notes three unconscious aims of acting. First, acting is rooted in the selfish or narcissistic need to show off, or *exhibitionism,* which is an instinct that is present in all children. When fascination with this instinct occurs during development, the child "shows off" to feel pleasure and ward off anxiety. Second, applause provides narcissistic satisfaction and temporary self-esteem. It represents the early bonds with caretakers and acting is an unconscious wish to revive the attention that was felt in these relationships. Third, the actor receives intense satisfaction from having a sense of "magical influence" (p. 147) over the audience and having control of how they will feel. The magic threat of a display or "show" is a determining factor in both the unconscious aim of acting and the origin of theater. According to Fenichel, these aims result in characteristics generally associated with actors including vanity, the need for glory and applause, and the will for power. Furthermore, by playing "parts," actors conceal their true personalities or they reveal hidden aspects of themselves when they fully identify with a role. Actors may also play themselves as they fantasize how they might have developed and behaved under different circumstances. Actors are characterized by having diverse fantasies that allow them to portray a wide variety of roles. The actor engages in the profession to obtain, by deception, narcissistic gratification from the audience. Shame and anxiety are generated when the actor fears being exposed as a fraud and fears the withdrawal of hoped-for assurance and approval from the audience.

Rumors fly: other psychoanalytic theories about actors

> *A therapist told me that being an actress was a sign of immaturity and narcissism and that I should grow up and find a more adult profession.*
>
> —Kathryn

Other theorists have contributed to the discussion about actors. They relied on earlier psychoanalytic studies to develop their own ideas. Because there is scarcity of studies with grounding in contemporary psychological theory (Robb, Due, & Venning, 2016), these theories still may be influencing how actors are thought of today. Bergler (1949) describes the long-held notion that in the actor-child, a narcissistic and forbidden desire to focus on the self is transferred to the desire to exhibit the body or to "show off." Another perception is that the actor-child was left feeling bewildered and guilty after witnessing disturbing events in the adult world, and concluded that the events were not real but "a play." It has been theorized that denial of reality has become a guiding and repetitive pattern which extends to acting. Many early psychologists also believed that the actor is compensating for flawed development of the self when creating a role. There is a long-held psychoanalytic notion that actors have a defective sense of self-image and identity. Weissman (1961) states that the underlying meaning of "the show must go on" is "I, the actor must go onstage" to relieve anxiety. The child-actor may have felt deprived of play, resulting in emotional instability, a lack of body image, separation anxiety, and a lack of self. Performing before audiences provides the actor with a temporary respite from the depressive suffering of the nonformed empty self. Blum (1976) theorizes that actors manifest several personality characteristics. First, they are more open to feelings and emotions. Second, actors are driven by exhibitionism and need applause to gratify this desire. Third, distinct ego systems in the actor allow the actor to engage in activities onstage that are inhibited offstage. A fourth characteristic is actors' "love affair with the world" (p. 182), where they wish to give creatively to the world or leave a personal legacy. Applause from the audience represents the world's acceptance of their "gifts." Blum also theorizes about the genesis of the choice of acting as a career. He posits two possibilities. The actor's parents either: (a) failed to teach the child emotional control or (b) were overly strict, resulting in the child's rebelling.

Just you wait: a psychoanalytic rebuttal

> *A good actor is more aware. They hear, they see, they smell. I'm more interested. OK, let's get down to that! An interested person, who is really watching and listening. If I say some people are more alive, that would be it. They smell that you are more alive. That would be it. Jealousy. Pure and simple. And then that makes them shrink up and feel smaller. It makes them feel somewhat like a failure. Isn't that why we must set up our celebrities and then rip them down?*
>
> —Kathryn

These theories form the basis of how actors have been perceived. Some have been critical of psychoanalytic theorizing with regard to actors' personalities. Reciniello (1991) believes that the usual analytic explanation that the actor "seeks to merely identify the similarities of the performer and the madman" (p. 96) is an error. She believes that the authors cited earlier shed no light on the abilities necessary for creative dramatic performance but instead tend to emphasize "the similarities between performers and deviants rather than to search for distinguishing characteristics" (p. 96). She notes that many of these theorists assessed only psychopathology, which necessarily resulted in descriptions of artists in pathological terms. She questions why actors are judged so harshly and offers her own psychoanalytic interpretation of what she feels is a prejudice. She suggests that psychoanalysts so strongly despise actors' "narcissistic displays" (p. 100) because they despise their own. Reciniello notes that unlike personality researchers who focus on the whole person, psycho-analytic writers have almost exclusively attended to the actor's limitations. She interprets Fenichel's opinion of the actor: "… he is held in contempt, but secretly envied" (1946, p. 156), as a "moment of self-confrontation" (p. 101). Reciniello believes that psychoanalytic theories reveal more of theorists than of the actor and his or her art. Hammond and Edelman (1991a) also con-tend that psychologists have formed a negative stereotype of actors. Their study investigated the way actors perceive themselves on several personality dimensions. They assert that it would be inaccurate to conclude that an actor personality type per se exists, and that pathological factors alone cannot account for the choice of acting as a career. They conclude that although there are per-sonality dimensions that distinguish actors from nonactors, the differences do not support the negative stereotype of actors. Novick (1998) notes that actors are perpetually stereotyped as exhibitionists and narcissists and have failed to develop a normal sense of identity. Novick remarks that "insecurity is where you find it" (p. 20) and that these stereotypes actually may contribute to an actor's poor sense of self.

So they say: alternate personality profiles of actors

> *But I didn't tell anybody I wanted to be an actor because in the Bronx, you don't screw around with no drama, you know, all that crap, you know?*
>
> —Marty

A few studies have investigated actors, but systematic and rigorous psychological studies of actors still are uncommon (Robb & Davies, 2015). What motivates the actor has been the subject of debate (Kogan, 2002). Although the presumption exists that acting is attractive to people with certain personalities (i.e., the theater's traditional freedom from convention attracts nonconforming personalities), there are no longitudinal studies on performing artists beginning in childhood that support this idea (Novick, 1998; Kogan, 2002; Robb & Davies, 2015). Moreover, whether personality traits are antecedents or consequences of participation in the performing arts is unclear. However, some studies have investigated the personalities of actors. In *Psychological Profiles of Professional Actors*, Nettle (2005) investigated the psychological characteristics of professional actors, and found that actors are higher in extroversion, openness, agreeableness, and empathizing than nonactors. Phillips (1991) studied a group of actors and found that they uniformly had a deep connection to acting and possessed optimism that was not related to how successful they were. Actors remain strongly identified with the acting profession even though they rated themselves as leading stressful, difficult lives. They tend to continue in the unstable profession because of their intrinsic passion and the pleasure of practicing their craft. Novick (1998) focuses on actors' insecurity. He theorizes that although actors are not necessarily more insecure than others, actors' insecurity may have specific causes, namely: (a) the lack of job security and (b) routine rejection. An additional contributor to actors' insecurity is the sexuality inherent in performance. Novick believes that at the core of what the actor reveals—whether it be transformation, intense emotion, or the ability to make people laugh—is sexuality. To make a living and to display the self sexually—even in a distanced and disguised manner—has often been considered shameful and undignified, which diminishes the actor's self-esteem. Maxwell, Seton, and Szabo (2015) studied actors' sense of well-being and found that actors studied had a positive level of satisfaction with their lives. They hypothesize that actors generally have an optimistic view of life. Robb, Due, and Venning (2016) explored the psychological well-being of actors. With regard to actors' inner lives (i.e., beliefs, thoughts, feelings, and personality) they found that (1) actors pursue improvement and have a high level of dedication to their work; (2) they see themselves as possessing inherent strengths (i.e., the desire to explore, heightened empathy, and the ability to improvise and be flexible in a variety of situations); (3) they are "called" to acting; (4) they feel a sense of mental precariousness (i.e., entering and leaving the inner world of the character); and (5) that they are highly self-reflective.

A very dramatic fashion: the presentational school of acting

I wanted to find out if I could do it or not, so I went to New York and stayed there for 18 years. I did several Broadway shows, a lot of off Broadway, a lot of regional theater. That's really where I got my training.

—Jake

It is a common notion that actors are merely "playing" and that acting does not require the depth of technique or craft necessary in other performance domains. We can see, however, that acting has been observed from various viewpoints historically. But what does an actor do, and what are their careers like? Acting is an ancient art form that has its roots in the teachings of Aristotle, who believed that acting should possess two forces: *action* and *passion*. These opposing forces seem to be reflected in opposing styles of acting. For many centuries, "the great argument in acting" has been between the Presentational versus the Representational styles of acting (Brestoff, 1995, p. xi). In the Presentational school, sometimes referred to "the Brechtian School" (Konijn, 1991), the actor presents or simulates the character and utilizes various and specific physical and vocal techniques, which can take years to learn and perfect. This "outer directed" style of acting is often associated with British and French "classical" acting (Aaron, 1986). In this approach, the subjective experience of emotion is deemphasized, technique is heightened, and the actor acknowledges the presence of the audience. With an emphasis on the physical act of delivery, the actor experiences the distinction between self and the role. The philosopher Diderot called this the *actor's paradox* (Worthen, 1984, p. 89). The Presentational style of acting is associated with Shakespearian, Commedia, and Restoration drama. Actors associated with this school are Lucille Ball, Jim Carrey, Laurence Olivier, and Robin Williams. Modern comedies, especially television sit-coms, are rooted in this school. Teachers of this school include Augusto Boal, Anne Bogart, Roy Hart, Karen Hensel, Joan Littlewood, and others.

At least I didn't fake it: the representational school of acting

I was very shy as a young man. And all of a sudden, I'm onstage and I'm expressing myself beautifully, and I'm getting angry and I'm getting loving … and there's no … nobody's gonna hurt you for it, you know? So, I liked doing all these things onstage I couldn't do in life.

—Marty

In the Representational school, the actor "becomes" the character using inner-directed psychological techniques, and experiences and expresses organic emotion that the character would express in the given circumstances of the play (Brestoff, 1995). This is often associated with American and Russian "naturalistic" acting (Aaron, 1986). In this approach, the actor ignores the audience and creates a psychological and imaginary "fourth wall" which blocks his or her connection to the audience. Rather than focusing on the presentation, actors using this approach focus on their emotional and psychological processes which motivate behaviors.

The most recognized form of this approach is "Method acting." It was first popularized in the 1930s by the Group Theatre in New York City (Garfield, 1984). Later, Lee Strasberg refined its techniques and developed an acting approach called "the Method" (Bates, 1987). Both are derived from the theories of Constantine Stanislavski, who is known as "the seminal theoretician of the modern stage" (Worthen, 1984, p. 143). Stanislavski's "System" is based on systematic and deeply analyzed motivations and emotions of characters, with the goal being psychological and emotional authenticity (Stanislavski, 1936/ 1986). This type of acting requires empathy and a subjective understanding of the character to the degree that actors embody the character's life (Nettle, 2005). Stanislavski believed that there should be no distinction between the self and the character. When the two combine, the *aristo-rol*, or "the third being" is created (Benedetti, 1998, p. 10). Method acting requires an actor to use a wide variety of complex emotional exercises including *substitution*, where an actor vividly remembers a past event and applies the reactions to the dramatic situation, *emotional memory*, where an actor recalls emotional sensations from his or her own life, and working through *actor transferences* to the character, to name a few (Stanislavski, 1936/1986). Actors associated with Method acting include Marlon Brando, Robert DeNiro, Dustin Hoffman, Daniel Day Lewis, and Al Pacino. Teachers of various forms of the Method include Stella Adler, Herbert Berghoff, Michael Chekhov, Uta Hagen, Sanford Meisner, and others.

Any way you look at it: the wisdom of balance

> *Well you might call it charisma ... you have the ability to communicate your passion and make others feel it. You have the gift to make people feel it. No matter what your training is, this goes above that. It's a gift.*
>
> —Kathryn

Actors adapt to the acting styles that are popular in any given time, and they must be flexible in their emotional, physical, and psychological abilities to play various roles in a range of styles. Naturalism in acting emerged as a reaction to the perceived falseness that preceded it. Silent films, from our current perspective, may seem overly acted. Acting that is more naturalistic may once have been considered artless because the use of technique is diminished. Like all art forms, the pendulum swings. From our current perspective, naturalism is likely to be overturned by presentationalism (Brestoff, 1995). Aaron states, "most truly fine acting has always represented a unity of the polarities defined in the contrast of these two styles" (1986, p. xv). The paradox of acting—whether to feel or to present—applies to genuinely great actors, according to Diderot (Konijn, 1991), and this seems to be a widely held perspective. As common aims, both perspectives assume that the actor takes on the attributes of the character and responds to the circumstances of the play from the character's subjective perspective. The unity of and application of both poles of acting is seen in actors such as Judi Dench, Phillip Seymour Hoffman, Derek Jacobi, Helen Mirren, Geoffrey Rush, and Meryl Streep. To understand and portray a character from a script, actors often engage in in-depth research of a character's historical, cultural, emotional, psychological, and physical characteristics to augment and refine their portrayals and interpretations of a role, and their unique performances support, enhance, and illuminate the theme and overall message of the play or dramatic text. Most current Western theories propose the integration of the body, mind, voice, emotions, imagination and the psyche to expressive ends (Brestoff, 1995).

That's what makes it an art: the actor's training

> *I trained at Lee Strasberg, so there was an onus on relaxation and sensory work. It was very American-based. I worked in England and it's more about the voice and the delivery and that sensory work is kind of frowned upon a bit. I did a lot of Shakespeare there as well. So, on the one hand, there was this technique of saying it's from the inside-out, and the English technique was more from the outside-in. And so, there was a bit of a clash there. In both worlds you can find the same results.*

—Jimmy

We know that classical musicians undergo rigorous training to achieve the level of mastery required to perform professionally. Most actors today undertake formal training in a university or conservatory setting (Bureau of Labor Statistics, 2019). Related bachelor's degree programs include majors in theater, drama, communications, dramatic literature, and film studies. Many stage actors continue their academic training in Master of Fine Arts (MFA) programs. At the graduate level, advanced actor training may include courses in acting, voice, speech, movement, directing, singing, and playwriting. The *National Association of Schools of Theatre* (NAST) accredits 160 programs in theater at the associates, bachelors, masters, and doctoral levels (NAST, 2019). However, because acting is not a profession that requires formal education or certification, many actors pursue their craft based on talent alone. Furthermore, many actors, regardless of formal training and experience level, participate in ongoing classes and workshops to continue to deepen and broaden their range. Often actors must engage in specialized training including dialect coaching, music lessons, movement lessons, and sports training in order to portray their characters more accurately. Actors must be able to memorize lines and follow direction. They must have stage presence and the ability to affect an audience and to go physically and emotionally beyond the "civilian" boundaries of affective expression. Finally, they must possess the talent and imagination necessary to create and portray characters (The Bureau of Labor Statistics, 2019).

Heck, I'd even play the maid: actors at work

> *Real jobs. That always kinda ticked me off. Real jobs? This is a real job.*

—Bill

Actors are likely to experience unpredictable working conditions. The unemployment rate at any given time is in the 90 to 95 percent range (The Bureau of Labor Statistics, 2019). Actors appear in a variety of venues, including theater, film, television, radio, nightclubs, cabarets, theme parks, internet, and various other performing arts media (Actors Equity, 2019). Acting jobs are typically short term, ranging from one day to a few months, resulting in erratic income and intense competition for jobs. Actors may supplement their incomes with other forms of employment. When performing, actors usually work long and unpredictable hours. For example, actors in a *repertory theater* company may perform in one show in the evening and rehearse another show during the day. Actors in *touring companies* travel with their productions, keeping them far from home base, family, and friends. Actors in film and television often travel to *location*, which may involve adverse environmental conditions and long waiting times. Television work requires appearing on camera with little time for preparation as scripts tend to be revised repeatedly. Regardless of the medium, actors must be in good physical condition to endure performance schedules, to maneuver around numerous technical elements of various studios, sound stages, and theater spaces, and to remain in character and use their emotions and voices appropriately (The Bureau of Labor Statistics, 2019).

Putting it together: how you see your craft

> *The purpose of acting is to educate the audience … have them reflect on their own life based on what they see onstage, and that the actors are participating in that. Even if it makes people laugh, and it makes them forget their troubles at home, then it's meaningful.*
>
> —Elizabeth

We have looked at the fact that many actors have faced ambivalence from others regarding acting as a profession. It has been documented that actors often feel devalued. It has also been documented that actors feel proud of their craft and have a passion for acting and the approach to the work despite these societal pressures. Navigating these attitudes from others however, it not always easy. In fact, societal preconceptions about what it means to be an actor may have influenced our self-concept. It is important to acknowledge these, and to know that society—and loved ones—may merely be viewing acting through a corrupted lens. In the next chapter, we will look at stage fright objectively and review its emotional, physical, and psychological aspects. But for now, let's look at any preconceptions you may have had to deal with when either announcing that you wished to be an actor or living life as an actor. Before we move on, please look at the questions below and try to answer them as truthfully as possible. As before, your answers are not being exposed for judgment and are serving to reveal the presence of how preconceptions about acting may have influenced *your* life. Keep in mind that as you address these questions, your honest answers are contributing to a balanced and sincere construction of what it means to be an actor in your world and in the greater world.

To the actor:

- What kind of support did you receive when you announced to family and friends that you wanted to be an actor?
- Who was positively supportive?
- What can you take from that now?
- Did you receive any negative messages?
- What were they?
- Do they still influence you?
- Have you felt that as an actor, you are expected to behave in a "certain way"?
- Have you enjoyed positive support from others?
- Have you internalized any of the negative assumptions about actors?
- What attitudes have you noticed in the greater world about actors/acting?
- What other messages did you receive about being an actor?
- How do you feel about being an actor?
- What method(s) of acting do you use?
- What training/classes/preparation have you had?
- How do you see your craft?

3   The actor's anxiety

High anxiety: anxiety in history

I was really a mess up there. I couldn't function at all. I really couldn't, you know. I was tied up in knots.

—Marty

Underlying the actor's experience of stage fright is *anxiety*. Anxiety varies from person to person, and it has been wrestled with throughout history. Onions (1996) states that the term *anxiety* is rooted in the Latin word *angere*, which means, "to choke" (p. 41). Johnson (2009) investigates the etymology of the term and notes that it has historically meant "anguish," "sorrow," "pain," and "strangulation" (p. 144) and that it first appears in the English language in 1525 in a play by Sir Thomas More. Anxiety is part of being human, and it has been present throughout history and understood through various viewpoints, depending on where the lens is located in history. Before Freud, the issue of anxiety was wrestled within the realm of religion and philosophy. References from the Bible indicate that anxiety was a condition of body, mind, and soul that was to be resisted and replaced with faith (Kierkegaard, 1980). Medieval thought included embracing collectivism, the divinity of man, and the centrality and certainty of a divine creator. This allowed for an acceptance of the ineffable and offered spiritual explanations and remedies for the problems of fear and anxiety (May, 1977). Emerging sciences in the Renaissance began to shift philosophical attention away from the centrality of the divine and toward that of the autonomous and rational individual. Descartes (1596–1650) formulated the link between medieval thought and the succeeding precepts fundamental to modern Western thought (Ponterotto, 2005). His maxim, *Cogito, ergo sum*, "I think, therefore I am," articulated the separation between mind and body (Tarnas, 1991, p. 277). Now individuals could determine their state through their minds. This shifted philosophical attention toward observed, mechanical, and logical phenomena to define what was true. Consequently, it shifted attention away from indefinable phenomena considered "irrational" including anxiety, which had no place in the reasoning world (May, 1977, p. 21). However, the Cartesian Split (i.e., the philosophical separation of mind and body) is now thought to be coming together. The fields of philosophy, psychology—and the field of acting—are thought to be undergoing a monumental change in thinking—*a paradigm shift*—where emotion, the body, and unconscious processes are again being considered holistically and fundamental to experience and meaning (Seton, 2006; Schore, 2011).

The dream that you've had before: perspectives on anxiety

> *Live theatre involves danger. Live theatre involves taking risks. And actors who are theatre actors take that risk night after night after night. It's very dangerous out there, because basically, even though you have other actors out there, you are on your own.*
>
> —Jake

Freud (1856–1939) highlighted the importance of the dynamic unconscious and he contended that he could demonstrate its influence on conscious processes and behaviors (Hampden-Turner, 1981). He agreed with the psychological separation of fear and anxiety. Freud's exploration of neurosis led him to theorize that anxiety is its fundamental problem (May, 1977). In the *signal theory*, he proposed that anxiety is produced by the personality which has three parts: the *Id* (which seeks gratification), the *ego* (which tests reality), and the *Super Ego* (which imposes moral and ethical limits to behavior). The ego alerts the system to the presence of threat and arbitrates the struggle between instinctual drives of the Id and the moral concerns of the Super Ego. This struggle is the source of anxiety. Furthermore, *repression* banishes anxiety from consciousness. Additional *defenses* and symptoms may arise to limit the impairing effects of anxiety (Zerbe, 1990). May (1977) addresses various theories of anxiety. Carl Jung (1875–1961) believed that it is "the individual's reaction to the invasion of the conscious mind by irrational forces and images from the collective unconscious" (1977, p. 158). Western culture holds these forces at bay by emphasizing rational constraints against them, resulting in additional symptoms like panic or neurosis. Otto Rank (1884–1939) believed that anxiety stems from "apprehension" (p. 149) caused by inevitable and lifelong separation experiences required for autonomy. Alfred Adler (1870–1937) uses the term "inferiority feelings" (p. 153) to describe anxiety. These are rooted in an inherent sense of inadequacy which is overcome by the strengthening of social bonds. Karen Horney (1885–1952) believes that anxiety is inherent in being human. It is the reaction to a threat to any developed pattern that an individual depends on to feel safe. May proposes that anxiety is "the apprehension cued off by a threat to some value that the individual holds essential to his existence as a personality" (p. 205). Threats may endanger physical, ideological, or psychological safety. *Normal anxiety* is a reaction to an actual threat that is not disproportionate, does not involve repression, does not need neurotic defense mechanisms, and can be confronted consciously and constructively (p. 209). However, *neurotic anxiety* is a reaction that is disproportionate and involves repression (i.e., dissociation), and is managed by various defense mechanisms and the development of symptoms. Here we see wide ranges of the possible sources of anxiety: a visit from irrational forces (i.e., an inner critic), a normal sense of apprehension about living, human feelings of inferiority, and reactions to any threat to feeling safe. The actor's struggle with stage fright is the human struggle with anxiety in the spotlight. As actors apprehend this state to enact stories, their dance with being human can be more deeply appreciated.

Waving through a window: the anxiety disorders

And it's there in all of us... all actors at some point... I know this...I have dealt with this demon.

—Jake

Anxiety disorders have various features thought to exist in two forms: *state anxiety* and *trait anxiety*. State anxiety is a transitory or situational form of anxiety that is a reaction to a particular threat—resembling fear. Trait anxiety is a stable part of the personality which interprets a wide range of stimuli as threatening or dangerous (Kenny, 2011). An actor's unique experience of stage fright would be influenced if they are an anxiety-prone individual, as compared to an actor who does not encounter the world in this way. In either case, anxiety disorders are among the most prevalent forms of diagnosable emotional conditions in the United States (Reichenberg & Seligman, 2016). Nearly 25 percent of the population has experienced an anxiety disorder, which is the primary symptom in 20 to 25 percent of all psychiatric disorders. Connors (1994) describes anxiety disorders as characterized by a sense of vulnerability. Anxious individuals feel threatened and fear internal or external catastrophe. The feared stimulus may be (1) a thought, as in *obsessive-compulsive disorder*; (2) a sensation, as in *panic disorder*; (3) an external object or situation, as in *simple phobia* and *social phobia*; or (4) a reaction to a past traumatic event as in *posttraumatic stress disorder* or *acute stress disorder* (Reichenberg & Seligman, 2016). Anxiety may be pervasive, as in *generalized anxiety disorder* (GAD) and may be induced by substance abuse or medical conditions (Vasey & Dadds, 2001). These factors are present in various degrees in varying forms of stage fright (Naistadt, 2004). In all these disorders, the individual will experience distressing anxiety without a functional solution other than avoidance (Seligman, 1998). The anxiety disorders vary widely in their frequency of occurrence in the general population, at age of onset, in family patterns, and in gender distribution. Furthermore, a diagnosis includes a criterion of severity, which must be severe enough to interfere significantly with an individual's occupational, educational, or social functioning (Vasey & Dadds, 2001). An actor who fears performing is certainly compromised professionally, and this could spread to other areas of life if left unattended.

Inside my mind: stage fright diagnosed

There's some kind of terror—horror, not terror—horror of being found out for me. These people are going to find out that I'm a phony. They're gonna find out that I have no idea what I'm doing, that I'm a fake, that I'm a charlatan, that I'm Houdini.

—Alex

Stage fright is a specific type of anxiety. The first mention of stage fright appears in *The Stage Fright: or How to Face an Audience* (Kielblock, 1891). Not all actors who experience stage fright have a diagnosable condition, as it is a natural part of acting (Zakaria et al., 2013). However, severe anxiety that affects our functioning, artistry, and performances certainly deserves serious attention. The avoidance of anxiety is implicated in drug and alcohol abuse and in impaired interpersonal, work, and social functioning (Seligman, 1998). The terms *performance anxiety* and *stage fright* first appeared in the *Diagnostic and Statistical Manual of Mental Disorders (DSM)*—a manual used in the helping professions to categorize types of distress—in its fourth edition as a *Social Phobia* (*DSM*, American Psychiatric Association [APA], 2004). However, Kenny and Ackermann (2007) argued that those with performance anxiety are more likely to have excessively high expectations of themselves and therefore fear their own evaluation of their performances, as opposed to those with social phobia, who fear the scrutiny of others. Another difference is that those with performance anxiety demonstrate a continued commitment to the feared performance situation, while those with social phobia try to manage their anxiety by avoiding the feared situation. In the most current edition, the *DSM-V* (2013), stage fright appears as a *Social Anxiety Disorder* (Social Phobia), and is described in the *DSM-V* as follows:

> A marked fear or anxiety about of one or more social situations in which the individual is exposed to possible scrutiny by others. The individual fears that he or she will act in a way or show anxiety symptoms that will be negatively evaluated (i.e., will be humiliating or embarrassing; will lead to rejection or offend others).
>
> (p. 202)

This edition adds the *predominately performance* specifier, in which the fear is restricted to speaking or performing in public. This addition adds clinical awareness to the needs of actors, yet much more research needs to be done. Diagnostic labels remain a paradox (Hayes, 2017). Kenny (2011) cautions that the field has not yet developed universal, reliable and valid assessment instruments to conclusively test for music performance anxiety. Therefore, at this time we must keep these limitations in mind when looking to research for understanding stage fright when acting. In addition, it is important to remember, that the complete absence of anxiety would not be a normal reaction to performing in front of an audience. Some anxiety is considered *normal*. Most individuals find that they must face and embrace this anxiety at some point during their lives, and this is true for most actors.

That's why I'm a mess: general components of stage fright

I get a knot in my stomach and I feel like the blood in my veins has thinned out and I'm not getting enough oxygen. I shake, and my knees feel weak and unsteady.

—Peter

Stage fright is a complex response to the prospect of the actuality of performing before a live audience. Various researchers have articulated the various manifestations of stage fright.

Kenny and Ackermann (2007) believe that performance anxiety is a group of disorders that affect individuals in a range of performance settings such as examinations, competitions, and public performances. It can occur across several domains, including academic performance, public speaking, sports, and the performing arts in acting, dance, and music. Fehm and Schmidt (2006) list three main *components* of performance anxiety, which include: (a) cognitions (i.e., irrational, perfectionist or catastrophic beliefs); (b) physiological reactions (i.e., trembling, palpitations, or hyperventilation); and (c) behavioral responses (i.e., the avoidance of auditions and performances). Jangir and Govinda (2018) agree with these and add affects (i.e., emotional responses like feelings of loss, etc.). Naistadt (2004) notes categories of fear, including (a) fear of forgetting performance content; (b) fear of failure or success; and (c) fear of a repeat of negative past experiences. These negative components are daunting, and the type and number that are experienced by any given actor will be unique to them and may or may not occur in any combination (Meyer-Dinkgrafe, Nair, & Procter, 2012). Also, there is a fine line between anxiety and *excitement*, and stage fright in many is experienced as a positive element (Arial et al., 2011). As we will soon see in our interviews, our actors experienced some of these components. It is hoped that this list is experienced as informative rather than a script of what must occur.

When the dog bites: physical attack

My eyes want to tear up. And I get a little giddy. My stomach starts to churn, and my hands get sweaty… and shaky.

—Bill

Stage fright often causes us to feel physically unwell. It is our body's way of protecting us from danger. Central to the stage fright experience are physical manifestations that range from mild to severe symptoms. These spontaneous physical reactions are useful in response to an external threat but are counterproductive and even disastrous for an actor about to interpret dramatic literature in front of a live audience. Symptoms reported by performers include (a) blushing, (b) cold sweats, (c) difficulty breathing, (d) dry mouth, (e) mild to severe gastrointestinal difficulties, (f) heart palpitations, (g) lightheadedness, (h) physical and mental immobilization, (i) reactivity to stimuli, (j) shaking, (k) watery eyes, and (i) weakness in the limbs, legs (Witt, Brown, Roberts, Weisel, Sawyer, & Behnke, 2006). These and other physical symptoms have been well documented in the literature. These symptoms occur in a range from mild symptoms (i.e., butterflies, sweating, trembling, tension, etc.) to mid-range symptoms (i.e., choking, dry mouth, need to escape, tightness in the chest, weakness in the knees), to severe symptoms (i.e., feelings of impending death, diarrhea, dizziness, faintness, tingling in limbs, urination) to complete collapse (i.e., disorientation, fainting, fear of dying, panic). Jimmy described physical effects so debilitating that he had to isolate himself days before performance. Marty said he was so physically distressed that "I wanted to sit down and cry sometimes because I was trying so hard." Stage fright can and has been intellectualized and analyzed. However, our actors remind us that stage fright *hurts*. These symptoms can be very frightening. It is natural to feel that we are going crazy, that there is something wrong with us, or that we don't have the ability to cope and weather these symptoms, sometimes causing us to wish we could disappear.

That can cut like a knife: crazy thoughts

What if I'm not good enough? What if I can't remember my lines? What if I'm not really a good actor? Is the audience gonna laugh at me? It's that. It's exposing myself. It's contradictory, because I want to express myself. But that is ultimate the thing I'm so scared of. What if I'm not really good enough?

—Jimmy

The most distressing aspect of stage fright seems to be the negative messages (i.e., *cognitions*) that swirl through our minds (Clason, Johannsen, & Mortberg, 2015). Jimmy experiences general negative and attacking thoughts like "You're not good enough!" and "You're worthless!" Peter had the very same thoughts, but then his thoughts would become more specific. "Your nose is deformed." "Your jaw is too big." "Your voice sounds weird." "I'm not good enough!" "The audience will hate me!" and "I'm a fraud!" are only a few of the harmful messages we tell ourselves. "Crazy thoughts" like these are what psychologists call *cognitive distortions* (Beck, 1995). Some examples of cognitive distortions are: (a) *all or nothing thinking* (i.e., "I'm a total failure."); (b) *catastrophizing* (i.e., "I won't be able to do any of it right."); (c) *comparing* (i.e., "The other actor is better."); (d) *discounting* (i.e., "I'm not good, just lucky."); (e) *emotional reasoning* (i.e., "I know I got cast, but I still feel like a failure."); (f) *labeling* (i.e., "I'm a fraud."); (g) *magnifying/minimizing* (i.e., "Not getting a direction proves I'm a terrible actor."; (h) *mental filter* (i.e., "The one negative comment must be right."); (i) *mind reading* (i.e., "I know the director hates me."); (j) *overgeneralization* (i.e., "Because that line reading was bad I must be a terrible actor."); (k) *personalization* (i.e., "The producer didn't look at me because he thinks I'm a weak actor."); (l) should-statements (i.e., "I should always be perfect."); and (m) *tunnel vision* (i.e., "I can't do anything right."). There are errors in thinking that are usually not grounded in truth and are generated from our *core beliefs* about ourselves. These central beliefs are experienced as absolute truths and influence how we see the world. Core beliefs include "I'm not good enough.", "The world is unfair.", and "I will never have what I want." An individual's core beliefs—unique to them and their history—will determine the types of distressing cognitive distortions they will experience in a stage fright episode.

I'm afraid: our fears

> *I also feel isolated and alone as if no one has the ability to help me out of the overwhelming nature of it. And just afraid. Just afraid.*

—Peter

The emotional aspects of stage fright can be experienced in mild to severe forms, on a *fear spectrum*. We may be mildly preoccupied, tense, worried, or anxious. We may be moderately agitated, concerned or scared. At the severe end of the fear spectrum we may feel terrified, horrified, and panicked. The emotion of fear alerts us to potential threat or loss. Our eyes widen, our jaw becomes tense, our breath becomes shallow, and our muscles tighten as we watch and wait to be attacked. Common *fear categories* include: (1) fear of being *criticized*; (2) fear of *forgetting*; (3) fear of *humiliation*; (4) fear of *failure/success*; (5) fear of the *unknown*; and (6) fear of the *return of past negative experiences* (Naistadt, 2004). In a stage fright episode these fears seem to amplify, and we can become afraid of almost anything. Fear of being *ignored* by the audience, fear of *disappointing* others, fear of *failure*, fear of *fear*, fear that our preparation is *lacking*, fear of looking "less than" or *looking stupid*, and fear of being *unlucky* are some common fears. We can worry about *performance concerns* like entrances, costumes, remembering our lines, the *quality* of our performance, and if the audience will approve of us. Stage fright fears can spread to other aspects of our *professional* lives. We may fear we will *lose approval* from cast mates, other actors, producers, teachers, and other individuals in our lives and in our profession. Severe stage fright can attack our very *integrity*. We can fear total *annihilation* and fear that we will lose all emotional and physical *control*. One of our actors, Jimmy, tells us that his fear was so intense that he could not leave the bathroom. We may also fear we will lose our *minds*. Probably the most devastating and costly fear is the fear of the loss of our *dreams*.

I did what I had to do: coping with stage fright

> *Probably one of the best compliments an actor can get is being called a "trouper."*

—Alex

We might ask someone in any other profession how they persist in the face of such discomfort. The performing arts possesses a "norm" that encourages performing in pain and through injury (Nordin-Bates, 2012). While many professions are played out at a single scene, actors may be in a hospital setting one day or in a royal court the next. They may be enacting war battles or a violent or emotional scene. These intense performance demands may complicate anxiety before a performance. A recent study found that approximately two thirds of actors use some form of coping mechanism to deal with the physical and emotional effects of acting. Many use physical exercise, life coaching, psychotherapy, and physical disciplines like the Alexander Technique and yoga. Actors also use drugs, alcohol, prescription drugs like antidepressants and anti-anxiety meds and beta-blockers to manage their anxiety. Actors also use other legal substances like marijuana or naturopathic remedies, and a small percentage surveyed used illegal substances as a direct response to performance related problems (Maxwell, Seton, & Szabo, 2015). Sometimes nerves will kill an appetite and the remedy for needed energy might be a candy bar or a caffeine drink. Sometimes, actors may feel so desperate that they will engage in activities that may threaten their employment. One of our actors, Peter, admitted to needing a pre-show drink to calm his nerves. "No matter how much I prepare, do my warm-ups, run my lines, and do what I think is best, sometimes I break down and have a drink before I go on. Sometimes I have more than one. I'm terribly embarrassed about it. I do hide it…and worry if I'm not careful someone will smell it on my breath."

Putting it together: your anxiety

> *But as I went on, I realized that we all get afraid sometimes. If we don't there's something wrong. Everybody has it at one time or another.*
>
> —Elizabeth

We have looked at the history of anxiety, various theories which attempt to explain it, the components of stage fright, and the symptoms of stage fright. The causes have been entwined with theories of the actor's personality, and as we have seen, there is very little research conducted on actors specifically. In the next chapter, we will look at some causes of stage fright. But for now, let's look at any symptoms you may have noticed when you experience stage fright. They may be (a) cognitive (i.e., negative thoughts); (b) physiological (i.e., sweaty palms, racing heart, etc.); (c) emotional (i.e., feeling scared or sad); or (d) behavioral (i.e., not going to rehearsals, etc.), or a combination of the four. These symptoms may be mild (i.e. a low intensity, brief episode before performance), moderate (i.e., a more intense reaction that may continue into performance and may affect an actor's perceived range of ability) or severe (i.e., catastrophic reactions that prevent performance). Before we move on, look at the questions below and try to answer them as truthfully as possible. As before, your answers are not going to be criticized. Avoid criticizing your own answers. Your honest answers are continuing to bring awareness to the presence and manifestations of your stage fright, so keep going. Noticing these will help you to take charge of it. Sometimes naming a symptom can be uncomfortable. It is a part of acknowledging fear, which can be anxiety provoking. Take the perspective that you are beginning to research a character. You are simply gathering information at this point.

To the actor:

- Can you accept that anxiety is a normal part of life?
- Can you accept that anxiety has been investigated for centuries?
- Do you feel anxious only when acting?

- Do you feel anxious in other parts of your life?
- Do any of the following apply to you:
  - a family history of anxiety
  - a personal history of anxiety
  - a past diagnosis of anxiety or panic triggered by acting
  - a past diagnosis of anxiety or panic not related to acting
  - an overall anxious outlook on life
  - mood swings
- Are your stage fright symptoms physical, psychological, emotional, or a combination?
- Which of these physiological symptoms do you experience?
  - blushing
  - butterflies
  - choking
  - cold sweats
  - feeling like impending death
  - difficulty breathing
  - dizziness
  - dry mouth
  - feeling like escaping
  - feeling like fainting
  - feeling like fighting
  - gastrointestinal difficulties
  - heart palpitations
  - lightheadedness
  - physical and mental immobilization
  - shaking
  - uncomfortable physical sensations
  - watery eyes
  - weakness in the arms / legs
- What were you thinking immediately before, during, and after the performance?
- Which of these cognitive symptoms do you experience?
  - negative thoughts about yourself
  - negative thought about your acting
  - negative thoughts that escalate into panic
  - excessive worry about things out of your control
  - self-harming thoughts/behaviors
  - difficulty preparing for a role
  - difficulty focusing
  - difficulty completing actor tasks
  - overly self-involved
- What emotions were you feeling before, during, and immediately after the performance (sadness, anger, fear, sorrow, etc.)?
- Which of these fears do you experience?

- fear of negative reactions from an audience
- fear of not being good enough
- fear of embarrassment
- fear of being disliked
- fear of forgetting lines
- fears unique to you
- Does your stage fright feel?
  - slight (i.e., apprehension)
  - moderate (i.e., scared)
  - severe (i.e., terrified)?
- Name your specific fears regarding acting.
- How do you cope with anxiety?

4   Causes of stage fright

I can do that: searching for answers

And I've tried everything. Psychoanalysis. The pin thing … where they stick pins in you … hypnosis. Drugs. Herbal therapy. Uh … chanting. Nothing works. Nothing.

—Alex

Actors with stage fright look to causes to help them eradicate this painful and limiting condition.

Some actors point to early childhood experiences of being criticized, past performance failures, insecurity, lack of preparation, fear of criticism, and negative self-judgments, to name a few.

Many actors feel a sense of futility when addressing stage fright. Perhaps, like Alex, you have tried several ways to cope with stage fright without much success, and perhaps you blamed yourself. Katherine recalled how her therapist told her that wanting to be an actor was a sign of her "immaturity." Or you may have been told that your pain and suffering is part of your talent.

We must remember that when an actor seeks remedies from a therapist or a teacher for the painful state of stage fright, these professionals look to the existing research in their own fields to direct their attitudes and practices. The classic psychoanalytic literature states that stage fright is caused by an unconscious fear of attack, developmental arrest, narcissism, audience envy, and other forces. These perspectives have influenced how actors have been traditionally perceived, and traditions are passed down and entrenched until they are considered again. Perhaps you have heard these and other theories about actors. The actors that were interviewed conceded that their attempts to get help were mostly unsuccessful. If you believed these theories about yourself because you are an actor, and perhaps you even thought they were necessary aspects of your talent, then how is it possible to have the solid self-esteem it takes to be an "emotional warrior" in front of hundreds of people?

Applause, applause: psychoanalytic theories

We know stories of very famous actors who've been debilitated by this disease, and it's destroyed their careers, unfortunately. I think you would have to go back to those individuals and find out what it was that gave them such self-doubt. The stage is a proving ground. So, all our personality disorders, all our personal demons, all our torments from childhood on come into play in that arena.

—Jake

Psychoanalytic theories articulated the original attempts to understand ourselves— and stage fright—and form the basis of subsequent *psychodynamic theories.* These theories comprise the most available research on stage fright among theater actors (Meyer-Dinkgrafe, Nair, & Procter, 2012). Both emphasize the role of the unconscious, the hidden thoughts and feelings it holds beneath awareness, and past developmental events as catalysts for stage fright (Nagel, 2004). It is a common psychoanalytic theme that the actor—who is narcissistically driven— needs audience approval, affection, and appreciation. From this perspective, it is theorized that stage fright is caused by the fear of being disliked and negatively scrutinized by the audience.

Stage fright is also thought to be caused by *exhibitionism* (i.e., the need to "show off") and the actor's fear of retaliation by the audience in the form of being attacked for their infantile nature (Bergler, 1949). Stage fright has been called the "actor's neurosis," which is thought to be caused by an exhibitionist's unconscious fear of castration and shame, which are remnants of developmental arrest that are activated in the acting situation (Fenichel, 1946, p. 360). Stage fright is also thought to be caused by the restriction of gestures imposed by blocking, past messages that fear is cowardly, the loss of composure, and the fear of being exposed as a fraud (Kaplan, 1969). It is also theorized that stage fright occurs when an actor fears that his or her selfish and infantile impulses (i.e., fantasies of omnipotence and accompanying exhibitionism) will be revealed to the audience which will activate their hostility, jealousy, and revenge. The actor fears that their success will additionally provoke these reactions, generating feelings of being unworthy of success (Freundlich, 1968). Acting is also thought to provide a temporary sense of another identity in the actor, but stage fright is the threat of losing this possibility (Blum, 1976). Stage fright has also been thought to originate in the relationship between the director and the actor, which parallels the relationship between a parent and the child. Opening night requires that the director leave the actor to perform alone, creating a sense of abandonment and loss, which activates stage fright (Aaron, 1986). Stage fright is also attributed to unique childhood conflicts that reemerge in individual actors when onstage (Gabbard, 1979, 1983). Nagel (1993) states that stage fright is a complex symptom with several causes: (1) it is the result of desired but limited opportunities to perform; (2) it is due to the fact that performers must face the paradox that they must retain control of memory and technique and at the same time lose artistic control; (3) it is caused by the conflict between a need to show one's artistry and the fear of being rejected by an audience; (4) it is the emergence of unresolved conflicts experienced in earlier meaningful relationships; and (5) it is caused by the presence of exhibitionism, castration fears, and narcissism. Nagel (2004) states that stage fright is caused by "the unconscious conflicts associated with attachment, rejection, competition, envy, loss, and the affects and fantasies they engender" (p. 39). Nagel cites the theories of Bergler, Freundlich, and Kaplan regarding the causes of stage fright, which include theories of voyeurism, narcissism, exhibitionism, and psychological development.

What's the story: alternative theories

> *I was very shy as a young man. And all of a sudden, I'm onstage and I'm expressing myself beautifully, and I'm getting angry and I'm getting loving … and there's no … nobody's gonna hurt you for it, you know? So, I liked doing all these things onstage I couldn't do in life.*
> —Marty

As the field of psychology began to incorporate cognitive, behavioral, end emotional theories to explain human life, theories of the causes of stage fright expanded. Vasey and Dadds (2001) state that empirical work has focused on single factors regarding the causes of performance anxiety. These include (a) genetic factors, (b) neurobiological factors, (c) temperament, (d) emotional regulation skills, (e) cognitive biases and distortions, (f) early control experiences, (g) parental responses, and (h) levels of exposure to feared stimuli. Jangir and Govinda (2018) list the causes of stage fright in speakers as: (a), fear of judgment, (b) previous failures, (c) poor or insufficient preparation, (d) narcissism (i.e., self-absorption), (e) dissatisfaction with abilities, (f) discomfort with body and movement, (g) improper breathing (h) expectation of perfection, (i) fear of being criticized by the audience (j) fear of embarrassment, and (k) fear of forgetting.

Kenny and Ackermann (2007) reviewed a number of theories that have been proposed to explain the cause of stage fright in particular:

- *The Yerkes-Dodson Law* is based on "the most quoted figure in the history of psychology" (p. 4) the Yerkes-Dodson Inverted U Curve, which describes the relationship between anxiety and performance. It illustrates that a moderate amount of arousal (i.e., anxiety) results in the highest level of performance. Impaired performance is caused by arousal states that are too low or too high. While anxiety that is too high impairs performance, extinguishing all anxiety, (even if possible), would also impair performance. Kenny (2011) notes that levels of optimal arousal vary between different musicians based on individual levels of state and trait anxiety, coupled with levels of task mastery (i.e. practice/rehearsal). Identifying optimal arousal levels in individual performers would therefore involve individualized assessment.
- *The Multidimensional Anxiety Theory* states that cognitive components (i.e., negative thoughts) contribute to performance anxiety more than somatic components (i.e., negative physical states). An actor who is self-critical will experience stage fright more intensely than an actor who has physical discomfort only.

- *The Catastrophe Theory* states that performers' worry combined with high physiological distress leads to a catastrophic drop in performance. Fear of not acting well combined with moderate to severe physical symptoms will lead to the interruption and likely failure of the performance.
- *Emotion-Based Theories* involve past experiences which cause the building of an internal "fear structure" (p. 7). This is reactivated in the performance situation either directly, imaginatively, or symbolically. The task of performing or the content of the performance (i.e., the role being played or the story being told) can trigger unresolved past traumas in the actor, exacerbating their stage fright experience.
- *Humanistic Theories* focuses on insight, conscious processes, and human potential. Lloyd-Elliot (1991) offers a model of stage fright based on the concept of the *life-script*, which originates from early childhood experiences and it is supported by internal messages. Stage fright is a consequence of a *defeating life-script* (i.e., "This is bound to be a disaster."). This "failure prophecy" coming from an "inner critic" provides the script—and emotions—for the scared, powerless person the actor becomes before performance.

My nervous system: autonomic responses

> *I get light-headed, I lose the ability to focus on what's around me, and it's like webs of darkness start spinning around in my head and in my eyes, and I lose the ability to function tangibly right then. It's almost like I'm shutting down. So, it's like a death experience.*

—Peter

From a biological lens, stage fright can be seen as caused by the body's reaction to threat. The body's response to fear and anxiety is synonymous (Marshall, 1994). It is regulated by the body's *autonomic nervous system* (ANS), which is comprised of the *sympathetic nervous system* (SNS) and the *parasympathetic nervous system* (PSNS, Wehrenberg, & Prinz, 2007). Traditionally, it was thought that the SNS responds to immediate threat, then *arouses* and mobilizes the body's physical "fight or flight" responses (i.e., increased heart rate, increased metabolism, etc.). Once the immediate threat has passed, the PSNS *inhibits* arousal, manages the body's physical responses, and returns the body to a calm state. These two systems were thought to work together in a "gas and brakes" like manner to respond to danger. The biological aspects of stage fright have been understood in this way. A more recent theory, the *polyvagal theory*, adds a third dimension to the functioning of the ANS (Dana, 2018). Rather than working in a teeter-totter-like fashion, the ANS works in a three-part hierarchical fashion, like a ladder. The *vagus* nerve, which runs from the brain to the body, operates the PSNS in two branches rather than one. The first branch is the lowest rung of the ladder—the *dorsal vagal* branch—and it is responsible for activities like heart regulation, digestion, and breathing. It initiates the freeze response (i.e., "playing dead") to overwhelming threat. The second branch is the highest rung of the ladder—the *ventral vagal* branch—and it is responsible for facial expression, vocalization, regulation of the heart and lungs, the initiation of communication, social engagement, and the expression of emotion. The middle rung of the ladder—the SNS—mobilizes the body to deal with threat. A dorsal vagal (PSNS) response would characterize the type of stage fright that Peter described (i.e., total collapse, "So scared I wanted to pee my pants.") and a ventral vagal (PSNS) response would characterize the exciting and "transcendent" aspects of performance along with the desire to communicate that Katherine describes. The feeling of wanting to fight or flee is an SNS response. Peter's earlier description describes a more intense form of stage fright where *dissociation* occurs. This experience allows a person to detach mentally and emotionally from a threatening experience, even to the point of losing contact with reality. These autonomic responses are encoded into our biology and are the foundation of our survival as a species and our lived experience.

To know somehow you are near: attachment issues

> *Stage fright is fear of a loss of love. That's it. That's my accumulated wisdom of all the actors I've ever talked to and worked with.*
>
> —Kathryn

Some believe the causes of stage fright are rooted in our very earliest relationships. Stage fright is typically understood to occur within a range of severity from mild nerves or even excitement which can improve a performance, to devastating forms that can destroy performance and even careers. Kenny and Holmes (2015) describe this as *stress* on the low end to *stage fright* on the high end. They add to the discussion by noting the depth of performance anxiety found in musicians. They theorize that musicians' performance anxiety has three forms: (1) a focused anxiety with no other emotional disturbance; (2) performance anxiety with other anxieties like generalized anxiety or off-stage social anxiety; and (3) performance anxiety with panic and depression. They believe these subtypes are related to an artist's developmental history as it intersects with talent, technical proficiency, preparedness, performance demands, and so on. The more disturbed the history, the more severe the performance anxiety. They frame an artist's *attachment history* as a way to conceptualize stage fright in a given performer. *Attachment* is a biologically-based motivational system that ensures an infant's survival by (1) maintaining proximity to a caretaker through crying, searching, crawling, and so on.; (2) using the *attachment figure* (i.e., the caregiver) as a means of attaining security; and (3) using the attachment figure as a safe harbor to return to after exploration or experiencing danger. The availability of these ensures that an infant will feel secure and experience a sense of trust that will become ongoing. The types of availability correspond with *attachment patterns*, which Kenny and Holmes believe correspond with the subsequent development of specific forms of performance anxiety.

They describe four types of attachment patterns: (1) se*cure attachment* resulting from responsive caregivers, which develops a sense of security; (2) *avoidant attachment* resulting from unresponsive caregivers, which develops apparent self-sufficiency accompanied with elevated stress hormones; (3) *ambivalent attachment* resulting from inconsistent responses from caregivers, which develops preoccupation with the caregiver, intense distress, and an inability to be consoled during reunification with the caregiver; and (4) *disorganized attachment* resulting from frightening experiences with the caregiver, which develops freezing, confusion, and other difficult behaviors. These early relational dynamics are implicated in the development of later maturing brain structures (i.e. the hippocampus), resulting in unchecked fight or flight responses of the autonomic nervous system. Kenny and Holmes contend that the *attachment system* remains active in adulthood and influences our responses to perceived threats. By addressing a performer's specific symptom presentation (i.e., cognitive, physical, perceptual, etc.) and viewing their unique type of performance anxiety through this lens, a specific treatment plan may be created to ease and eradicate specific symptoms. For example, fear of being a fraud is associated with anxious attachment, difficulties with emotional control may be associated with ambivalent attachment and self-sabotage and immobility may be associated with disorganized attachment. Our intrinsic sense of safety and security, which is influenced by how these were developed during our formative years, can shed light on the feelings of security we bring to the stage. It is natural to think that these formative experiences are so entrenched in our personalities that they may never be changed, but with proper support and guidance, an individual may attain *earned security*, thereby mitigating the effects of these difficult attachment patterns.

Break a leg: past performance traumas

> *Now every time before I go on, I get anxious that something is going to happen. I know I took that fall years ago, but I still get nervous in the dark.*
>
> —Peter

Sometimes we can feel fear while acting even when the actual danger is not onstage, but caused by our own performance histories (Grand, 2008). This can manifest in several ways. First, past performance traumas that have not been resolved may be reactivated in subsequent performances. For example, if an actor forgets their lines during a performance, the fear of forgetting again may resurface and the problem can take on a life of its own. Jimmy recalls forgetting his lines during an important performance.

> After that, my stage fright was worse. The lines! The lines! The more I worried about them the worse it got for me. It was a nightmare! And each performance got worse, until I finally got a handle on it. But it was terrible.

Second, actual physical trauma can resurface as a "body memory" even after the actual injury is healed. Peter recalls taking a tumble from the edge of the stage into the front of the audience area when a light cue was missed.

> I was playing a busker—you know a street performer. I was doing a hand-stand when the lights went out early. I remember hitting the floor, but not feeling anything else except that I *had* to get back onstage to finish my scene. I automatically jumped up, hoisted myself back up to the stage and did—are you ready for this—a cartwheel—to make it look like the fall was part of the show … and I just kept going! Afterwards, the producer found me backstage and literally knelt down before me and kissed my feet!

He found out later he had broken his collarbone.

> Even though ultimately, I was fine, every performance after that gave me terrible stage fright. Even though I knew I was safe I felt that some unforeseen bad thing would happen again. And later, even though my collar bone was OK, sometimes it would ache a bit. It finally went away.

Third, the art of acting itself may exacerbate stage fright when the role is particularly demanding. Seton (2006) has coined the term *post-dramatic stress* to describe intrusive thoughts and avoidance tendencies of acting students exposed to material that required them to enact a violent or difficult scene. Employing "emotional recall" or imagining difficult events can cause an actor to feel apprehension about performing. These examples remind us that stage fright may have ancillary aspects and we can lessen our stage fright's impact by carefully and compassionately taking our histories into consideration.

Losing my mind: negative thoughts

> *I thought to myself, "I'm boring the audience. I'm not doing my job. I'm just a bad actor."*
> —Jake

Some believe that stage fright is caused by negative thoughts. Like Jake, Jimmy tells us that before he was about to go onstage, he would experience general negative and offensive thoughts like "You're not good enough!" and "You're worthless!" Peter had the very same thoughts, but then his thoughts would get more specific. "Your nose is deformed." "Your jaw is too big." "Your voice sounds weird." These attacking thoughts cause anxiety, distress and, damages self-worth. During a stage fright episode, these kinds of thoughts feel so *true*. And our *ego* insists that we be right, so there is no being "talked out" of them. Self-critical thoughts such as these are central to the stage fright experience. As the performance time nears, these negative thoughts seem to accelerate in frequency and intensity. Peter tells us that by curtain time he was "in a frenzy."

Jimmy describes feeling "out of control" due to the impact of these escalating negative thoughts. Elizabeth berated herself mercilessly and was convinced her entire performance was a failure because she paraphrased a line. Her fellow actors didn't even notice, and the positive feedback from the director and the enthusiastic audience applause was hard evidence that her performance was moving and effective. However, she could not control her negative thoughts, and she dwelled on and magnified this one small detail. She could not see the overall positive picture and she suffered from a distressing and distorted version of reality. These types of negative thoughts are probably the most difficult aspects stage fright, and they contribute to the formation of stage fright in return.

Putting it together: because, because, because

I'm not sure why I have it, and I've thought about it a lot. It could be childhood, it could be that what we are doing is so larger than life and it's just plain frightening, and then all the bad stuff happens.

—Alex

Stage fright seems to have several causes. Its presence will be unique to each actor and unique to each performance. Depending on one's theoretical point of view, stage fright can be thought to be caused by unconscious forces, negative beliefs, specific attacking thoughts, specific fears, past relationships, past criticisms, and past performance issues. Some actors may carry unconscious beliefs that will affect them. Others will still be carrying the emotional burden of destructive words or actions from a significant person from the past. Others will be harassed by self-generated negative judgments that fuel their anxiety. Still others might fear the repeat of difficult or injurious past performance experiences. In the next chapter, we will look at some ways stage fright may manifest in class, in rehearsal, and in our performance approaches. But before we move on, please look at the questions below and try to answer them as truthfully as possible. Here we are trying to get to the "root" of your particular stage fright. In many cases the underlying fear is about not feeling *worthy* or *safe*. These primary fears may generate a cascade of symptoms, thoughts, and behaviors. Keep in mind that as you address these questions, reviewing childhood issues and past trauma may be more emotional than naming symptoms. Remember that there are many causes for stage fright. Identifying them in you will help loosen its grip. If you feel negative emotions by reviewing past events, those feelings are understandable reactions to events you likely did not cause. As you answer the questions, tell yourself that you are delving even more deeply into *you*, the way you would delve into a character. As you will see, stage fright and self-worth are intertwined, and the foundation of how we value ourselves rests in the answers to some of these questions.

To the actor:

- What are your responses to the theories about the causes of stage fright?
- Have you been told that actors are neurotic?
- Do you think this is true?
- What have you been told about your fear?
- Do you think your stage fright is rooted in a childhood experience?
- If so, describe the experience.
- Is your stage fright related to loss of approval from a specific person?
- If so, describe that experience.
- Does each performance feel like too much pressure?
- Is your stage fright related to fear of audiences?
- Is your stage fright related to an important person criticizing you?
- If so, describe that experience.
- Do your stage fright experiences feel like you have too little or too much energy?
- When you have stage fright, do you want to run away? Collapse? Feel the fear?
- Do you feel your stage fright is rooted in family relationships?
- Describe how you believe this may be so.
- Did you experience a difficult relationship(s) where you felt criticized or bullied?
- Is that happening now?
- Is there past criticism that still bothers you?
- What was the specific criticism?
- Who said it?
- What was your relationship?
- Can you let go of the effect it had on you?
- Do you feel your stage fright is rooted in a past performance failure or trauma?
- Describe the event in as much detail as possible.
- Have you had a teacher or director ask you to "use" painful feelings?
- Is your stage fright mainly comprised of negative thoughts?
- What is your best explanation of your stage fright?

5 Stage fright off-stage

You're so unprofessional: anxiety behaviors

But I was so nervous, and I just felt so unprofessional and so bad, because I didn't hold up my end.

—Elizabeth

Stage fright has several facets and they can emerge beyond the actual performance situation. As we know, stage fright is a common reaction to performing, and most nervousness we feel indicates that we care about our work and our craft and want to do our best. No one wants to feel anxiety—or stage fright—and we will often adopt strategies to *not* feel it. However, the anxiety may emerge in unwanted behaviors and performance strategies that we often condemn in others and ourselves. Being "professional" is introduced early in actor education and is a highly regarded ethic in the field. Being on time, taking direction, knowing lines, having the skills appropriate for a role and expanding acting abilities to fit character needs are just a few of the behaviors expected in actor training and in the acting world. Mishaps in rehearsal, a diminished level of ability or commitment, and a host of other aspects of fear are usually taken at face value. We may label behaviors like lack of preparation, contrariness, and not knowing lines as not only unprofessional, but lacking in talent. That may be true in some cases, but these behaviors may be mechanisms used to deal with anxiety about acting instead. Conduct that we may chalk up to "unprofessionalism" may in fact be stage fright in disguise. Yet, if the calling and the ability is there, than can we can see how crucial it is to see stage fright in all of its forms so that an actor's true artistry may be revealed. Acknowledging the signs in rehearsal as well as performance can help us in seeing what possible effect stage fright is having off-stage. Have you noticed any of these feelings or behaviors?

- feeling afraid to ask for a letter of recommendation
- not asking for letters of recommendation
- feeling afraid to get up in class
- not getting up in class
- noticed that you can't find the right monologue

- made excuses to not perform
- avoided auditions
- found you are not ready to audition
- not participated in rehearsal fully because you are not feeling well
- chronic forgotten lines
- feeling threatened when a direction is given
- inability to take direction
- argued with directors or scene partners
- not wanting to attend to role preparation
- not attending to the requirements of the role/production
- focusing on performance mistakes
- blaming others
- disparaging yourself
- not appraising performances realistically
- judging others' performances
- sabotaging artistic relationships
- made excuses that were not based in reality
- set yourself up for failure before you tried
- avoided hearing any feedback or criticism
- over prepared to the point you are constrained by information

I start to feel defensive: stage fright maneuvers

> *Stage fright is your defense. And if you go out there, there's always a chance that you're gonna fall on your face… so why go out there?*
>
> —Bill

Maybe you have an upcoming audition or performance. You know you should read the play, learn the monologue, practice the dialect, and get ready. You honestly think the date is much farther off in the future than it actually is, and by the time you realize it, it is too late to prepare adequately and there's not much you can do. It could be that you did not really want this role, or it could be that you used what psychologists call a *defense mechanism* to deal with underlying anxiety about the audition. By missing the audition, you may have felt relief in the short term, but your sense of self weakens, and you feel bad about yourself for missing the opportunity. Defense mechanisms are unconscious thoughts and behaviors that protect our personality and *self-image* from painful feelings including anxiety (McWilliams, 2011). They are learned in childhood and they can be categorized by how early they are formed in our development. Early (i.e., *primitive*) defense mechanisms help young children cope with stress. As we mature, our defense mechanisms evolve along with our ability to handle more complex life issues. Primitive defense mechanisms (i.e., *acting out, denial, dissociation, introjection, projection, reaction formation* and *regression*) are considered to be less mature and while they work well in the short term, they become less effective over time. More mature defense mechanisms (i.e., *displacement, intellectualism, identification, rationalization, repression,* and *undoing*) are considered to be psychologically more advanced. Mature defense mechanisms (i.e., *assertiveness, compensation,* and *sublimation*) are the most constructive, adult, and helpful ways to deal with anxiety (Merino, 2011). These help to ward off anxiety, but unlike the less mature defenses, they do not subvert acting and performance goals. Defense mechanisms are complicated, because they seem so logical and so rational at the time they are used, yet they are unconsciously driven. It is only when you see that your goals are not being met and your artistry is not progressing, that you suspect that something is wrong. Our actors give us insight into the complexity of the fear we are defending against: fear of the unknown, of loss of control, of failure, of success, of scrutiny, of rejection, and so on. Defense mechanisms are not necessarily negative. They exist to protect us. Almost everyone uses defense mechanisms to negotiate stress. But if we can see how they may be operating, we can be sure that we are addressing our stage fright completely and allowing our artistry to flourish. Let's look at the following defense mechanisms:

- *Acting out.* This defense mechanism is at play when we literally portray an inner conflict. It is usually an unconscious behavior that expresses what we are incapable of saying. In the case of stage fright, consciously we wish to perform, but unconsciously our fear may cause behaviors that prevent the performance from happening, like not being prepared for the role, arriving late to rehearsal, causing production mishaps, and so on.
- *Denial.* This defense is the refusal to accept reality and acting as if a painful event or fact did not exist. For example, an actor may not acknowledge that an audition, rehearsal, or performance is looming because to face the fact creates intense anxiety. They may engage in thoughts and behaviors that preempt their attention like watching TV or surfing the internet. An actor managing stage fright may *deny* that certain maladaptive coping mechanisms like overusing alcohol are a problem. They may refuse to accept that certain behaviors (i.e., *avoiding, isolating,* etc.) are manifestations of stage fright or that their stage fright is a real concern that needs attention.
- *Dissociation.* When an individual loses track of time or forgets who they are, they may be *dissociating.* They may be able to continue functioning, but they are lost in another representation of time and space. This is one of the more difficult types of defense mechanisms and actors with a history of severe trauma or abuse may dissociate. It is an automatic response to severe feelings of anxiety which the actor cannot tolerate. An actor with stage fright may "space out" or "numb out" and forget where they are.
- *Introjection.* When an external thought or behavior is threatening, incorporating it into our own set of values gives us a sense of protection and proficiency over the danger they present. For example, if an actor has been criticized, the actor will become critical themselves. Observed behaviors may also be introjected. For example, an actor who copes with stage fright and uses alcohol or drugs to cope may have *introjected* this poor coping skill

from childhood, as they remember family members using alcohol during times of stress. The alcohol fuels depression and self-criticisms increase, creating a downward spiral.

- **Projection.** This defense is a maneuver that places negative aspects (i.e., unacceptable feelings, thoughts, and desires) within the self onto someone outside of the self who does not have that aspect. *Projections* are often used when there is little insight and acceptance of one's' own feelings. Projection often comes in the form of assigning blame to others. An actor with stage fright may project fears of failure onto other actors, directors, teachers, and so on because they cannot acknowledge their own feeling of inadequacy.

- **Reaction Formation.** When we convert a negative or unwanted thought into its opposite, we are using the defense *reaction formation*. An actor may begin to ridicule acting or actors to avoid managing the anxiety that arises when engaging in the craft that they love. This maneuver gives the actor a sense of proficiency over anxiety.

- **Regression.** Reverting to an earlier stage of development, or *regression*, is a way to manage overwhelming fear. In the case of stage fright, an actor may regress to earlier levels of functioning. For example, an actor may adopt childlike attitudes like not understanding, pouting, and so on. An extremely frightened actor may stay in bed and refuse to engage in activities related to getting to class, rehearsal, or performance.

- **Displacement.** Commonly known as "kicking the dog," *displacement* occurs when negative or unacceptable thoughts or feelings are taken out on a non-threatening person or object rather than the true person or object causing the emotional upset. An actor trying to manage ongoing stage fright may dispel converted anxiety by hitting or slamming objects or may divert their anxiety to other "safe" targets.

- **Intellectualism.** When emotions are too painful, we will "over think" or *intellectualize* and place our attention on cognitive aspects rather than accessing emotions. An actor with stage fright may over-focus on theories of acting and details of performance rather than acknowledging the fear and committing to the emotional obligations of the role. "Being in one's head" means that feelings are cut off from expression, including the character's feelings.

- **Identification.** Sometimes if the sense of self is not strong, *identification* with a famous person or entity can enhance the sense of self. An actor may act like a particular star in all of their auditions, never really believing that they possess their own unique talent that is worthy of development and expression. An actor may magnify even brief interactions with well-known individuals or institutions to ward off feared personal failure and to impress others. An actor with stage fright may put more importance on a relationship with a director, outer authority, or association to lessen anxiety and to divert feelings of low self-worth.

- **Rationalization.** When we must accept an occurrence that is painful, we might *rationalize* or invent another point of view to lessen the anxiety it causes. For example, if an actor is having difficulty with a role, they might say that the difficulty is in the direction or with other actors rather than their stage fright.

- **Repression.** Actors may *repress* past performance failures and therefore be unable to learn from the experience. If a difficult event or episode causes anxiety, we may "forget" the experience, so we do not have to feel the discomfort it causes.
- **Undoing.** When behaviors or thoughts are uncomfortable, we may attempt to *undo* or nullify them as if they never occurred. For example, if given a challenging direction, an actor may not apply the direction because doing so will reveal that they didn't do it "right" the first time. By acting as if the direction never happened, the actor can temporarily avoid the discomfort it caused.
- **Assertiveness.** This is a healthy balance between being too passive and not taking one's own needs into account versus being too aggressive and crossing others' boundaries. When feeling vulnerable or frightened, asserting one's needs for clarity, safety, and confidence—from ourselves and others—are clearly known and stated.
- **Compensation.** This defense mechanism has a quality of awareness. It attempts to balance a perceived weakness with an acknowledged strength. An actor might offset the pain of not being cast in a role by focusing on their social skills, becoming a great networker instead. An actor with stage fright might overcompensate for feeling fragile by using other skills that bring praise, but their stage fright remains unchecked.
- **Sublimation.** Painful or unacceptable feelings and impulses may be converted into something more acceptable and useful, which reduces anxiety. An actor with stage fright might use fear to motivate backstage physical exercises, more study of lines, or helping other actors as a way to channel their difficult feelings.

As we stumble along: stage fright styles

> *I knew I was supposed to be ready to understudy, but I just couldn't do the lines. The lines! The lines! I kept putting it off and it made me sick! It would have been easier if I had just learned them, but I just didn't!*
>
> —Jimmy

The behaviors associated with *stage fright styles* are often viewed as unprofessional, but they are ways of managing covert forms of stage fright. In class, rehearsal or in performance, stage fright may manifest in a particular *way of being*. Naistadt (2004) describes three types of stage fright in public speakers and these can be expanded into *styles* of how actors engage in class, in rehearsal, and in managing their acting lives.

- **The avoiding actor.** For example, some actors *avoid* performing. Although talented, their eyes are always downcast in class, they do not volunteer to present, and are almost always the last to perform, if they are there at all. They miss departmental auditions, do not keep up with class work, and do not progress in the rehearsal process. They are rarely solid with lines and are often late which makes others feel frustrated, think that they are unreliable, and concerned that they may need to be replaced. If we asked the avoiding actor about their behaviors, they would passionately profess that acting is their life's calling. The avoiding actor may say, "I'm trying!" with little to show. Actors who avoid the work generally fear *criticism*, which they invite. By sidestepping their responsibilities, they are managing their stage fright. It is easy to feel frustration with this style, but it is this actor that is feeling the most anxiety. By understanding an *avoiding actor*, his teachers and directors can reframe their responses as reactions to fear and come from a compassionate position to help break this artistically destructive cycle.

- **The anticipating actor.** Other types of actors *anticipate* actual and hypothetical mistakes and focus so much on the details of performance, that they have difficulties with finding joy, spontaneity, or flow in their acting. An anticipating actor may become so consumed with different acting techniques and stay so mentally focused on applying them correctly that they are rarely in the moment when acting and cannot respond organically. They will over prepare to ease their chronic worry. Even within a scene they will direct themselves and act a "result." While their teachers and directors appreciate their intellectual grasp of acting theory, when these actors try to foresee and control their performances their creativity and believability are restricted. The anticipating actor wants to "not do it wrong" and letting go of strict controls prevents the very freedom in performance they state they desire. Actors who adopt this style generate frustration as they appear so willing and conscientious about the work. But their fear of looking bad makes directing them or scene partnering with them creatively stifling. These actors must be encouraged to "dare to be bad" to break this style.

- **The procrastinating actor.** Some actors manage their stage fright by putting acting tasks off until tomorrow. This causes an increase in adrenaline, which is needed to assist their nervous system in negotiating the conflict between fight and flight responses. They have less fear of criticism, and less fear of "doing it wrong," but they put off preparing their performances to manage their anxiety. A procrastinating actor may have several key speeches to research, memorize, and work through for an acting class. They may appear productive by engaging in activities like creating worksheets for the research and highlighting their script. As time passes these actors cannot delve into the work. Peter described applying this style. "I just couldn't get into the work. I couldn't even explain why or come up with an excuse if I had to." These actors can be helped by knowing that sometimes just by starting the effort without knowing the outcome is more productive that waiting for every detail to be preplanned.

- **The unprepared actor.** Some actors unconsciously feel that challenging work and preparation means that there is a chance they will be exposed as less talented if they fail. They will not employ these and rely on "winging it." Because this is usually an unconscious maneuver, they generally don't report any anxiety and seem easy-going and good-natured. If they get through a performance well, they feel a sense of proficiency and conclude that their natural abilities are intact. If the performance was lacking, they can then conclude that lack of preparation rather than lack of skill or talent was the cause of the failure, rather than fear. These actors may receive accolades for their quick thinking—and may wish to cultivate this reaction in others—but their artistic development is stalled as they do not incorporate technique or craft. These actors can be helped by being urged to see the value in the process rather than the result of work, which will lessen their fear.

- **The self-sabotaging actor.** When stage fright is present, some actors may engage in *self-sabotaging* behaviors, which disrupt long-term goals of performing and performing well. A self-sabotaging actor might self-medicate with drugs or alcohol, overeat, initiate conflicts with others in rehearsal or become addicted to activities or substances that divert their attention away from their craft. These behaviors bring short term relief from anxiety but create long-term obstacles to moving ahead. Disrupted relationships, less than optimal health, and missed opportunities are the outcomes of self-destructive behaviors. These actors may be adamant that they wish to work, but their outside difficulties derail their progress. This often causes lower self-esteem and increased anxiety in the actor, which fuels the need to continue or even heighten these behaviors. These actors are helped by encouraging them to not see acting as separate from their life, but that their healthy life choices only strengthen their acting.

- **The critical actor.** Sometimes stage fright is managed by an overly *critical* style of being that protects an actor from feelings of vulnerability. The critical actor holds almost everyone in disdain: teachers, directors, other actors, and cast mates. They are often deeply knowledgeable, and others may fall into the trap of wanting to please them and manage their scrutiny, even teachers and directors. They often initially impress others with their knowledge, but their ongoing critiques keep them safe from letting go emotionally and appearing foolish. It is a form of the defense mechanism *intellectualism*, but it becomes such a pervasive part of the actor's way of being that it influences almost all acting activities. These actors can be helped by redirecting their focus to their inner work as actors and stopping the need to direct others.

- **The unknowing actor.** Actors who adopt a chronic sense of "trying hard" but never "getting it" can be a using a style of *unknowing* to manage the fear associated with coming in contact with the emotional depth and vulnerability needed as an actor. The unknowing actor has difficulty internalizing direction, and difficulty building to the next step of characterization, yet they are consistently pleasant and responsive. There is a sense that they are "playing" at not understanding, and it feels like they are stalling the momentum of the work. These actors can be helped by appealing to their talent and holding them accountable to higher standards.

- *The negotiating actor.* At times, some actors are so fearful in class or rehearsal that any piece of added information or direction feels like a threat. Because they have difficulty accepting novel methods or new ideas from others, they must negotiate with the teacher or director before they will accept and follow a direction or internalize and apply a new technique. This negotiation will come in the form of questions, reasons why they are unable to understand or apply the direction or technique, or seeming contradictions from other teachers or theories. Masked in the guise of discussion, the actor is unwilling to collaborate due to the shame they feel for not already possessing the information. These actors can be helped by feeling trusted by their teacher or director, which help them take in and incorporate added information to deepen their artistry.
- *The inhibited actor.* Some actors are so bound with anxiety and worry that they become restricted in every way. They have difficulty expressing themselves emotionally and physically and find it difficult to respond to scene partners or complete acting objectives. The inhibition will be apparent in their acting, but it will also physically manifest in poor posture, a faint voice, uncoordinated breathing, and difficulty moving with ease onstage. They will appear shy and withdrawn. These actors may be helped by feeling encouraged by their teacher and director and being supported to express themselves, even in small non-acting ways, like expressing their opinion, assisting with props, being made responsible for a production issue, and so on.
- *The dreaming actor.* Acting has the potential for rich rewards. Some actors may *fantasize* about imagined outward career success to avert the focus needed to prepare for a role. Some actors have not yet built their true self confidence. They may focus on the future, dreaming of red carpets and awards, but avoiding the challenging work needed learn a craft and gain experience. These actors may frequently be focused on going to the next noteworthy class, school, or company, with less attention paid to the current role or production. These actors can be helped by holding them accountable to the work at hand and completing it to fulfill today's obligations.
- *The isolating actor.* Actors may feel shame regarding stage fright and may use *isolation* to avoid acting. They love acting and desperately wish to perform, but they are incapable of getting too close to any audition or performance where that may become a reality. They may appear as stage managers or crew members so they can be near acting, but they have not yet developed the confidence to try. In class, they may be withdrawn, yet watchful. These actors can be encouraged by being accepted and validated for their love of acting to help them to feel part of the world.

Nothing but a fraud: stage fright thoughts

> *Stage fright wants you to think about your inadequacies, and wants you to be filled with self-doubt, and wants you to fail. "You're not good enough to do this. You're a failure."*
>
> —Jake

We have looked at the fact of the *presence* negative thoughts in stage fright. A cognitive orientation can shed light on the origin (i.e., *core beliefs*) and specifics (i.e. *cognitive distortions*) of our negative thought processes (Beck, 1995). Beck contends that these negative thoughts appear in specific and consistent *forms*. When stage fright is active, these turn our attention from positive and productive outlooks to negative, harmful, and destructive biases. These thoughts begin to emerge when we are stressed, when we feel vulnerable, or when we feel exposed. These cognitive distortions are *mistakes* in thinking and can usually be dismantled by *testing* their content. Review the types of cognitive distortions below:

- *All or nothing thinking.* This mistake occurs when a situation is viewed in only two categories: good or bad. There is no "in between" or "gray" in this thought process. An actor may characterize a performance as a disaster if only a minor mistake—like dropping a line—is made. Or if an audition went badly, the actor will conclude that they are not talented at all (i.e., "I'm a total failure.").
- *Catastrophizing.* When the future outcome is predicted negatively without factoring in any other alternatives, this is an error. There is no taking "one step at a time." There is the conviction that the audition will go badly, that the performance will be terrible or that there will never be another role (i.e., "I won't be able to do any of it right.").
- *Comparing.* Judging oneself against others and assuming that they are automatically more competent, more talented, and more effective is also an error. This happens frequently in class, in auditions, and in rehearsals. Whether it be surface qualities like looks, more internal abilities like talent, or simply that another is more competent or more valuable, comparing ourselves to others will almost always activate unnecessary anxiety (i.e., "They are so much better.").
- *Discounting.* This error in thinking occurs when positive experiences and abilities do not register as meaningful or do not "count" at all. When we devalue what is good, we prevent ourselves from gaining anything worthwhile from the experience. From negating other actors to not being able to accept compliments, this error in thinking keeps our negative state intact (i.e., "I'm not a good actor. It just comes easy to me. I'm lucky.").
- *Emotional reasoning.* Emotions are powerful influences on how we navigate the world. However, when we place more importance on what we feel is true more than the facts, we are not taking all of reality into account. This mistake in thinking occurs when actors with stage fright report that they feel like a fraud (i.e., "I know I got cast, but I still feel like a failure.").
- *Labeling.* Another mistake in thinking occurs when we put a fixed label on ourselves or others without regard to evidence to the contrary. Negative

labeling of the self is almost always counter-productive. It may be a maneuver to gain encouragement from others, but the content of the thought is rarely if ever useful (i.e., "I'm a fake.").

- *Magnifying/minimizing.* When we take a specific event and either blow it out of proportion or minimize its importance we are not thinking in a reality-based, balanced way. We apply this mistake to avoid registering the true impact of an event. However, it directs us to make future mistakes and view things unclearly. (i.e., "Not getting a direction proves I'm a terrible actor." / "Not knowing my lines is no big deal.").
- *Filtering.* Seeing the "big picture" gives us direction and a way to navigate our experiences. When we pay attention to one small detail as evidence for the negative rather than seeing the whole and possibly positive scenario, we create anxiety and lose our sense of purpose in a role (i.e., "The one note means I'm a bad actor.").
- *Mind reading.* Believing you know what others are thinking without evidence is a common, but incorrect way of dealing with others. We mentally "jump to conclusions" about what others think without acknowledging that they may be thinking something completely different than what we assume (i.e., "I know the director hates me.").
- *Overgeneralization.* Making overly broad and general negative conclusions about a situation without considering all of the facts is another misinterpretation of reality (i.e., "Because that scene was bad, I must be a terrible actor.").
- *Personalization.* This error occurs when you believe that others are behaving negatively toward you because of you, without consideration of other evidence to the contrary. A director, teacher, or scene partner may be having their own inner thoughts, difficulties, or preoccupations. Assuming that their behavior is personal is a common but unnecessary error (i.e., "The producer didn't look at me because I'm a weak actor.").
- *Should-statements.* The word "should" is absolute and implies a drive toward perfection, which can never be attained. A fixed idea of how events *should* go, or people *should* behave negates the human factor, and creates anxiety (i.e., "I should always be perfect.").
- *Tunnel vision.* When we see only the negative aspects of a situation and do not see anything neutral or positive, we are making this mistake (i.e., "I can't do anything right."). An actor with stage fright will focus on perceived negative aspects of a performance like a paraphrased passage and will not see any neutral or positive aspects, like the fact that the audience didn't notice, or that the paraphrase saved the scene.

Do you recognize any of these *cognitive mistakes*? They are almost—if not always—present in a stage fright episode, so it is crucial that they be addressed. Beck (1995) tells us that they can be *challenged* by asking: (1) is the statement true?; (2) is there evidence to support the statement?; (3) what is the specific evidence that supports this idea?; (4) is there an alternative explanation?; (5) what is the worst that can happen if this statement were true?; (6) what is the effect of believing the negative thought?; (7) what if you thought differently?; (8) what should you do about it?; and (9) what would you tell a good friend if they were in the same situation and having the same thought? When you challenge these negative beliefs in this way, you will likely have emotional responses to them. It is crucial that you feel the emotions that come up as each belief is challenged. That the negativity feels true, right, and correct is *why* it stays intact. Allowing yourself to feel the emotional responses to these challenges will begin to dismantle the negative thoughts that contribute to stage fright.

But it sure isn't pretty: negative core beliefs

I just froze! I thought I was the worst actress in the world! But then I got off-stage and I was OK, but I had to go through the same thing all over again. And that went on for, well, that entire run of that show. Me, blaming myself.

—Elizabeth

There errors in thinking are usually not grounded in truth and are generated from our *core beliefs* about ourselves. These core—or *central*—beliefs feel like absolute truths and influence how we experience life and function in the world. Core beliefs are the content of cognitive structures in the mind called *schemas*. They function as guiding principles out of which our emotions, thoughts, and behaviors flow. They develop in reaction to patterns of interactions with significant others or to noteworthy events that form the conclusions about the self. An individual's core beliefs are unique to them and their individual history. Core beliefs can be positive or negative. *Positive core beliefs* guide us to negotiate the difficulties of life, survive, and even thrive in our relationships and professions. *Negative core beliefs* are usually global, absolute, and general. They can have an effect on our entire life, can color our artistic and professional endeavors, or may emerge abruptly during a stage fright episode. Their content will determine the types of distressing distortions that are experienced in a stage fright episode. Negative core beliefs are not necessarily the truth. They can be strongly felt and believed. But, like with cognitive distortions, their "reality" can be tested and refuted. Beck (1995) states that negative core beliefs fall into two broad categories: (1) beliefs associated with *helplessness* and (2) beliefs associated with *unlovability*. Although stage fright may be considered a specific fear of a specific event, a predisposition of negativity toward the self is common in the stage fright experience. However, positive core beliefs can inoculate us against the negative thought processes and feelings of stage fright by positioning our sense of self to deal productively with threat. Replacing unloveable core beliefs with *loveable core beliefs* and helpless core beliefs with *autonomous core beliefs* is a necessary step in dismantling stage fright. Even if the exercise feels foolish and the new beliefs feel untrue and counterintuitive, doing so will help you to gain power over this particularly distressing aspect of stage fright. Below, see if any of the *negative, unloveable,* or *helpless* core beliefs apply to you. If so, consider holding an alternative *positive*, *loveable*, or *autonomous belief*. Identifying your core beliefs related to acting and stage fright may take some time, or they may be evident to you now. Take some time to consider if negative core beliefs are part of the stage fright experience for you.

Negative core beliefs include:

- "I'm a fraud."
- "I can't function."
- "I'm not good enough."
- "Others are better than me."
- "I can't achieve what I want."

Positive core beliefs include:

- "I can do most things competently."
- "I am substantially in control."
- "I will land on my feet."
- "I am worthwhile."
- "I am capable."

Unloveable core beliefs:

- "I am unloveable."
- "I am unlikeable."
- "I am undesirable."
- "I am unattractive."
- "I am unwanted."
- "I am uncared for."
- "I am bad."
- "I am unworthy."
- "I am bound to be rejected."
- "I am bound to be alone."
- "I am different."
- "I am unloved and unloveable."

Loveable core beliefs:

- "I have likeable qualities."
- "I am appreciated."
- "I am unique and interesting."
- "I am valuable."
- "I care for myself."

- "I am rightfully here."
- "I am worthy."
- "I have my own self, and my tribe."
- "I am with others and with myself."
- "I am my own self."
- "I am valuable."

Helpless core beliefs:

- "I am helpless."
- "I am powerless."
- "I am out of control."
- "I am weak."
- "I am vulnerable."
- "I am trapped."
- "I am inadequate."
- "I am ineffective."
- "I am incompetent."
- "I am a failure."
- "I am defective."
- "I am not good enough."

Autonomous core beliefs:

- "I am able to handle things."
- "I have control."
- "I am able to focus my energies."
- "I am capable."
- "I can rely on my inner strength."
- "I am free and unrestricted."
- "I am enough."
- "I am effective."
- "I am skilled and capable."
- "I am able to overcome setbacks."
- "I am perfect as I am."
- "I am worthy as I am."

Putting it together: careful the things you say

> *Stage Fright really wants you to fail. And so, the battle with Stage Fright is to tell the beast that it's not going to win. And you must battle that beast and say, "I'm better than you. I'm better than all those voices who tell me to fail. I can do this."*
>
> —Jake

Stage fright is painful. One of its core aspects are negative thoughts and beliefs about the self. It is natural to employ a defense mechanism or a style of life to avoid facing these distressing notions. Remember that defenses and styles are used to avoid pain. However, negative thoughts and beliefs are rarely constructive, rarely augment our performance abilities, and rarely contribute to our growth. They are almost always destructive, inhibiting, and lessen or even destroy our goals and the expression of our talent and artistry. The types of negative thoughts and beliefs will be unique to each individual actor with stage fright. Some actors may be guided by negative core beliefs that will affect their performances. Others will be tormented by self-generated negative thoughts about themselves and their talent. In the next chapter, we will hear from eight professional actors who will reveal their experiences of stage fright. All of them experienced negative thoughts and beliefs about themselves. But before we move on, look at the questions below and try to answer them as truthfully as possible. Again, your answers are not going to be evaluated. They are intended to reveal what negative thoughts and beliefs are driving your stage fright, your use of defenses, and your adoption of rehearsal styles that are holding you back.

To the actor:

- Have you ever felt anxious in class or in rehearsal?
- What triggered that feeling?
- Have you ever been labeled "unprofessional"?
- What behaviors have you observed in yourself that generate this label (not memorizing lines, not taking direction, not doing work, etc.)?
- Have you become ill to avoid performing?
- Have you questioned your talent?
- Have you had difficulty preparing? (memorizing lines, choosing the "right" monologue etc.)?
- Have you made excuses to not perform?
- Have you had a pattern of conflicts with directors?
- What is the nature of the conflict(s)?
- Have you had a pattern of conflicts with scene partners?
- What is the nature of the conflict(s)?
- Do you sometimes shut down?
- What discomfort do you need to avoid?
- Is there another underlying issue that you know of that could account for these behaviors besides stage fright?
    - a *diagnosis of a learning issue* (i.e., information processing disorder, ADD, dyslexia, etc.)
    - a *diagnosis of a mood or other disorder* (i.e., depression, anxiety, bipolar disorder, a personality disorder, etc.)
    - a *substance abuse issue* (i.e., alcohol use/abuse, stimulant use/abuse, prescription drug use/abuse, nonprescription drugs, etc.)

- a *lifestyle issue* (i.e., not eating or sleeping properly, financial issues, living situation issues)
- a *relationship issue* (i.e., conflicts with friends or family or verbal abuse) that is causing distress?

- Do you know that you are talented but feel blocked?
- Do you focus on mistakes?
- Is it difficult to take feedback or criticism?
- Do any of the *defense mechanisms* ring true to you?
- Which ones? Describe a time when you used them.
- Do any of the *stage fright styles* ring true to you?
- Which ones? Describe a time when you used them.
- Do any of the *mistakes of thinking* apply to you?
- Which ones? Describe a time when you used them.
- Can you identify a *negative core belief* related to your acting or stage fright?
- What is it?
- Is it an *unlikable* or *helpless* core belief?
- Will you challenge your *mistakes of thinking* and core beliefs?
- Will you accept that *mistakes of thinking* can be corrected?
- Will you accept that issues contributing to your stage fright can be resolved?

6   The stage fright experience

Delving into stage fright: the interviews

The actors in this chapter—Alex, Bill, Elizabeth, Jake, Jimmy, Katherine, Marty, and Peter—generously offered their time to discuss this painful event. Their voices have been heard throughout, and here are their accounts of their experience of stage fright. All have had significant experience working as actors in the professional theater. All have played what would be considered the "great" roles, ranging from parts in plays written by Shakespeare and Moliere to Ibsen, Shaw, Odets, Williams, Miller, Mamet, and more. Their experience includes work in Equity Waiver theater, Equity theater, regional theater, Broadway, and international theater. The oldest actor aged 88, completed the run of a professional play only a few months before the interview. Their experience also included roles in musicals, TV, film, radio, industrials, voiceovers, and webisodes.

The interviews focused on their stage fright experience when performing in the live theater. The actors were asked to describe—in as much detail as possible—how stage fright felt emotionally, physically, and how it impacted their acting. The central experience—stage fright—was framed between the actors' *draw to acting and the acting experience* and *the nature of stage fright* in their lives. This organization was intended to reflect how stage fright was positioned in the literature and to reveal how stage fright exists within the context of acting.

The material is presented here in two parts. The first part begins with an introduction in which each actor is briefly described. This is followed by the *themes* that emerged from each interview. The themes are titled, are described, and under each identified theme, verbatim material from the interview that is the basis for the theme is provided. The inclusion of this material allows the reader to get a sense of the depth, the richness, and the texture of the experience and provides a form of validation of the themes. Following the individual themes is an *essential description* of stage fright for each actor. The description mirrors the general composition of the interview and attempts to present a description for each actor that could come as close as possible to how they experience stage fright. Therefore, it is written in the first person, in the form of a monologue.

Interview with Alex: introduction

These people are going to find out that I'm a phony. They're gonna find out that I have no idea what I'm doing, that I ... that I'm a fake.

Alex is a 48-year-old actor. She has been enacting professionally in the theater since the age of seven. She studied acting in New York City, London, and at several major repertory theater companies. She names Uta Hagen, Anne Bogart, Sanford Meisner, Alec Guinness, and others as primary teachers. She has performed in regional theater, off-Broadway, and on Broadway. She also works in film and on TV in award-winning guest starring, starring, and series regular roles. In addition, she worked as a cabaret singer, as a theater director, and as a teacher of physical acting. Alex has experienced stage fright all of her life. It remains "debilitating" for her. During the interview, Alex began to have the sensation that her ears were starting to close up and her breath was becoming shorter. She attributed this to discussing her stage fright. She stated that in her experience, most actors do not discuss stage fright. She also said that when actors do say they have stage fright, they are often referring to "normal nerves." Most actors, she believes, do not discuss the presence of more serious forms of stage fright. She stated that she has never discussed it with anyone because, "Nobody's ever asked me."

Below are the themes that emerged from Alex's interview. An essential description of her stage fright, monologue style, will follow.

- expression
- freedom
- communication
- expansion
- inherence
- service
- the color red
- physical attack
- inhibition
- shame
- fraudulence
- the unexpected
- permanence
- courage
- necessity
- familiarity
- responsibility
- coping
- duality

Interview with Alex: themes

Expression. Alex acts because she wants to make known the many "voices" (i.e., characters) inside of her. Alex described a very powerful performing experience that occurred when she was approximately six years old. She had decided to record the audio portion of the film, *The Wizard of Oz* on cassette tapes so she could listen to and memorize the movie script and the songs so she would not have to worry about when it would be broadcast on TV "cause I could imagine the movie, you know, in my head." At the time, her father was the musical director of a well-known musical being rehearsed in the city where she lived. She told her father that she could perform the entire movie. He assembled his cast to view her performance during a lunch break.

Surrounded by legends in the theater, Alex stood on a rehearsal table, and performed all the parts and sang the songs from the film, from memory. She felt great joy and relief expressing her inner experience of the movie. This event made her certain that she was going to be an actor.

> At that moment, as I was standing onstage, I knew I had to do this for the rest of my life … that there were a whole bunch of people inside me, and if I didn't get them out, I would implode.

Freedom. This important experience was freeing for Alex. It changed her experience of being in the world. The relief she felt expanded into a feeling of being liberated from the heaviness she felt.

> Because it was the first time in my life that I felt free, and I felt lifted, and I felt light. I spent a lot of times just, even that young, feeling very heavy.

For Alex, the sense of freedom had a quality of release. Speaking text that contained content and meaning that she could relate to contributed to this quality.

> It, for me, when I was young, it was a release. It felt like a breath. I had felt like for most of my young life, I was inhaling, and it was the first time I think I felt like I exhaled. Like something came out of me. It didn't feel like a purge. It felt like a release. Literally as if all of the words that I wanted to say that were stuck in my belly finally went *(exhales)* and came out.

> And I also feel like when I got older, into my teens, that there were a whole bunch of writers … that when I read them, I went, "ooh that … I feel like that! Oh, that's how I feel!" So, if I spoke them, there was a sense of freedom.

> And so, I would gravitate toward these people and find these pieces of text and go, "Oh, I can say this!" And as I exhale, I'm breathing. I'm releasing. I'm changing.

Communication. For Alex, acting as a means of self-expression has extended to expressing something to and then receiving something back from the audience. She feels this progression has made her less selfish and more expansive as a person. When she expresses herself to and receives responses from an audience, a "breakthrough" may occur. Alex experiences this exchange as a physical "shattering," which opens her up and lowers her defenses so that she can receive deeper responses from audiences and give more of herself emotionally and psychologically back to them. Experiences in front of audiences continue to fulfill her artistically as well as expand her as a person.

> Now that I'm older, now I feel like when I exhale, they exhale. And so now, I'm receiving them more. When I was younger … it was very selfish for me. It was really about, "I need to get this to you." And now I feel like I need to get this to you so that I can get what you have, because that fills me up.

> I believe that we have moments. You know when people talk about, like, breaking down the wall or having a breakthrough? I understand that, but for me, it's about shattering. When you "shatter." Shatterings come in all different kinds of sizes. All different sizes. There can be a large shattering, or there can be millions of small shatterings, and these shatterings happen in your vessel. In your body. And instead of it being like a glass that's broken on the floor and that kind of disperses like that, that you have to clean up and throw away, when your vessel, in my opinion, when your vessel shatters, you expand. So, you receive more information. You receive more gifts from people. And you keep shattering throughout your life, as long as you allow it to happen.

Expansion. For Alex, the consequence of communication is expanding her viewpoints as a person.

> L: You keep expanding.
> A: That's right! And you keep receiving more gifts and those gifts get bigger. So, for me now, it's about when I get up onstage, or when I'm on set, I do my work in order to shatter. So that a release happens, and I exhale, and then, either from my scene partner if I'm on set or from a live audience when I'm onstage, when they exhale, I receive them. So, I hopefully expand. It doesn't always work, but that's my goal, and why I can't stop doing it.

Inherence. Alex feels that her ability and desire to perform are inherent. She feels that performing is something that she was born to do. She also credits her father with supporting her, as he was also in the profession.

> This thing that happened to me because of my father's belief in my ability to communicate changed my life. I was born to it. I still have those cassettes, by the way.

Service. Alex believes that the purpose of acting is to create a place where people can come together to connect, to ignite their imaginations, to entertain what is possible, to feel differently, and to "shatter" or expand as people. She believes that these kinds of experiences are required for healthy human existence, as they meet a universal need for community.

> As human beings need a place to go where we can commune ... even if it's in a movie theater ... where we can all go off into imagination land, because anything is possible. All of our dreams come true. Even in things that shatter us.

> People on the planet will pay money in order to have their lives changed ... they'll say, "I will pay for this ticket, because I wanna feel differently. Not better or worse. I wanna feel different when I leave."

> So, there's a great need for us as human beings to commune with each other. We don't have to fight. Doesn't matter what political party you belong to. It doesn't matter what religious belief you have. What's the color of your skin, the sexual orientation, nobody cares. We're all there together to be changed by this piece of art that's in front of us. And I think that's required for the human existence.

The color red. When asked if stage fright were a color, Alex responded that it is "hot red." She associated that color with "horror."

> There's some kind of terror—horror, not terror—horror.

When reflecting on the color of her stage fright—red—Alex stated that that she has the sensation that stage fright is running after her and trying to "get" her. This feeling shifted into an image of a Devil face, chasing her.

> A: I feel like it's trying to get me. I feel like it's chasing me. Yes! I think that's right! I feel like it's running to get me. And that it's bad. It's a bad ... this just popped into my head and now I don't remember what movie it's from, but one ... some actor played the Devil, and he's got this big, long moustache on, and he's got one of those really fake red, like, cowl things with little horns on it, but he's got these really evil eyes, and that's what I think he looks like.
> L: Like the Devil?
> A: Yep! And he's running toward me!
> L: What does he want from you?
> A: I don't know. I don't know. I don't know.

Physical attack. Alex states that physical symptoms of stage fright arose in her teens and worsened as she moved into her 20s. These included difficulty breathing, a racing heart, a sensation as if she were running, and the impulse to not speak.

I would get physically sick to my stomach every opening night. And then my stage fright happened right before the first entrance I had to make. After that, I was fine. But the very first entrance, I would go into my pause—and now this is in my teens—I would have a shortness of breath. My heart would race. And I was still in the pause, but it felt like I was running for my life. And if someone would come up to me and go, "A., you … ." I could not answer them. I would not answer them. Not I could not. I would not answer them.

Later in her career, Alex began to experience an upset stomach.

And by this time, now, there's a stomach thing added to it, where it kind of feels like my stomach is like a clothes dryer!

Alex experiences extreme physical reactivity when having a stage fright episode before an entrance.

It's off the charts. So, I'm standing backstage and … the orchestra's going up and I go into my pause, but I feel like I'm running really fast. I have a shortness of breath. My stomach is a clothes dryer and it's tumbling really fast. So, I'm back there and I'm in my pause, and the guy who's playing C … had never seen me backstage. I try to hide myself backstage, so people don't see me, so they don't get worried, and they don't worry about me, 'cause I don't … I know I'll make my entrance. I always do. But I don't wanna worry any of the actors, like, "Why is A … What's happening?" So, I was off in a corner, but so I could still see the conductor's baton, so I knew when my entrance was. M., the guy who played C., found me for some unknown reason and came up to me and touched me. Now we have, you know, head mikes on that are on, 'cause we have an entrance in two minutes. So opening night, off-Broadway, New York City, right about three, maybe five seconds before we're about to go on, before all of this disappears for some unknown reason, I go, *(expletive)*! Simply because someone touched me. He just touched the back of my shoulder and this text flew out of me.

Inhibition. Alex describes stage fright as being in a state of inhibition and immobility called a "pause." She describes it as "literal blankness."

Where it's not a freeze, it's really a pause. Where like, you know you see people at a bus stop and they're waiting for a bus? And they're just in a pause. They're not, like, frozen stiff like they can't move. They're just in a pause. And that's what would happen to me. Right before I would go onstage, I would pause. For a really long time. I would never miss my cue, but I would come out seconds before I was supposed to. It felt like nothing. It felt like I was in a closet and someone had closed the door and turned off the light. Not in a scary way, just nothing. Blankness. Literal blankness.

So, there was no, like, shaking or sweats or even fear attached to it. I just paused. Like ... that's it.

Shame. Reflecting on the meaning of the "hot red terror," Alex stated that she feared being ashamed, of "being found out for *me*."

Fraudulence. In addition, Alex's stage fright contributed to a fear that she would be found out to be a fake and that she was misrepresenting herself. She experienced the audience as powerful and being able to define her to herself.

These people are going to find out that I'm a phony. They're gonna find out that I have no idea what I'm doing, that I'm a fake, that I'm a charlatan, that I'm Houdini. And that really all of my stuff is smoke and mirrors.

As she described this experience, Alex began to have physical reactions during the interview.

Something is happening to me, like my ears are starting to close up a little bit. Wow. This is really weird. Um ... that there's a feeling of, I'm gonna be found out.

The unexpected. Alex described backstage experiences in which even though she knows she will experience stage fright and that the symptoms will ultimately arrive, when stage fright does occur, she experiences it as a surprise. It always happens yet it is always unexpected.

And I got my first off-Broadway show. Now, I had done this show for about a year and a half, so I knew the show like the back of my hand by the time I got to New York. So, we're backstage and I knew it was coming, and it was opening night, it was New York City, famous people. Even though I know it's coming, and I know it's going to happen, it's always a surprise when it happens.

Permanence. Alex states that her stage fright has existed since she was a small child and that it happens in front of any audience. Who is present, the venue, or the size of the audience makes no difference in triggering her stage fright?

Any time there's an audience. Anything. Anything ... there could be a room full of five people, the pause is still there. Same pause. Same pause.

Alex feels that her stage fright is permanent and there is no remedy for it. She has tried to cure it medically, psychologically, and spiritually. Failed efforts contribute to a sense of resignation.

And I've tried everything. Everything. Psychoanalysis. The pin thing ... where they stick pins in you ... hypnosis. Drugs. Herbal therapy. Uh ...

uh … chanting. I've tried everything. Nothing works. Nothing works. Nothing. It doesn't even stop for a short period of time. Nothing works.

Courage. As Alex reflected on stage fright and how it affects her physically and emotionally, she considered the idea that going onstage was an act of courage and heroism. She wondered whether her going onstage was a way to elicit admiration from the audience for being brave.

A: You know what? I wonder if part of it, if the reason I go out there, is so that people will think I'm a big hero.
L: Because of the fear?
A: I think maybe. Even though nobody knows, maybe there's something in me that when I get out there, I think to myself, "That was pretty heroic."
L: Wow.
A: I've never thought of that before. Because if everybody with stage fright didn't go out onstage, nobody would be out onstage.
L: Right.
A: So how do we get past it? I think that we need … I need to congratulate myself for something. So when I make it out onstage, I go, "Huh. Nice work. Good for me."

Necessity. Alex enthusiastically agreed to participate in the interview. She described her stage fright as long-standing and "disabling," and hoped to gain some insight into the experience. In the interview, she states that she now believes she actually needs stage fright to go onstage. It has become a pattern and is now a part of engaging in the ritual of acting. As she spoke during the interview, she revealed that she does not think she can perform without it. She also says, "stage fright is not hurting anything," as if she held compassion for what she earlier described as a "bad" Devil.

A: No, but I'll tell you something. If it ever went away, I don't know that I would go onstage.
L: Because?
A: I have a real … thing about, um, patterns. Once I find a route, that's the way I go. If something were to change right before I went onstage, something inside my brain would shift.

Familiarity. Alex feels that her stage fright has an element of familiarity that accompanies the feeling of it being necessary for her to perform.

L: So, it feels familiar?
A: That's right. It's part of the process. 'Cause that's what I do. So, if that stage fright goes away, I don't think I'd make it. I really don't.
L: Really?

A: I don't think so.

L: In spite of how uncomfortable it is.

A: Yes *(whispers)*. That's weird.

A: It feels ritualistic now … but it feels ritualistic. It feels like a ritual. Yeah. I mean, I don't like it, so I guess there is a part of me that wishes it would go away. And I'm almost 50 now, so you would think, "All right. Come on." But at the same time, it's not really hurting anything, and it's not really hurting anybody else. And it's for a very short period of time. It's not, like, doesn't last for an hour. It's, you know, clomp, clomp, clomp … you know, like a couple of minutes of horror.

Responsibility. Alex strongly believes in her responsibilities to her fellow actors and to the audience. This feeling allows her to put their needs before her own so that she can fulfill her duty onstage.

> I'm a firm believer that I have, and I learned this from my father, I have a responsibility to the people who came to see either me or the world that all of the ensemble is creating. And I have a duty. And no matter how frightened I am, no matter what's going on with me, I have to go out there.

Coping. Alex copes with stage fright by remembering her sense of responsibility as a performer and by "going" onstage, which she experiences as "launching." She moves forward.

A: You know, it's interesting. When we were talking about, you know, responsibility?

L: So, you cope with it by …

A: By going.

L: By going.

A: By going. I was gonna say, I talk to myself, but that's not true. I—I'm present, and I know what's going on, and I know there's a … there's like a countdown, like, 5, 4 … like a rocket launching. And, like a rocket, I go. I just go out of the pause and I go forward.

Duality. When asked to sum up what stage fright meant to her, Alex initially described her stage fright in terms of a visual image of a supernova about to explode. Stage fright is the intermediate place before the moment when something awful will happen, yet this event produces something wonderful.

A: The essence of it feels like, you know when a star is just getting ready to explode and it puffs up and it's really bright? That's what it looks like. That's the essence of it. Right before the supernova. But seconds before. Like, you know it's going to break. You know something awful is going to happen. But at the same time, you also know there's gonna be a rebirth. So there's this weird dichotomy that I live in for this moment in time.

L: Is the rebirth those positive things you were saying about acting?

A: Yeah. So you know, I'm standing there in my pause and going, "This is gonna be great! I am so frightened right now. I do not want to move. But it's gonna be fantastic! But I don't want to move!" Well I know it's gonna be fantastic … That's bizarre. But it's never gotten in my way. It's never prevented me from performing. You know what I mean?

Essential description of stage fright: Alex

When I was a child, I knew inherently that I was to act. It allows all of the people inside of me to come out. But before I knew this, I felt as if I was always holding my breath. When I finally knew this, as a young child, I felt as if I could finally exhale. At last, I could express all that I felt and innately knew! What I knew was true! As an actor, by speaking text and sharing with others, we commune! We grow. We give and receive gifts! We "shatter!" When we shatter, we physically break apart, we take in something new, it becomes part of us, and we expand as humans. The anticipation of this is like considering the awe and beauty of the birth of a supernova. Yes! It happens in the stars and it happens onstage! But! Before they attain their destined beauty, supernovas are silent.

There is nothing.

And that is what stage fright does to me. I am in blankness. I am in nothing.

I am in a pause. But! The supernova *must* horribly explode. And that is what stage fright does to my body. As the arrival of the explosion nears, I sweat, my breath shortens, my stomach churns, my heart races! I am in nothing. But I have to get onstage! I have to go! But I feel shame, and I feel like a fraud! There is a red, evil face. I know it will always be there, but I am always surprised when it appears. It chases me! I need to run for my life! I need to make my entrance, but the face—Stage Fright—chases me. The face of the Devil is chasing me—onstage. I explode!

I know my duty. I will run onstage. And I will perform. I will fulfill my responsibility as an actor. And he won't get me. This time. But he will try again. And again. And I will pause, and run, and explode. And I will pause again, and run again, and explode again. It is a pattern. So, it is comforting in a way. It is what happens to Me. It is My Happening. It is part of the ritual. After all of these years, the Devil, which is Stage Fright, is familiar. I don't know that I could go on without the horror, without the chase, without the explosion. If he were not there, I don't think I could go on. In a way, he makes me feel heroic. He gets me onstage. We are in a necessary partnership, the Devil face and I. The explosion happens.

And it is wonderful.

Interview with Bill: introduction

Because we've always been looked on as the fly-by-night devil-may-care Puck entities that people think we are. And it's just something that's been handed down through the centuries.

Bill is a 52-year-old actor. Although he appears in film and on TV, he feels that the theater is his home. After discovering he had a talent for entertaining others, he decided to pursue acting first as an amateur in high school productions and then as a professional when he became an adult. Bill completed an actor conservatory program at an internationally known institution. He has been a member of several repertory companies and he has played a variety of roles, from character parts to leading roles. Several years ago, Bill began directing. He brings his expertise as an actor to this position. Bill has experienced stage fright before going onstage as well as during performances. Although these experiences were very uncomfortable, Bill accepts stage fright as permanent part of his process as an actor. He feels that as a group, actors tend to be met with disrespect. Discussing his stage fright experiences made him feel valued.

The 22 themes that emerged about Bill's stage fright are listed below. An essential description of stage fright from Bill's perspective follows these themes:

- safety
- freedom
- expression
- clarity
- danger
- courage
- inherence
- difference
- service
- the color orange
- motivation
- necessity
- protection
- physical attack
- feeling alone
- doubt
- fear of failure
- death
- permanence
- changes
- responsibility
- coping

Interview with Bill: themes

Safety. Bill describes himself as shy and withdrawn child. He had difficulty making friends and connecting to others. However, his experiences in a junior high school speech class led him to his high school drama department, where he realized that he was good at entertaining people. Through speaking and acting, he felt a sense of self-worth that he had not experienced before. He was able to hold the attention of others. Their response made him feel valued.

I was a very shy and withdrawn child. Um, I wasn't … I was good at making friends, but I wasn't really good at … at approaching people or anything, and when I got to junior high, I decided to take a speech class. And through that speech class, it kind of led into, uh, the drama department there in high school, and then I … it just snowballed from there. I realized I was pretty dang good at it, so that's what I did.

I also realized I was able to entertain people through … through speaking. And, uh, hold them. They would listen to me, and I would have something, you know, I would have … I realized I was worth listening to. Let's put it that way.

Bill states that "he" has not been onstage for 40 years. It is the "character" that goes onstage. In this process, Bill states, "everything fades away." Bill feels that the stage is a safe place for him.

Freedom. Bill states that being onstage and being able to tell someone else's story is liberating. He feels more freedom onstage than he does in everyday life. He describes acting as "therapeutic" for him.

B: It's great! It's great to be able to tell someone else's story. To take, uh, you know, to take a couple of hours out of your life for an evening and be someone else. Um, it's very therapeutic.
L: How is it therapeutic?
B: Therapeutic in the way that you're able to, uh, to live out scenarios and get out aggressions. It's freeing. It's a very freeing thing. I know when I'm up there, I feel free. I feel really free. I don't know any other way to put it.

When Bill feels free onstage, he describes it as "exhilarating."

Exhilarating. There's a chemical that the body releases when you get to a fear, to a fight or flight state. Adrenaline. It's an adrenaline rush.

I was doing *[name of play]*. And I recall being up there and actually, to put it in reality, I was just up on the back of another actor, but actually feeling, I mean, letting go enough to feel that I was riding horses in a field, and, uh, and that was a great feeling for me.

Expression. When acting onstage, Bill also lives out fantasies and expresses emotions that he would not explore or express in everyday life due to the repercussions that he feels might occur.

B: I can live out fantasies and other life scenarios onstage and not have the repercussions if I did something like that in real life.
L: You can embody experiences onstage that you couldn't every day.

B: Yes. That you wouldn't every day. I'm not saying that you couldn't, but you wouldn't.

Clarity. Bill states that the intense listening that must occur onstage translates to more concentration off-stage. This necessity has taught him to listen more carefully to others, which has given him clarity in his interactions with others in his off-stage life.

> It also gives you, through the words of really good authors ... the ability to listen, to truly listen and you can take that with you off-stage and truly listen when people are talking to you, and it makes things much more clear in life for me.

Danger. Bill described concerns about the many things that can go wrong onstage; an awareness which contributes to his feeling that acting is dangerous.

> There's always a chance that you're gonna fall on your face. There's always the chance that somebody's not gonna like you. There's always the chance that you're gonna forget your lines. Um, all this rehearsal has done—has done no good. You won't remember anything when you walk out there, so why go out there?

Courage. Stage fright is something that the actor cannot share with the audience. Those in the audience—representing non-actors—would not have the courage to appear onstage as actors do.

> And stage fright is the one thing you can't experience with them ... because they don't know what it's like, because they're too afraid to do it. A lot of your audience members would never go onstage ... that same thing that causes stage fright keeps them from wanting to do it. You know?

Inherence. Bill believes that actors "are born." He feels his capabilities are innate and inherent.

> You don't choose to be an actor ... well I guess some people choose it, fall into it as a career but you don't become an actor ... you are born an actor. I am an actor. There really was no choice for me. I feel it is what I was born to do.

Difference. Bill believes that non-actors are different from actors. He believes that their differences as a group make them a distinct "culture."

> It's how we see things ... getting the story of things ... getting the meaning ... seeing how things fit together ... because we try to be what ... others are not ... so we've had to stick together.

I think that is a sign of an actor. You can see it, when young actors walk in to audition. You can tell in five seconds who has it, who is an actor. Actors are not like ordinary people.

Bill feels that the actors' opinions are not respected. He feels this personally and notes it has happened historically. Therefore, discussing his stage fright made him feel valued.

Well first of all, I think it's really cool that someone cares enough to do something like this ... where my opinions and the opinions of other actors really matter. It's nice to know someone wants to know what causes this. I feel a lot of times, actors, unless they're movie stars and in the media and people know who they are, I don't feel they get a lot of respect.

Bill feels that actors have been historically viewed with some suspicion.

Because we've always been looked on as the fly-by-night devil-may-care Puck entities that people think we are. And it's just something that's been handed down through the centuries. I mean, you know—the little hoop earrings—that's the way they would tell actors back in the turn of the century ... if you had an earring, you were probably an actor, and you could ... you had to pay up front. And people wouldn't let them have credit.

Actors wore earrings because of their kinships to gypsies, I believe. I think that's where it came from originally ... that that's the way people could separate them. 'Cause the common man wouldn't wear them," but "those—those hedonistic bohemian actor types— ... 'cause what they do is not work. I think that that has been propagated throughout the centuries, and now we're kind of stuck with it. We're kind of stuck with it."

Bill believes that although people go to the theater to see actors, they do not want to associate with them.

L: Yet people go to the theater to see actors.
B: Absolutely. But we don't want to hang with them.

Bill feels that actors are viewed by others as not embarking on a path of valued work.

Real jobs. That always kinda ticked me off. Real jobs? Well, what I have is a real job. This is a real job. You have to earn that respect. People don't seem to give it to you readily. We've always been looked on as shysters, fly-by-night shysters.

Although Bill feels that others do not understand the actor's job, he feels that other actors and artists do understand that their path is of value.

People can't understand it unless they've done it, or they're in the business, or they've been around. It's hard to explain. I don't wanna do to other people what people have done to actors, so I'm not going to pigeonhole anyone.

Service. Bill believes that his job as an actor is not only to entertain audiences, but also to assist them with feeling and to educate them about different life scenarios.

Oh, as with any art, I think it's to put a mirror up to your audience's face and say, "Is this you?" When people go to the theater, they go to feel something. They go to the theater to be moved ... for entertainment.

There're many different reasons people go to the theater. And, as to, "Art imitates life," you're showing people different ... ah, wow ... different scenarios. Different life experiences ... it's an escape for them, and I think that that's a valuable service.

People pay millions of dollars for that service every year. They just go to the movies. So it's obviously a service, or ... it wouldn't be such a huge business.

The color orange. Bill associated the color orange—then an actual orange—to his experience of stage fright. He explained that when eating an orange, the body reacts with a sensation in the throat that he cannot control. When he is about to appear onstage, his body similarly reacts. However, at this stage in his life, the reaction is one of positive excitement.

Orange. It's exciting. It's exciting.

Motivation. Bill acknowledges that despite the discomfort, there is a motivating aspect to stage fright that prompts him to get onstage and perform.

As much as it can hamper, it's—it's a helper as well. Because it's part of the springboard that gets you out there.

Another aspect of motivation that Bill experiences is anticipatory "excitement." This feeling has evolved from earlier preoccupations with the feeling of danger.

But at this point in my career, and in life, it's more of a ... it's more of an excitement of what I'm about to do.

Necessity. Bill feels that his stage fright is a necessity. It allows him to perceive danger and to be focused on and handle his task.

I'd be afraid if I didn't have it ... then I wouldn't know where the danger is ... it's like a hunter needs to be focused to get the bear ... he can't be relaxed ... no fear means you don't get hurt.

Protection. Ultimately, despite the discomfort, Bill feels that his stage fright has a protective function. It is there to safeguard him from the perceived dangers of performing. Bill sees it as a defense.

> I think it wants to keep you safe. It's your defense ... I don't think I ever realized that until just talking to you, but I think yeah.

> Oh, I think it's protection. I think it's protection. Absolutely. Self-preservation. It protects me from ... from the audience attacking me.

He imagines the protective aspect of stage fright as a "Relaxed Fellow."

> B: He tells me that, "If you go out there, they will hurt you ... stay with me ... stay here where it is safe with me ... I'll protect you ... you don't need to do that."
>
> L: You called stage fright "he." Is it related to a real person?
>
> B: To me? No. But he is a Relaxed Fellow ... he wants me to stay backstage with him. I don't think because I think those things about myself, because I know I can take care of myself out there ... the doubts are there to protect me.

Physical attack. When Bill is about to perform, his stage fright manifests in uncomfortable physical symptoms. His mouth gets dry, his eyes tear up, he gets light-headed, and he experiences an upset stomach.

> I want to say in severe stage fright, for me, cottonmouth happens. Especially if ... it's opening night. My mouth will dry right up. Not crying, but just my eyes will water. Giddy. A little giddy. Stomach ... you know, is that a good description?

He described one experience in particular where he felt he was going to be sick before making an entrance. The feeling intensified as the time for the entrance neared.

> And I remember standing down in the stairwell, getting ready to go up and go onto the stage, and truly feeling like I was about ... to lose my lunch, my neighbor's lunch, I was going to lose my lunch from three weeks past, I was going to lose it all right there. And it built to such a climax that just before I went onstage, I was actually ... my gag reflex started to work.

Feeling alone. Bill also experiences stage fright as feeling as if he were falling through the air with nothing to hold on to. He called this, "true fear."

> Oh yes ... when I was younger, it was like Wile E. Coyote ... remember the cartoon? Yes you do! He was falling in the air grasping at the air ... panic ... he has nothing to hold on to ... when I had stage fright when

I was younger it was like that. I had nothing to grab on to … it was like I was falling in the air.

You are on your own … you have to figure it out yourself.

Doubt. Bill feels that the function of stage fright is to cause him to doubt himself and his abilities.

Oh, to break you down. To break you down. To tell you that you're not worthy. It's to tell you that you're not … that you can't do it.

Fear of failure. Sometimes he experiences these negative thoughts as an "inner voice" telling him he will fail.

"You can't do it … you're no good … you'll screw up."

Death. When Bill was discussing the protective aspects of stage fright, one of the dangers he described was the potentially destructive audience. He used a metaphor of "death" to explain his feeling about the audience.

To keep you from going up there and being eaten alive by that monster we call the audience.

Bill feels, however, that without the audience, he would not be able to do what he does.

I mean, I—I love the audience, or I wouldn't—I wouldn't be doing it.

Permanence. Bill states that despite how much he enjoys acting, he experiences stage fright to some degree every time he goes onstage. He feels it is permanent.

To some degree or another, I experience it every time I go out onstage.

Changes. Bill states that his stage fright experience has changed over the course of his career.

Now I'm old … I can take care of myself out there … I can handle myself when something happens … onstage or inside me … I am confident that even though I don't know what is going to happen, I know what to do.

And I realize that now, later in life, that I just didn't know the difference between excited and fear because they're so close together.

Responsibility. Bill has a sense of responsibility to his fellow actors. Bill notes that despite the forms of stage fright—"true fear" or "excitement"—he always made his appearances. He described a stage fright experience where he felt he was going to be sick. He focused on his responsibility to the other actors in the show.

> I knew that I had to go on the stage because there were other people out on that stage depending on me to get there or I would ruin their chances as well. So, I took the step out, and as I took the step out and spoke the first words that I was supposed to speak at that time … it all left me. It all left me, and I went into what I was doing.

Bill feels that this sense of responsibility extends to having no choice but to make his stage entrance when the time comes. Although responsibility to his fellow actors is a factor, he says that it is only a part of the experience. There is another element to this feeling which Bill has difficulty verbalizing or describing.

> I never felt like I had a choice to *not* go onstage when it was time to go onstage. I just have to go. You can't leave. You can't leave. So, when I'm standing in the wings getting ready to go on, I'm aware of what I'm about to do, and I—I find that I've had the thought, "I can either turn around and walk out that door, or I can go onstage."

> And what is keeping me from turning around and walking out that door, I can't tell you what that is, but it's something very tangible.

> If you built a wall behind me, you could keep me there no stronger than my feet planted on the stage, getting ready to go out. Don't know what it is.

Coping. Bill copes with stage fright by controlling his breathing, concentrating on his acting tasks, connecting with other actors, and noting what he *can* control and what he *cannot* control.

> I know I'm not going to get hurt. And I give myself all these questions. "What is there that you can do about this right now?" Then usually the answer is, "Nothing." I ask myself, "What have you done to prevent this?" Well, I've rehearsed. Do something about everything you have direct control of. If you don't have control of it, you have to kind of let it go.

> I don't have control over the lights. I don't have control over the soundman. I don't have control over the traffic outside … while I or my fellow actors are in some type of monologue. You know, I have no control over that. So, what I have to worry about is what I have direct control over. And what I have direct control over is my concentration to keep me where I need to be.

Bill feels that ultimately, he has coped with his stage fright by incorporating the feeling of fear into his experience. Rather than fighting it, he gains a sense of mastery.

Then accepting the fact that you're fearful and going, "OK. I'm a little nervous tonight. I wonder what that is." And then going on with your life. Don't let the 'little spook' get you down. As scary as stage fright is, there is nothing else in my life I would rather do more than what I do. Absolutely nothing.

Essential description of stage fright: Bill

Actors are born. Actors are different. I am an actor. Our job is not often respected. What we do is "not real." It kind of makes me angry. But look at the millions of dollars people spend every year to go to the movies and to go to the theater. Why?

Because people go to the theater to feel something. To be moved. To escape. We hold a mirror up to you and say, "Is this you?" We have been doing this for centuries. And actors have been disrespected for centuries. It would be cool if people understood us more, but they don't. It's OK. When I do these things for audiences, I feel free. I am up onstage as the character, in the safest place in the world. I am exhilarated! I do what I have to do. Being onstage helps me see the off-stage world more clearly. And I'm doing what I love to do. I was born to it.

When I was younger, I really had a lot of fear before acting. Stage fright made my heart race, and my eyes would tear up like I was gonna cry, and I would have trouble breathing. I would have these negative thoughts, like I was worthless, and I would think that I wasn't good enough to get onstage. All of the good stuff was gone. The stage became a dangerous place! A dangerous place! The fear of going onstage was like falling in the air and having nothing to hang on to. It was true fear. It was panic! But for some reason, I would never run. The choice to run was never an option. I don't know why. There was like this wall behind me that kept me planted at my entrance. I always went onstage. No matter what. People are depending on me, you know?

Even though stage fright made me feel so terrible, he really is a Relaxed Fellow. He was just trying to keep me safe backstage with him. He was just trying to protect me from the audience! From being judged by you. And from all of the dangerous things that can happen onstage, that as a non-actor, you probably wouldn't get. But I used to tell him that the audience—you—are not so bad. I'd be the same way if I were in the theater. So, I don't fight with stage fright anymore, that "little spook." I can only control what I can control, and stage fright is not on the list. I just accept that he is there and move on. This calms him down. Now the feeling I get before acting is excitement. It's excitement that gets me out there to do my job. I can't say I like the feeling all of the time, but if I just accept that he is there and that I can't do anything about it, it just becomes part of the performance. I just concentrate on what I have to do, and I go onstage. And I get lost out there. I feel free in that world. Don't you feel it?

Interview with Elizabeth: introduction

Yeah, when everything's cookin', being onstage is like nothin' like it in the world! It's like the most expensive caviar and champagne all at once.

Elizabeth is a 77-year-old actor. She has been acting professionally for 61 years, having started in radio when she was a teenager. She has been acting in the professional theater for 48 years. She completed drama training in her early 20s and moved to the United States soon after. Elizabeth has performed leading and supporting roles in various types of productions including contemporary and classical comedies and dramas, as well as film and TV. Elizabeth has also been a drama coach for the last 30 years. In addition, Elizabeth is a member of a repertory company where she continues to perform on a regular basis. Last year she appeared in five plays. Elizabeth has experienced stage fright throughout her career. Her most recent experience occurred a few months before the interview. She described it as "Unbelievable. Petrification. If that's a word." She stated that she felt embarrassed discussing it and that she should have completely conquered stage fright by now.

The themes that emerged from this interview are presented below. An essential description of Elizabeth's stage fright will follow.

- attention
- communication
- safety
- excitement
- service
- the color white
- physical attack
- inhibition
- fear of failure
- shame
- control
- death
- the unexpected
- permanence
- changes
- responsibility
- coping

Interview with Elizabeth: themes

Attention. Elizabeth was drawn to acting because she "loved the movie magazines." She felt that she was not suited to anything else. She chose acting because she felt she would not get attention otherwise.

> I was about 13 and I wore Coca-Cola bottle glasses, I was 5'7½, and I weighed about 95lbs. So, I looked at myself in the mirror one day and I said, "Well, there's nothing else you can do. You have to be an actor because nobody will pay any attention to you if you're not."

Communication. Elizabeth's earliest performance experiences took place during her father's performances as an orchestra leader when she was a small child.

> My father had a Saturday night gig every ... during the winter in this dance hall, and at 8 o'clock every night, they would bring the microphone down front, and the chair, and everybody would stop dancing and my father would lift me up on the chair and I sang two songs.

Elizabeth loved seeing the faces in the audience and now feels that what she loved most about being onstage was the sense of "communication" she established with them.

> E: And I looked out at all those faces—there was probably maybe max-imum a hundred people, but when you're 4 years old, that's a lot of faces. And I loved it, and then I went to bed.
> L: Do you remember what you loved about it?
> E: The faces. 'Cause they were just like ... I was an only child, so it was really nice. I felt like I had a whole lot of people to ... of course, I didn't know the word at the time ... but communicate with.

Safety. Elizabeth feels that being onstage is lovely and safe.

> L: You mentioned earlier what it was like to be 4 years old and put on the chair in front of the audience.
> E: Yeah. Yeah.
> L: You're still acting and very busy. What's it like to appear in front of an audience now?
> E: Well, the first word that came into my head was "lovely" *(laughs)*.
> L: What's lovely about it?
> E: Oh, it just feels so warm and nice and cozy. You know, it's like being in mother's womb again. Do you know, it's interesting, because I think it's not only the audience. It's the lights. The lights are so warm. And I did *Gypsy*, played Gypsy Rose Lee from the age of 17 to 25, and I was 36, so I used Erase a lot *(laughs)*. And when I went out there and sang and looked up, even though I was taking off my clothes at the same time, when I looked up into that spotlight, it just felt like I was in the safest place in the world. That light just was like a shield for me, and it was wonderful. And it was a very successful production. But that's how it felt.

Excitement. Elizabeth feels that acting is an exciting peak experience for her. It has been a life-long experience.

> Yeah, when everything's cookin', it's ... nothin' like it in the world. It's like the most expensive caviar and champagne all at once *(laughs)*.

It's exciting. It's still exciting. It's still exciting. I still get on a high when I get a, you know, when I get a role, I can't wait to sit down and start memorizing the lines.

Elizabeth feels that being someone else is central to this positive feeling.

I'm gonna be somebody else. I'm me all the time. It's nice to be somebody else for a change … Hey, I've lived with me for a long time *(laughs)*. I mean, everybody needs a change, you know? And the challenge. The challenge. To be somebody else.

I did a show a couple of years ago … And I played two different characters, one in the first act and one in the second act. And I worked really hard to make them two different people. You know, I wore a wig and did an accent, and then the other one I was just, you know, fat old me. And I enjoyed that one immensely. I had absolutely no problems any night ever. I had more fun in rehearsals. I laughed all the time. And it was just a terrific experience. But they're not all like that.

Service. Elizabeth feels that acting has a purpose in helping the audience to have a broader perspective about the world and to be less focused on individual problems.

It helps to make people face the fact that there are other things in the world worse than what they've got. It may help them to deal with what they've got. And it may help to make their outlook sunnier, and stop thinking about self, maybe. Hopefully.

Elizabeth believes that acting also educates audiences. She believes acting and theater are effective means for delivering information.

The best thing that the school district could do is to hire actors and do history in play form, and children would never forget their history, because they'd be entertained at the same time. Instead of just reading the boring words about what their clothes look like at the time. That's a bore to a boy. But to see a woman in—in 16th-century dress that's cut down to here and her whatsits hangin' out, you know, they'd pay attention, and they'd remember.

Elizabeth feels that the entertaining aspects of theater also provide a benefit to audiences.

And I think that there's, you know, so many times you read a critique of a film and people say, "Oh, this is just a piece of fluff. There's nothing meaningful in it." Well, I'm sorry, but if it—especially during times like this— when we have the recession, if it makes people laugh, and it makes them forget what they've got waiting at home, then it's meaningful.

The color white. When asked to associate a color to her experience of stage fright, Elizabeth responded that it was white, "like icicles." This association allowed her to connect her feeling of stage fright with an experience of almost being physically attacked. She was in a public restroom in a place that was familiar to her. She heard a loud bang and suddenly the door opened. A strange "homeless-looking man" bounded into the room waving his arms. Elizabeth feared for her life. She stated that she was "completely frozen."

Physical attack. Elizabeth experiences physical symptoms in the stage fright episodes she described. When describing her experience in the restroom, she stated that during the intrusion she became so fearful that she could not talk or yell. She moved her hands up to her throat and made a choking gesture and stated that she felt like she was being choked to death and could not speak. She uses this event to describe how she feels when experiencing stage fright.

> And this man who looked homeless was going like this *(motioning arms)* and I just like ... I—I mean, I couldn't talk. I couldn't yell *(motioning both hands up to throat in choking gesture)* ... and I was completely frozen.

> The same fear. Yeah, it was ... it affected my body the same way. I wouldn't say it was the same type of fear, but the same ... it had the same effect on my body.

Elizabeth experiences a sense of panic that she registers as pain in her stomach.

> L: Where did you feel that panic in your body?
> E: Right here! Right here! Right here! Right in my core.

Inhibition. Elizabeth described her stage fright as feeling and being "frozen." Its physical manifestation inhibits her from moving. Her first experience occurred in her 20s. She was appearing in a successful comedy. Before she was to make her entrance, she "froze" backstage and was unable to move. Another actor—whose character was in a wheelchair—came to her rescue and literally kicked her onstage from his chair.

> I was completely immobile. I mean, I was frozen. And I was supposed to make an entrance between a pair of French doors. And I played the nurse, who was the comedy relief ... and I just stood there.

> And he was in a wheelchair because he had broken his leg ... and the actor playing the part just lifted his foot and put it in the small of my back and just gave me one big push, and I almost literally fell through the doors. But, of course, when I came through the doors, because I was so ungainly because of his push, everybody laughed.

Being immobile before entrances became a pattern for Elizabeth after this experience.

> I had to go through the same thing all over again. And that went on for, well, that entire run of that show. And for the next two shows, I had that.

Elizabeth's experience of immobility, which affected her physical movements, spread to a type of mental inhibition that she calls "brain freezes." She described how this occurred in a recent production.

> And in this play, I would get "brain freezes," so that everything was going along swimmingly and then all of a sudden, I was totally blank. This never happened to me before.

> It was like the very first time when my outer body went frozen, only this time it was the inner body that went frozen. In the early days, the total immobility.

> Now, at least I've gotten past the immobility, but my outer parts are moving but my inner parts are still frozen. I haven't been able to get all the way through yet.

Elizabeth feels that this aspect of her stage fright is the most disturbing.

> It was, uh, it was very scary, because ... I went up, just ... I mean, I've gone up on lines, but I've never been completely blank. And that's the way I was. So, to me, that's stage fright.

> Oh, my brain was frozen, and this was, you know, like, locked. Very, very, scary.

Fear of failure. Elizabeth feels that the fear of failure is central to her stage fright. For Elizabeth, failure means not fulfilling the requirements of her job.

> E: Well, the fear was failure. You know? I mean, yeah, I guess failure. Failure.
> L: And what would happen if you failed?
> E: Nothing. But to me, it would, you know ... I'm very, um, I'm old-fashioned. I'm loyal and I'm steadfast, and it would be such a slight on my character, for myself ... if I weren't able to fulfill my job. And that's what getting those words out is: fulfilling my job.

Shame. Elizabeth feels that feelings of shame and inadequacy are also central to her stage fright.

You know when you have dreams, and you're running down the street and you're naked? That's stage fright to me. It's just being … afraid of being caught in your underwear, so to speak.

And I think the real reason people feel stage fright. Well, I shouldn't say that. The real reason I felt stage fright was that I felt inadequate. And if I go out there, everybody's gonna know it. And I'll never get to do this again, which is like the worst thing in the world.

Elizabeth felt embarrassed discussing her stage fright.

L: So, what's it like for you to talk about this?
E: Embarrassing.
L: Really?
E: Yeah. After all this time, I should be better than that.

Control. Elizabeth feels like her stage fright is controlling her. It is a part of herself that she does not know.

E: It's controlling you. Yeah. And, I don't know whether there's a boogieman inside of those of "us who have it" that says, "I want you to do what *I* want you to do, not what *you* want to do."
L: What would it want you to do instead?
E: God knows. I don't know, 'cause I don't know this person. This is not me. This is maybe another part of me that I don't know, but I—I don't know.

Death. Elizabeth describes a time when she feared for her life. She states that the feelings she experienced during this event parallel how she experiences stage fright.

But that feeling I had when that man walked in was exactly the feeling I had when I was onstage in this play and I went blank. And I just … my whole body froze, and I just … everything froze.

The unexpected. Elizabeth states that her stage fright experiences are unexpected.

L: Did it seem to come out of nowhere?
E: Yes. Absolutely. Yes. Which is what made it so frightening, 'cause I never knew when it was gonna happen … I finally admitted to myself at the end of the run, I did know all the dialogue, because if I didn't, it would always happen at the same time … but it never did. It always happened somewhere different.

Permanence. Elizabeth does not experience stage fright in every show. However, she believes its presence in her life is permanent.

And there are times when I do shows, and I have absolutely no stage fright whatsoever. I'm nervous, but no stage fright. But then every once in a while, it'll pop up, and I think it has to do with the character or the role I play. And sometimes the people I'm surrounded with.

Changes. Elizabeth's stage fright has changed over time. She has moved past the physical manifestations. The mental manifestations are still present.

In the early days, the total immobility. Now, at least I've gotten past the immobility, but my outer parts are moving but my inner parts are still frozen. I haven't been able to get all the way through yet.

Responsibility. Elizabeth's stage fright caused her to have difficulty performing. When that happened in a show a few years ago, she considered leaving the cast of the show. Her sense of responsibility to them kept her committed to the show and caused her to perform despite distress.

E: I could've dropped out of that thing. But I wouldn't do that, because I had given my word that I would do it, so I'll do it.
L: Who did you feel a responsibility toward, in terms of keeping your word?
E: My fellow actors. And it was really terrible, because, um, I was in such bad shape that, uh, they cancelled the opening and moved it back one month because everybody in the cast had said to their friends, "Don't come opening night. It's gonna be … ." I mean, they didn't tell me this, but I knew. 'Cause I told everybody I knew, "Don't come opening weekend."

Elizabeth draws strength from other actors being committed to her when she needs help. She feels this support onstage as well.

I've worked with people who had stage fright. I worked with one guy, playing … he played my husband, and he would walk up and down and walk up and down and say, "Why am I here? Why am I here? What am I doing this for?" And I finally got to the point where the second night, I went over and hit him on the backside and said, you know, "You're here to support me. Come on, let's go!" *(laughs)*.

But I wasn't, you know, I wasn't onstage alone, and they helped me immensely in the moments when I needed them.

Elizabeth feels a sense of responsibility to the audience. She believes she must perform despite the discomfort in order to fulfill her responsibility to the audience.

I mean, what can I do? Look at the audience, say, "Sorry you guys, you can go home now."

Coping. Elizabeth copes with her stage fright by viewing it as a part of her that tempers feelings of self-importance.

> Or maybe, maybe show that I'm not all as important as I think I am about my own self. That there's another part of me that's equally important, and … you know, I'm not sure. I don't know. I never thought about it that way before. But, uh, yeah. It's an interesting thought.

Elizabeth has had to find ways to cope with her stage fright experiences before a performance. One way is to check the "feel" of the audience so she can prepare.

> The greatest thing for an actor is if you could have some kind of a mental thing in your brain that would go out and see what, you know, like Friday nights are good audiences because it's the beginning of the weekend, and they were at work, so they haven't had to go out to dinner yet, or they just ran home and had a dinner that came out … and they're excited and happy and looking forward to the weekend. Saturday nights, audiences are not always that good. They've had a bite of dinner, and they sit there like lumps, but they're usually good clappers *(laughs)*.

Elizabeth developed a meditation practice where she internally focuses and asks for strength from a higher power.

> Well, after that first show, when I couldn't move, I said, "I'll have to find … something so that that doesn't happen again." Because there's not always gonna be a nice, kindly old man to stick his foot in my back. So, I started doing this … I guess you could call it meditation exercise … wasn't even an exercise. I just find a place, preferably dark, and I do it at the same time every night, depending on if I'm not the first one onstage, and I'll do it like five minutes before I do go on. If I am the first person onstage, I will go into a bathroom when they call five minutes or 10 minutes, and I'll turn off the light in the bathroom. And I just concentrate and it's, um, it's a philosophy I have, and I think if you don't believe, it might not work. But I just call for a power and strength, and let me fulfill what I have to do, and I always know if it's going to be OK because my hands start to tingle, so I know that there are friends there helping me and I'll be fine. And I go out and bingo!

Essential description of stage fright: Elizabeth

I just love being onstage. I love looking out and seeing all of the faces in the audience. And really communicating with them. I love being under the warm lights. It feels like a shield. To me, being onstage is the safest place in the world. It's like being back in mother's womb. It's lovely. And I get to be someone else. Not just old me. You know, sometimes people do need a change. And when I get to be someone else, and it's all cookin' up there … well it's like the best champagne and caviar in the world! Bingo! And when it's cookin', hopefully it'll get your mind off things. Maybe make ya laugh. Get you to stop thinking about yourself and think about somebody else for a night. You might learn something too, but if you just get a laugh, well that's OK too.

When my stage fright hits, well, it is very, very scary. One time I was in the ladies restroom and was almost attacked by an intruder—thought I was gonna die!—and I froze. I couldn't move. I couldn't talk. That exact same thing happens when I get stage fright! It's so frightening because I never know when it's gonna happen, but when it does, it's like my body turns into an icicle. I can't move. I can't think! I can't talk! I just freeze! I really feel like I'm gonna blow it out there, out there onstage.

Maybe it's some part of me that I don't know trying to control me—or choke me—yeah, that's what it feels like! Or maybe it's just a part of me that wants me to not feel so important. I don't know but it sure makes me feel inadequate when it happens. Like you're running down the street naked! I do know that you can't say to the audience "Go home, I'm frozen stiff back here." You gotta do it. One time—when I was frozen—an actor had to literally kick me onstage! We do that for each other. Gotta get the show up.

I don't know about other people but acting is what I am supposed to do, because it makes me so happy. Hopefully, you too. So, I have to deal with this thing. When this stage fright hits, I just get very quiet and I concentrate. I concentrate on what I have to do and ask for power and strength so I can fulfill what I have to do. To say my lines and do a good job. Sometimes by getting out there I can help another actor do their job. Even though I'm scared to death, I'll be fine. I'll do my job. It will be lovely out there.

Interview with Jake: introduction

It takes tremendous courage to do that night after night after night, to put yourself out there, naked onstage, not knowing what's going to happen … In an open amphitheater, with all eyes on you. That's terrifying! That's terrifying.

Jake is a 60-year-old actor. He has acted for 42 years. Jake's earliest experiences in the theater were in community theater productions with his family. Jake received a bachelor's degree in performing arts, and subsequently started a theater department at his college. However, he wanted to know if he could "do it" in the professional theater, so he gave up academia and moved to New York to pursue acting professionally. Although most of his training occurred in regional theaters, he studied the Sanford Meisner Technique in New York. Jake has a wide range of experience acting in TV, film, regional theater, on Broadway and off-Broadway, and in roles in musical theater, dramas, comedies, and classical plays. He is currently a member of a nationally known repertory company where he regularly performs. Jake is also a director, an acting teacher, and a theater historian. Jake has experienced stage fright before going onstage and during performance. He believes that theater actors with stage fright must cope with it in order to survive in the profession. He described discussing his stage fright as "releasing."

The themes that emerged are listed below and will be followed by an essential description of Jake's stage fright:

- communication
- transcendence
- danger
- courage
- inherence
- difference
- service
- the color maroon
- motivation
- physical attack
- feeling alone
- fear of failure
- self-absorption
- inhibition
- doubt
- conflict
- death
- the unexpected
- changes
- responsibility
- coping

Interview with Jake: themes

Communication. From an early age, Jake wanted to release his "inner clown." He was a "bit of a showoff," had the ability to make people laugh, and wanted to be "center stage." However, his family expected him to maintain this role in the family. At puberty he protested this assignment, and desired more control over how he was perceived, and wished to be taken more seriously. His "inner clown" merged with his serious side to form how he wanted to be seen by others and how he sees himself as an actor. He wished to communicate a deeper and more serious side of himself through acting.

> I remember one time, when I was around 11 years old, coming to the dinner table protesting the fact that I had gotten this image of being the clown in the family. And I didn't talk. And this went on for about a week. I was the silent, sullen teen. And my parents realized something was wrong, and my dad took me out to dinner and said, "What's up?" And I explained

I didn't like this label of being the clown. I wanted to be taken seriously. He said, "Well, that's OK. This is all part of growing up." I didn't want to be perceived as just a clown, as just someone who could imitate people and just someone who could make people laugh. I wanted to, you know, to let them know that I was someone who could think good thoughts, think big thoughts, and philosophize and communicate in a—in a serious way, not just a humorous way.

So, there's two sides of the equation here, which is the clown that always wants to be center stage, but also the performer and the person that wants to be taken seriously. I think I've been able to blend that, and its still part of me, I think, as a performer.

Jake sees acting as his life path not only as a way to express himself, but also as a way to deepen aspects of himself.

It's growing as a person. You know, it's sort of why we're here, isn't it? To grow? To learn? To evolve?

Transcendence. Jake loves acting. He describes it as, "your soul is awakening." This going beyond himself involves catharsis, emotional breakthrough, emotional attachment to others, and being connected to the present moment, which he calls, "the now of now." It is a state of being where nothing else exists. He credits this experience as being one of the greatest in his life.

J: I have to say, some of my greatest experiences as a person have taken place either onstage or in a rehearsal … some of your best work may never be seen by an audience. Some of your best work may be in a rehearsal with a director and a couple of actors and a stage manager, watching you find your way to create a character. And there will be moments of catharsis, of breakthrough, in rehearsal that are profound and moving and deeply felt, and you have to remember that process and then bring it to life, recreate something like that, for an audience.

L: What does that great moment feel like, physically, mentally, emotionally? What is that like for someone who may have never experienced it?

J: It's being in the now of now. It's being so connected to the present moment that nothing else exists, and if … well I'm just gonna say it. I guess it's like orgasm … You are there with another person or people, um, and, you are so in touch with who you are in that moment that you are the full expression of that being, of that entity, and, depending on the dramatic material you're doing, your soul is awakened.

L: Your soul is awakened.

J: Your soul is awakened, and you get to fly. One of my earliest experiences was seeing *Peter Pan*. And I think one of the other reasons I became an actor was I wanted to fly. I wanted to learn how to fly. And, um, there've been a few incidents, a few moments in my career where I've really felt that I have soared, that I have flown above the ground, free, connected to myself, but disconnected and free almost from the Earth.

This feeling keeps Jake acting. He states, "That's why we do it. That's what we live for." Jake believes that in addition to the love of the craft and the positives experienced when performing, actors ultimately act for love.

And, you know, actors do this for love. We go out there onstage to be loved by a lot of people.

Danger. Jake feels that acting in the theater is dangerous. Live theater presents the possibility of the unknown, which can be terrifying for him.

It's not like in the movies or on TV, where we could just edit that mistake. We can just do another take. Live theater involves danger. Live theater involves taking risks. And actors who are theater actors take that risk night after night after night.

It's very dangerous out there, because basically, even though you're dealing with other actors out there, you are on your own. You are in charge of your own instrument and how your instrument's going to respond to the other actors ... You could fall down. You could fail. You could forget your lines. Props could get missed. Something could happen and accidents might happen ... it's terrifying.

Courage. Jake believes that actors have a more difficult time engaging in their profession than others do because of the public exposure required of them and the potential criticism. This necessitates courage in the face of terror.

It takes tremendous courage to do that night after night after night, to put yourself out there, naked onstage, um, not knowing what's going to happen ... In an open amphitheater, with all eyes on you. That's terrifying! That's terrifying.

Inherence. Jake grew up in a theatrical family. His father was an actor turned college theater professor/director and his mother was a dancer. He performed in community theater with his family. After wanting "to change the world" in the 1960s as a philosopher, a political scientist, and a political activist, he realized that his acting talent was inherent and that his passion for the theater was in his "blood." He feels that acting is his life's purpose.

Difference. Jake feels that because of the nature of the profession, actors face more difficulties than those in other professions.

And I think actors, you know, have a more difficult time than a lot of people, because they're in public, because they're being judged by an audience.

Service. Jake remembers coming to the conclusion that actors "inherited the responsibility not only to entertain, but to educate the audiences." He sees acting as a responsibility and a service.

> I realized that being an actor when I was young wasn't just about making people laugh … there was another aspect to all of this, which was to make people think, to make people cry, to get them to hold the mirror, as it were, up to nature and get them to think about their own lives, by what they were witnessing onstage.

> That's it. To take your audience on a journey, enlighten, entertain. As George Bernard Shaw has said, in any great work of art, does it raise their level of thinking? Does the work of art significantly contribute to one's better understanding of humanity? If you've done that, if you've somehow reached those people and touched those people, then you've succeeded as a performing artist, as an actor.

Jake feels that this service is sacred. He experiences acting as taking audiences on a "sacred journey."

> It's a sacred journey. If we go back to the Greeks and even before them into ritual, it was the shaman and the medicine man and then eventually the actor's responsibility as a senior member of society, as a respected member of society, to explain the supernatural forces in the universe to the tribe. This came out of ritual, and then the Greeks, you know, adapted that form of ritual so that actors then had an exalted place in the society in which they lived to perform the works of the great playwrights, and to be, as it were, a priest in a way, to communicate a story to an audience, (to) get them to participate somehow in that story and come out, as Aristotle would say, at the end of that story enlightened through that catharsis and changed somehow so that their soul was in harmony. That's a great responsibility for a performer.

The color maroon. When reflecting on this feeling of stage fright, Jake was asked if a color could be associated with the feeling. His answer—maroon— opened up an avenue of deeper reflection on the meaning of stage fright. For Jake, this feeling of stage fright contained a sense of lifelessness.

> Just the color of blood of some kind. A puddle of blood and, you know … if the blood has gone out of an animal or a person. There's just a puddle of lifelessness, of, um, the life-force exiting from your body, so that it's not a bright red … almost a burnt blood or a blood that's old, that's been let out, that … it's like it's too late to get back in and refresh and turn red again. Interesting.

> Well, I'll go ahead and say it. When my children were born, here in this house, on the bed that I built—both our kids had home births—the color

of the placenta when it comes out of the womb has a maroon color. It's not bright red; it's deep, dark, black red. It's maroon. The color of the placenta. The color of the afterbirth.

This association helped Jake articulate a deeper meaning of this feeling; it is a desire to return to the life-force. Stage fright is the absence of the life-force.

It's a feeling of wanting to get back in the womb, where strength derived from, where the life-force, you know, existed.

Jake described a stage fright experience that occurred before going onstage during the run of a Broadway show when he experienced this feeling. As an understudy, he was called to go onstage within an hour before the curtain. He had the feeling that the blood was draining from his body.

I get a phone call ... and the stage manager said, "Get down here. You're going on tonight." I felt my heart sink to my feet. I will never forget that physical feeling of the blood draining from my body.

Motivation. Jakes feels that there is a motivating, "daring" part of stage fright that challenges him to succeed. It exists alongside its debilitating aspects.

The essence of stage fright is that psychological and physical debilitation of who you're trying to be, of what you're trying to do. It's taking away from something that you love. It's stealing your focus. It's stealing your stamina. It's daring you to do your best. It's challenging you to, uh, succeed. It's asking you to fail. Does that make any sense?

Physical attack. Jake's stage fright is accompanied by physical symptoms. His heart races, he has cold sweats, his breath becomes very shallow, his vocal apparatus becomes pinched, and he loses control of his voice.

When you're backstage, ready to go on, the heart starts palpitating and you breathe very, very high ... cold sweats ... You are not centered; therefore, you're not breathing low. And when you breathe high, from your neck, from your chest—you know this—your—your vocal apparatuses are pinched, you don't have full control over your voice. Um, when things are pinched and contracted, you're not emotionally connected to your instrument. You are hampered. You are, you know, halfway there ... less than halfway there. You're ... you know, you're using about 30% of your full capacity as a performer.

Uh, yeah, that's ... that whole physiological aspect of stage fright would be, you know, a whole 'nother conversation and a whole 'nother aspect to all of this.

Feeling alone. Jake described stage fright as a place of transition. It is the intermediate place between not being connected to anything and the place where
he can rely on his own powers and instincts to survive on his own in a fearful
world. This place is characterized by acute aloneness.

> You're on your own now, aren't you? You're not connected to anything
> here. You're on your own. You're out in the world, by yourself. Good luck.
> And I think that's, um, that's a great explanation, or one possible descrip-
> tion of stage fright … entering a world where there is fear, where there
> is no umbilical, where you have to find your own strength and trust your
> instincts, your primal instincts to breathe on your own for the first time.

Jake described another nuance of feeling alone which is the result of being
disconnected from the life-force: the dramatic situation. Jake describes the
ultimate positive acting experience as being "in the now of now." In the theater,
this is often referred to as "being in the moment." When he experiences stage
fright, this positive experience vanishes, and he loses the "moment-to-moment"
connection that is part of the "now of now." Jake described one particular stage
fright experience as a "disconnection." He was cut off from what was happening
onstage. Instead, he felt as if he were watching from the audience. These feelings
contribute to an emotional disconnect which diminishes his performance.

> You're almost a part of the audience who's watching. You're not really talking
> to the people onstage; you're not really behaving moment-to-moment.

> So, it's never your best performance when you're afraid … You are the far-
> thest thing from being in the "now of now." You are somewhere else …
> you are not a part of the play. You're not a part of the performance.

Fear of failure. Jake experiences stage fright as an entity that wants him to
fail; it wants to keep him from being successful onstage and fulfilling his task of
enlightening audiences.

> Very, very interesting of what stage fright wants. It really wants you to fail.
> You know, it's—it's not just parental demons. Its self-identity demons. I want
> to be a success, I'm wanting to be that performer that truly enlightens an
> audience. It wants you to fail.

> If fear and … stage fright had an objective, it really is to undermine the
> work that you have to do as an actor. To undermine the process. It's a mon-
> ster that wants some part of you to fail.

Self-absorption. When Jake experiences stage fright, his focus is averted. He
is not "in the moment." He becomes self-absorbed rather than being engaged
with the dramatic circumstances of the play from the character's point of view.

For an actor, we call that "going into one's head." Becoming mental. Going out of the moment and watching yourself.

> Being self-conscious and, um, putting your attention on yourself and thinking of, "OK what do I have to do now? Why can't I remember my line?" It's getting yourself out of the moment of the play.

Self-absorption causes him to blame himself when something goes wrong onstage. Jake described an example of this experience. He exaggerated his part in a mishap before he could recover.

> There was another big experience … in the beginning of the second act, this other actor and I were onstage, and from the back of the audience, someone yells out, "This is boring! This is boring!" I thought to myself, "This is my fault. I'm boring the audience. I'm not doing my job. I'm a bad actor." Then I heard a disturbance in the audience, and he was ushered out. He was drunk … but the man wasn't enjoying the play … I blamed myself. That's when actors' insecurity creeps into, again, the responsibility of entertaining the audience. That and … that "maroonness" sunk in at that minute … I thought, "Well this is my fault." And then just that fraction of, "Don't be nuts … .there's someone crazy in the audience. Just continue." And we continued with the scene. We didn't stop the show.

Inhibition. In addition to being self-conscious, Jake experiences stage fright as restricting and inhibiting. He states, "It's the absence of release. It's the absence of freedom." Jake feels that stage fright inhibits him from doing his best work.

> Stage fright wants to prevent you from being the best that you can be. Stage fright wants to prevent you from doing your job … it steals your stamina. Because, you know, so much of an actor's life is getting in touch with that inner child and being a child again and being free to play in the sandbox. Stage fright puts up rules. Stage fright almost becomes the parent, the authority figure, saying, "You can't do this." Your instrument is—is being wrapped up somehow. Your instrument is being constricted, so that you're not at your best and you're not at your fullest.

Doubt. Jake feels that the function of stage fright is to devalue the actor. This manifests in self-doubt.

> Stage fright wants you to think about your inadequacies, and wants you to be filled with self-doubt, and wants you to fail.

> And, um, when self-doubt creeps in, whether it's an actor or whether it's an accountant, you know, it prevents us from doing our best work.

Jake associated the feeling of stage fright with the feeling of being strangled by "that self-doubt demon." He describes stage fright's voice:

"You're not good enough to do this. You're a failure."

"Grow up and do something more worthwhile."

Jake experiences self-doubt when he feels he does not meet the audience's expectations.

Knowing that something could go wrong. Knowing that you might be laughed at and booed off the stage. Knowing that fruit might be thrown at you and you might get a tomato in your face. Not fulfilling the requirements of the performance, of the expectations of the audience.

Jake is philosophical, however, about the audience's judgment. He seems to accept it as part of the job.

That's the history of the actor, isn't it? Being judged by society.

Conflict. When Jake feels the doubts, restrictions, and insecurities that stage fright brings, he tries to fight these negative feelings by strengthening his ego through positive self-talk. This experience feels like a battle between a "demon" and his actor-self that takes place on the "proving stage."

Reminding yourself that the demon's not gonna win. Having control over that fear. It alters your performance because you're trying; you're combating something that you shouldn't have to think about when you're onstage. The battle with Stage Fright is to … to tell the beast that it's not going to win. And you have to battle that beast and say, "I'm better than you. I'm better than all those people who wish me to fail. I can do this."

It's onstage, it's a proving ground, you know. The stage is a proving ground. Um, so all our personality disorders, all our personal demons, all our torments from childhood come into play in that arena. On that proving stage.

Death. When Jake was describing the physical aspects of stage fright, he made a "choking" gesture with his hands. Upon exploration, he revealed that stage fright feels like a literal physical attack, like strangulation.

Something's about to strangle you or you're being strangled.

The unexpected. Jake's stage fright comes unexpectedly. He described an example that occurred onstage. It happened during an off-Broadway run. He had been performing the role for two years. During and after the experience, he was fearful about being able to recover and doubted his abilities.

I'd been doing a play for two years, and one night, for some reason, I could not remember what I said next. The grooves in the record, or the recording, or whatever it is these days, had become so deep that I couldn't climb out of it, and the other actress would have had to help me.

And then after I got back on track, I started thinking about, how could I possibly forget my line after being in a play for two years? The same thing happened, and I went up on the next line. Then I stammered and I struggled. That's scary when you think, "Oh, I can't do this. I can't, uh, I can't—I can't go on. I don't know what I say next."

Changes. Jake describes how his stage fright has changed over the course of his career. Early in his career, Jake's stage fright centered on being liked and judged by the audience.

I think early on in my career, that's where the fear factor came in, wondering whether they'd like you or not … dealing with self-judgment issues, audience judgment issues.

Jake believes that as the actor matures, stage fright is less focused on the self and more focused on the professional aspects of performing and wanting to meet those demands effectively.

As you mature as a performer, as you become a professional and get paid for what you do … that means not caring whether they like you or not, because you're gonna be in some plays that are very controversial and the audiences will walk out, or the audience may vocally protest what you as the actor are saying, because you are performing a text. A professional actor needs to know that despite the controversy, you're there to do a job, and it's not your job to control the audience in any way.

Furthermore, Jake believes that emotionally healthy actors suffer less from stage fright than emotionally unhealthy actors.

And perhaps those that, you know, have debilitating stage fright remain in that area of, "The audience hates me. The people who are judging me don't like me and are not gonna forgive me if I make a mistake."

I think a healthy performer, a healthy actor, an actor who's not debilitated by stage fright, doesn't deal with those issues. Takes a more positive approach to realizing that the audience is there to support you. The audience is there to love you.

Jake has seen that stage fright must be dealt with over an actor's career; the demands of the theater insist that an actor must cope.

You can't be a professional actor and perform eight performances a week and have that demon, um, in your life. I think performers who have not been able to conquer that demon are performers who have gone on to ... to do something else, or maybe do community theater, or maybe remain amateurs. We both know stories of very famous actors who've been debilitated by this disease, and it's destroyed their careers, unfortunately.

Responsibility. Jake feels that he has a responsibility to the profession to perform despite the discomforts of stage fright and other negatives of the job. He noted this after describing the positive aspects of acting.

You know, your entire career won't be filled with all those moments every time. There've been, you know, experiences I've had in regional theater where I hated being at the theater. I disliked the people I was working with, but I knew I had a contract, and I couldn't wait to leave. Um, but as a professional actor, you have to put that behind you and go to work every day. It's a job. Hopefully, it's a job that's filled with more joy than contempt ... that's what actors have to deal with sometimes, is dealing with personalities that you may have conflict with.

Coping. Jake described coping with stage fright. When experiencing it, he uses positive self-talk, mentally refuting doubts about his abilities by reminding himself that he is indeed capable of performing. He described a particular performance experience of feeling unsure and talked himself through the experience.

I had to remind myself of my experience. That I'd done this before ... I had to tell myself I have more stage experience than most of the people out there ... and to remind myself that I was an expert, and that I can do this ... I had to pump myself up. I had to be my own cheerleader. And, um, so it was just reminding yourself to be confident.

Another coping method Jake uses is to dedicate his performance to another person. This helps him to concentrate on the performance.

One of the things I do sometimes is to dedicate a performance to someone that I know and that sometimes helps me give a better performance or helps me concentrate a little more—and it could be a person that may not even be alive anymore—but dedicating my performance just hooks me in, sinks me down, allows me to center ... allows me to relax a little more, knowing that I'm doing this just for one person, rather than 1,500 people.

When stage fright attacks his confidence, Jake focuses on trusting himself to not fail and to deliver a good performance.

And trusting that the instrument that you've trained will somehow be able to take over and be released. Rather than the performer full of fear and self-doubt, the performer full of expertise and confidence.

Essential description of stage fright: Jake

Stage fright is like a demon, or a monster that attacks my purpose. As an actor, it is in my blood and it is my responsibility to educate, to enlighten, and to entertain an audience. In doing so, I engage in a kind of holy ritual that goes back thousands of years. My purpose is to help others understand aspects of the human condition so we may all evolve together on life's journey. I know I am answering my calling. When I act, I express my whole self. I feel as if my soul is awakening. When onstage, I feel like I am in the "now of now." Nothing else exists. It is one of the greatest experiences of my life. I am alive. I can fly!

When stage fright attacks, it attacks this awakening, this flight. It assaults me on many fronts, unexpectedly. My body registers its presence. I break into cold sweats. I begin to feel lifeless. Stage fright is draining my blood! I am marooned, separate from the life-force that nourishes me and propels me forward. I am separate. I am alone. As my blood drains out of me, stage fright strangles me! I cannot take a full breath. My voice is pinched. I cannot call out. My life-force is leaving. Stage fright steals what I have so I become only a small part of what I truly am. When I try to fight this demon, it taunts me. It tells me I will fail. It tells me I cannot proceed. It ridicules me. It twists my focus. I become self-absorbed. I blame myself for things that are not my fault. Stage fright tells me that I have no right to succeed. But it dares me to try.

And I do try. I fight. I trust my instincts. I trust myself. I trust my instrument and the sacred journey I that I am on. I know I can do this! And I do. I win the battle on the proving ground that is the stage. And after years and years of battles, I still win, even if stage fright wants to pick a fight. I am still here. My sense of duty and responsibility continues to fortify me. I am now strong *(breath)*. Stage fright was a formidable opponent. Sadly, I see colleagues who have been weakened by stage fright or who have ultimately lost the battle. They are off the stage now. But I continue. I go on. I do my duty. I live. I am alive! I fly! But I still watch.

Interview with Jimmy: introduction

For me, it's like, it felt like I was like going to the guillotine. But it's like—it's like, oh God … it's like terror.

Jimmy is a 46-year-old actor who was raised in Europe. He works regularly in American film and TV and has a recurring role in a European television series. He has trained in classes and workshops in Europe and completed a two-year program at a well-known studio in New York City. He has appeared in theater in Europe, in London's West End, off-Broadway, and on Broadway. He has appeared in classical, Shakespearian, and contemporary plays, and has a wide range of training and performance experiences to draw from. Before he became a professional actor, Jimmy aspired to be a professional musician. He realized that rather than play an instrument, he wanted to be onstage himself. He states that, as actors "we're using ourselves, the whole thing as an instrument." Jimmy experiences severe stage fright. It continues to affect him to the extent that his physician suggested that he stop acting due to the intense physical toll it takes on him. He has hoped to conquer his stage fright. However, he feels that if he faces it directly, he may have to account for the true level of his talent. He is not ready to do that.

Jimmy's interview yielded a number of themes. They are:

- expression
- courage
- inherence
- difference
- service
- the color red
- familiarity
- protection
- physical attack
- fear of failure
- shame
- doubt
- conflict
- inhibition
- death
- permanence
- changes
- responsibility
- coping

An essential description of Jimmy's experience of stage fright follows the presentation of themes.

Interview with Jimmy: themes

Expression. Jimmy believes that authentic self-expression is crucial for everyone. Without it, a person can become lost and vulnerable. His means of expression is acting.

So, acting was definitely really the thing I wanted to do.

Everyone should express themselves, who they really are. Even if you're a bank manager or you're an actor or whatever.

I'm interested in exposing myself. I was interested in myself, not as an ego-centric person, but I think we should all be interested in ourselves and be working on ourselves and acting was ... that's why I became an actor.

But if you don't do that, I think you can get in a lot of difficulties. You can start losing yourself, you can start losing confidence because you don't know who you are, and you lose references. And then you might drink some booze or take some drug, you know?

Jimmy feels that if he did not express himself as an actor, he would regret it in later life.

But I think if I hadn't have become an actor or done something in the arts, I think my later life would've been really, really tough.

However, Jimmy's desire to express his feelings and to expose his inner world is frightening for him.

I mean, it's so contradictory, because I want to express myself and expose myself, and I did thousands of exercises, and how many workshops have I taken to expose myself, and really just let myself be raw.

That's what I'm trying to find. But that is ultimate the thing I'm so scared of.

Jimmy describes expressing himself onstage as "fantastic." However, this is experienced only if he feels he was able to endure the fear of making a fool of himself, both of which inevitably occur in each stage performance.

If I got through it and I felt like I hadn't stumbled on any lines and I hadn't made an idiot of myself, and I felt like I wasn't too restricted by my own fear. I wouldn't even say fear. Terror, maybe.

If I had made it through, and, you know, the last scene had just finished and we'd do the bow, then yeah, there was nothing better. That was a huge high. It was fantastic.

Courage. For Jimmy, acting, and exposing himself emotionally, physically, and psychologically is a courageous act.

It's just so challenging for me in all aspects and such a courageous thing to do, I have to say. To be an actor and go out onstage or even on a film set and really expose yourself.

Inherence. Jimmy described coming from a family that had no interest in the arts. However, because he was a sensitive child and was extremely interested in other people, he associates sensitivity and curiosity with being an actor. Jimmy did not consider being an actor, because he had no reinforcement that a career in the arts was an acceptable choice. Looking back, he felt that being an actor was who he was inherently. When he decided to pursue acting, he knew that it was the right path for him.

I knew that I was destined to be an actor. I just knew it was right, and the right way to go.

Difference. Jimmy feels that actors are different from non-actors. Actors must be more aware of the human condition in order to portray it onstage.

> Because we have to be superhuman in some way, don't we? I mean, a really good actor has to be really very specific and very aware and very perceptive in what the world out there is. I mean, art reflects the life, doesn't it? We're showing a mirror to what's going on out there. That's huge. That's huge.

Jimmy believes that being an actor invokes some negative feelings from others. He had difficulty revealing to others that he wanted to be an actor because he would be viewed as being different from them.

> I didn't know how to tell people that I wanted to become an actor because I thought they'd go, "Ah, that's J. He wants to be center of attention. He wants to be cool. He wants to be different. He wants adulation." Or something like that.

Jimmy feels that non-actors do not understand the nature of stage fright and how difficult it is for him and for actors in general.

> I say sometimes, you know, most people don't—don't really understand it. They just don't really understand how bad it can be.

Jimmy feels that as an actor, he must be highly aware of other's perspectives; empathy is necessary in creating roles and providing a service.

> And acting made me very aware of people's emotions, people's dreams, hopes. Because every character has that. Their objectives, what they want, what they don't want. You know, their obstacles they need to overcome, what they can't overcome. All this made me aware. People fascinate me. People's mannerisms, where they come from, how they have become what they are, what they say, that fascinates me. That's why I became an actor.

Jimmy feels that the entertaining aspects of acting also have value to audiences.

> Even a lot of the dross that I do … a lot of … like romantic fare and stuff … there's no real depth to it, but it still makes people feel good when they watch it on a Sunday evening. And that's already worth it. I think you can really, really change people's lives as well. So … it's like a mirroring … for people. To have a reference as well.

> How much a part of it can change people's lives by revealing the truth about relationships, the human condition and people's motivations.

To tell the truth ...about the ins and outs of life. To shine a light on, you know, things like family and relationships and human mannerisms, conditions of, you know, why people react this way, why they act that way. A lot of people who do a lot of bad things really actually act that way because they really do believe that they're right. You know? Things like that ... I think you can change people's lives.

Jimmy feels that viewing live acting performances can be therapeutic for audiences.

J: But if you expose yourself and show who you are, then people ... I mean, we—we have so much in common. You know? So many people can then pick that up and use it for their own lives ... They can go, "I feel that way. Oh, it's great that someone else feels that way." You know? It's therapy.

L: Acting is therapy?

J: It's definitely therapy. I mean it's a great thing to be able to sit in front of a therapist and talk about your problems and if they're a good therapist, they'll be able to acknowledge, you know? And give you ... and tell you, you know, "I know exactly what you're going through." That is a huge thing, but not many people have that luxury, or even wanna do that. So, theater and film can do that to mass audiences. Can even do it subliminally.

Jimmy notes that acting can also be used as a disservice.

You know? I think it's huge. It's huge. I mean, you could even use it in bad ways. I mean, you know. TV and politics and all that. You can really influence people with a great story.

The color red. Jimmy associated feeling of stage fright with the color red. It is connected to the physical feelings of chaos that he registers physically in his stomach.

You know, at first, I thought white, but no. I think it's just fire red. It's just chaos in there. It's just ... it's like a washing machine, tumbling a tumble, tumbling and tumbling and tumbling and tumbling, you know?

Yeah, maybe exploding. Or maybe just disintegrating.

Familiarity. Jimmy expressed the idea that perhaps he facilitates his stage fright because it feels familiar.

When you have some habits and you know, they say, "You keep them, because you know them, and you feel safe in them." I don't know if I would go that far with this, because why would I torture myself like that? But there is something about them that … I don't know. I don't know.

It seems like I'm facilitating them a bit or something. Otherwise, it wouldn't be going on for 20 years like this. There's something about it that I feel I want it to be that way. But it's just instinctively I kind of feel that.

There's something about a comfort zone in there, or something familiar that I know.

Protection. Jimmy wonders whether his stage fright protects him from having to face up to the true extent and quality of his talent, which he fears might be inadequate.

I think it does have a purpose. It's just … it's a nightmare. And if you have something like that, wouldn't you try and fight it? And I haven't really done that. So, it has to have some purpose. I must be getting something out of it.

I wonder what it would be if it wasn't there. What would happen then? Maybe if it wasn't there, then I would really find out if I am really up to snuff or not.

Maybe it could be that. It could be, forget all these egocentricities and these, you know, stupid things, um … uh, these anxieties and all that. Forget all that, just, trivial stuff. Let it all go. What is there really? It could be that.

Physical attack. Jimmy describes the very intense physical symptoms that he suffers when stage fright is present. He experiences severe gastro-intestinal difficulties, stomach pain, and feelings of anxiety.

Well first of all … you could sit on the toilet all day. All day. And that's a problem when I did some plays, where the toilet was actually the public toilet. Downstairs in the pub or something. It was a nightmare. I mean, if you have your own toilet, which you don't normally, that was the best thing to have. You would have a stomach ache and then you would have a lot of, um, to be really honest, you'd have a lot of uh … what is it? Uh … Just a lot of movement in the—in the stomach and, you know. It just all goes on the stomach. But I'm having severe anxiety. Severe. Yeah, and it doesn't stop.

Fear of failure. An overriding theme for Jimmy is fear of making an error or of being at fault, especially regarding his lines.

But I'm always afraid of losing my lines, not knowing my … you know … um, making a mistake. It's all this … fear of doing it wrong. Yes. Yeah. Failing. Yeah.

> That's why I went through my lines again and again and again. Whereas that becomes a trap, because it's then all only about the lines, and you make sure that you don't mess up the lines.

Jimmy's fears manifest in negative internal self-references. He does not know the cause.

> And I'm whipping myself and yeah. Yeah. Am I good enough? Am I good enough? You know? I think … That's a great question. I don't know the answer to that question. But I'm definitely whipping myself. There's definitely some self-flagellation in there.

However, Jimmy attributes the origin of these fears to criticism from others in his past. He feels that he has now taken on their "critic" role.

> I think it's, you know, maybe four, five voices from a long time ago. Teachers 100%. Teachers and authority figures. Yeah. And then from earlier, at school. Maybe my father's in there. 100%, he's in there. Yeah.

> I don't think I had a good—got a good deal from people teaching me. And maybe they told me a lot, you know, "You're useless!" or "Shut up!" or whatever. And I think, you know, I think that's why I've taken over that role on myself. You know?

Shame. When having stage fright, Jimmy experiences internal negative questions concerning his ability to perform. One type of question involves being embarrassed if people think he is not a good actor. He also feels shame if he anticipates or is seen making a mistake.

> What happens if I'm not really a good actor? I'm ashamed if I made a mistake. I think it's about being … making a mistake. Is the audience gonna laugh at me? What are they gonna do? It's that.

Jimmy described his stage fright and fear of being shamed as having become centered on knowing his lines.

> And then it just morphed into that. The only way you can really shame yourself is when you forget the lines.

> That's what I feel. You're doing a scene and then all of a sudden, "I don't know my lines. Can you give me the line?" They give you a line, and then you do it again. "Oh, I don't know my lines again." That's the only way, really, you can, don't you think?

Jimmy noted that this experience is perhaps a common event.

But that's with everyone. If you're a bank manager or whatever and you're going to do a—a speech, if you forget the lines, or start stuttering, that's the only real time … real way you can really be ashamed.

Doubt. When experiencing stage fright, Jimmy questions his adequacy. He feels that central to his stage fright is a sense of not being worthy.

What happens if I'm not good enough? You just don't think you're worthy. You're not good enough. You're not sure.

And that makes sense, then, that you give yourself … that out. Of anxiety and all that stage fright. Because if it wasn't there, then maybe you will find out that you're not worthy.

Conflict. Jimmy experiences stage fright as an intense internal battle between a part of himself that is critical of his abilities and another part of himself that tries to encourage him to move forward and say his lines.

I don't know. I'm such in a state. I'm in such a state …

"Don't mess up the line. Do it. Do it!" Ah. This is what's going on between the lines. I've done a lot of work on the lines, of course … but what's going on is, "OK it's me. Is it me? Where's my … Oh God, it's me now. Do it. OK." I say the line. "Oh well damn! Well damn. Oh good. Good. Oh, gosh he said— … Ah! Ah! Do it! Now say the next line! Yes! OK, you've done it! Oh well done! Oh no, that was terrible!"

So that's what's going on. So, it's that battle again.

However, Jimmy notes that his feelings are not necessarily an accurate appraisal of his performances.

When I finish a take I go, "Argh that was terrible!" I really give myself a hard time. They always say those takes where I give myself a hard time are the best takes. So those takes where I'm battling are the best takes. Those takes where I'm actually feeling quite relaxed: dead.

Inhibition. Jimmy notes that his stage fright inhibits positive aspects of his personality from being expressed.

Anything that anyone says could be twisted around into stage fright. If someone says—says a joke. You know, I must say backstage—I'm actually a funny guy—backstage, there's no humor with me. I think people are pretty bored with me backstage, in the dressing room. I don't say a word. Because I'm dealing with this thing.

Death. Throughout the interview, Jimmy used the words "terror," "horrible," "terrible," and "huge" to try to express the depth and magnitude of his stage fright. He stated that it ultimately feels like impending death.

> For me, it's like, it felt like I was like going to the gubillotine. But it's like— it's like, oh God ... it's like terror.

When asked what objective it might have, Jimmy stated that it felt as if stage fright were out to destroy him.

> I mean, it's a huge ... well it's just ... objective is to, um, wow. It's to destroy me. It's trying to destroy me. Yeah. Definitely. It's trying to annihilate me.

Permanence. Jimmy feels that his stage fright is permanent. He said, "I even noticed it when I first started acting." He still experiences severe symptoms. Before recording the interview, he revealed that his physician had cautioned him about continuing with acting because of his extremely high levels of stress due to stage fright and the effects it has on his heart.

> I mean, it hasn't got much better with the stage fright ... No. No. It's right there. It's always there, that fighting and, "Can I say that line, right? Oh, I got that line out right." Or, um, very self-conscious. So self-conscious. But with plays, I have to say, nah. It's constant. Constant.

Changes. Jimmy noted that his stage fright has changed in terms of its duration. The intensity is still severe. When he was younger, he experienced symptoms when he awoke on the day of a performance. At this stage in his career he experiences severe symptoms an hour before curtain.

> And the last play I did was a catastrophe for me ... the moments before going onstage, the last half an hour. Now when I wake up in the morning, I don't have that Hell. But then it starts like an hour before. So that's come because of practice. But the hour before, the last play I did was just Hell. I was just in Hell.

Responsibility. Despite feelings of terror and dread as well as severe physical symptoms, Jimmy feels a responsibility to the audience. He feels he has no choice but to go onstage and perform.

> But there's no way to walk away. You can't. But, you know, you have an audience in the evening and you've gotta do it.

Coping. Jimmy uses various tools to cope with stage fright, including training, preparation, getting to the theater early, and calling his wife, who helps reassure him and coax him onstage.

It's—it's so strong that, um, that the only way I used to fight it—and this was a problem—was go through my lines again and again and again.

Basically, it was waking up in the morning, let's say … when the show was running already, waking up in the morning with a knot in my stomach, and then waiting and waiting and waiting, and then I always got really early to the theater. Like three hours early. Did all my voice and speech exercises, did my relaxation exercises, everything, in order to get this growing, growing fear away.

But I phoned my wife so often. I'm saying to her, "You've gotta help me. What do I do? What do I do? I don't know my lines."

Jimmy also copes with his stage fright by rationalizing its purpose. He feels his stage fright protects him from having to face the true nature of his talent and can also act as an excuse when his performances do not measure up to his expectations.

So at least I have a reason why I'm not succeeding that well, because of my stage fright. Thank God for my stage fright. You know? It's always tough. For me, it's always tough. It's tough for me as an actor. For other actors it's easy, but for me it's tough because of the stage fright. That's what I hang onto. I tell my wife as well, "Yeah I know it was good, but I had such stage fright. I don't think I really did the job I really wanted to do." Isn't that some way—somehow kind of an excuse?

You know all that stuff about fear of success. You know, it's all about fear of success or fear of failure. All that stuff. I don't really understand that all, but I think there's an element of all that stuff in there, you know.

I don't know if it's fear of success. But it is—it, uh, I mean, what would really happen? And that's the scary thing. What would happen if … because I always want people to think I'm a great actor, and I'm not? I can't be. I can't be with this Hell.

Jimmy does not feel that he has coped with his stage fright by addressing internal processes.

Because what you should really do is try and deal with what's going on inside you, and I never really did that.

Essential description of stage fright: Jimmy

I always wanted to express myself, you know? My family had no clue about the arts, really, so it took me a while to realize that I wanted to be an actor and to accept that it was OK. Looking back, I was a really sensitive kid. I really cared about why someone did certain things, or why people felt the way they did. When I realized that I was an actor, I felt I finally found the right way to express myself. And everyone has to express themselves, whoever they are. If people don't express themselves, they can get into a lot of trouble. They forget who they are. By expressing myself as an actor I provide a really important service. We change people's lives. We show you the ins and outs of life or just make you laugh. When audiences can see a performance and say, "I feel that way," it can even be therapeutic.

I think I am a really good actor. I like acting but my stage fright is terrible. It is just Hell. Pure Hell. It is like going to the guillotine. Before I go onstage, it is this red chaos that goes straight to my stomach. It just tumbles, and tumbles, and tumbles in there. I've spent entire days in the toilet, it's so bad. And I have so many negative thoughts going round and round in my head that I try to fight. They come from people in my past, yeah, but now they just come from me. I really worry that I am not good enough. What if the audience laughs at me? What if I do something wrong? I have always felt this since I began acting but stage fright has really affected my ability to memorize my lines. It's all about the lines now. The lines! The lines! As soon as I get one out, I literally panic about the next one. I tell myself, "Do it! Do it! Oh my God, is it me? I say the line! Oh good! Then it's me again! Oh God! Do it!" God! When my stage fright is happening, I am in such a state. I am in such a state. I try to deal with it, but it is always there. But when you have to go onstage, you don't have a choice. You have to do it, you know?

My career really could have been better if I did not have this Hell. It is the same Hell, even though it starts a little later in the day now. It is so bad. Why do I torture myself? I think there must be something that I am getting from it. I think I tell myself, "You know, if you did not have this stage fright, you would have to face if you were really up to snuff." I'd really have to face if I were good enough, talented enough. But I just can't face that right now. I think you have to really delve into what this fear is all about, and I haven't done that. What would happen if I threw all of this aside and just faced that question? That's the question. That's the question. Maybe someday I'll do that. Not now, though. I just can't face it now.

Interview with Kathryn: introduction

> *Well I'm very clear about what actors do. It is helping the audience to rehearse and to remember. We help the audience to rehearse for the big moments that are coming: love, death, and fear.*

Kathryn is a 62-year-old actress. She has worked in film, in TV as a series regular, and as a regular in soap opera. In addition, she has worked continuously in the theater for the last 36 years. She was trained in mime, Moliere, and Shakespeare in Europe, in conservatory in Australia, at the college level in the United States, and at the American Conservatory Theatre (ACT) in San Francisco. In the theater, she has played leading roles in classic plays on Broadway, off-Broadway, and in professional and regional theaters throughout the country and abroad. In addition to working regularly in the theater, Kathryn runs a professional training program for actors at an Equity regional theater and teaches classical theater acting at an acting conservatory. Kathryn grew up in various places, including California, East Africa, and Paris. She had a powerful experience when she first acted as a child. When Kathryn went away to school in her early 20s, she was told of an audition for a Shakespeare play. She auditioned and won one of the leading roles, even though it was her first serious audition. This experience caused her to connect with her early positive experiences of being onstage. She has been acting ever since. Kathryn's stage fright experiences have changed over the course of her career. In the beginning, they were more severe. Years of experience have given her insight into how it affects her and how to cope with it.

Kathryn's interview revealed the following themes. Following the presentation of themes, this section will conclude with an essential description Kathryn's stage fright:

- safety
- transformation
- transcendence
- communication
- danger
- trust
- inherence
- difference
- service
- the color red
- motivation
- physical attack
- feeling alone
- fear of failure
- shame
- fraudulence
- loss of love
- death
- duality
- dreams
- permanence
- changes
- responsibility
- coping

Interview with Kathryn: themes

Safety. For Kathryn, acting was a refuge. The stage was a place she found safety. She remembers feeling unimportant as a child. She was timid, felt she was ugly and small, and cried easily. She recalls feeling intimidated by others, especially by her older sister. Her first acting experience occurred when her parents put her in a children's acting program "to get me out of the house." She remembers playing her first role, that of the Wicked Witch in a Halloween play. Her performance brought her attention on the playground. Other children would run up to her to ask her to do the voice of the Wicked Witch. And suddenly she was popular.

> Look at me! Look at me! Again, I'm sure psychologists are right. I was a timid child. Many people that I talk to and have taught have said they were timid, they were shy, they had a speech impediment, who later became actors.

Transformation. Kathryn remembers feeling transformed onstage. "I had energy, power, and size. I suddenly had a power I hadn't felt before in my life. I was this character and not myself." The transformation also included feeling loved and special, as well as feeling "in the moment" and part of a fantasy.

> It's, "Look at me! I'm holding all of this together in front of 400 people!" Particularly if you're in a good play, a play that makes the audience weep, a play that makes them laugh at bad people *(laughs)*. Uh, for example, it's great to be in *[name of play]* because they are so ready for the transformation. That moment of transformation is holy.

Transcendence. When delivering emotional, psychological, and philosophical truths to an audience, Kathryn describes the feeling of doing so as "transcendent."

> If we dare use the word, *transcendent*. I have transcended my own self ... as Hamlet says, "I am myself indifferent honest, and yet I could accuse me of such things it were better my mother had not borne me." My own frailties, my own inadequacies have been transcended through the power of those words in front of that audience.

Kathryn says that this feeling is not unique to her; she feels it is common to many actors who have matured in their craft. She describes a famous and similar incident involving Laurence Olivier.

> K: The other was the famous Olivier matinee that he did of *Othello*, and after the first act ended, the cast came to him at his dressing room and said, "Larry, you have transcended acting today. You are in a different place." And he said, "I know, but why?" And he went into his dressing room to change his costume. He knew and they knew that he had gone to some level of acting that he hadn't been to before in this production, maybe not hit it again. They all had the sense of the awe. The magic. But even he didn't know why. And he was one of the great actors of the twentieth century.
>
> L: When you just said that, you got very emotional.
>
> K: Oh God, yes.

L: What was happening with you when you said that?

K: Because you want to … you touch that not often, but you touch it every once in a while, and then you wanna know why it doesn't happen every time.

Kathryn further described this feeling and how she yearns for it.

But no, 'cause when it does happen, it's better than sex. It's better than great food. It's transcendent. It's an out-of-body experience. That's why it's so ironic they kicked actors out of the Church for so many hundreds of years. Maybe they didn't like the competition. I don't know. I don't know, but no, I get very emotional about it. Why I love teaching it. When I see it happen to a student, when I see that they're in the moment and they're going and they're flowing and … I participated in that. I helped make that happen.

Kathryn described this feeling as something to be pursued.

Joseph Campbell talked about following your bliss. Sounds easy. I think many people never find bliss. They find hobbies. They find distractions. But if you stick with your bliss long enough, it is transcendent … and I know that it's not a given, that it doesn't happen every time, it's special, it can't be bought. How many things cannot be bought anymore?

Communication. Kathryn experiences a sense of connection and "communion" with the audience.

'Cause it's a silent communion with the audience. I don't have to hear you sob. I'd like it if you applauded at the end, but … you know, I need to feel your focus. I want you to be listening. I want you to be here with me.

The positive response from the audience has a reciprocal effect.

The more they laugh, the better we get. 'Cause there is nothing like the sound of live laughter and the actors getting better when they are playin' a crowd.

However, Kathryn feels that the positive response from the audience is not so much for her as a person or as an actor, but for the emotional, psychological, and philosophical truths she speaks as the character. The audience response to her deliveries makes her feel like she and the audience are in harmony.

I was in *[name of play]*. I played the sister, you know? And she has a great exit line. She said, "You want me to tell her that? I would not tell any young girl such a thing." My character turned and walked off—and I would get exit applause. And it wasn't for my performance. It was the audience saying, "Yeah! You told him, and that's true!" And we were in solidarity, the audience and I.

Danger. Kathryn feels very strongly about the difference between acting in theater and acting in front of a camera. Her experience of acting in front of a camera provides a great sense of safety, as scenes can be reshot, actors can take many breaks, and the relationship to the camera—a machine—is not at all the same as relating to another flesh and blood human being in front of a live audience. However, acting in film does not provide the immediate and visceral response that acting in the theater provides. Kathryn notes that the "danger, thrill, and vocal response" from the audience that are not present in other venues of acting.

> And I feel sorry for people who only act in front of a camera all their lives, because they're not really acting.

Trust. Kathryn also feels strongly about the sense of trust and camaraderie she feels with and among other actors. By going through stage experiences together, attachment bonds with other actors are strengthened. This feeling of ensemble creates personal and professional trust—and even love—onstage.

> K: We are comrades ... we're in this together, the way I'm sure soldiers do ... if I'm onstage with seasoned professionals that I trust, I am relaxed ... yes, it's a conspiracy. We're in this together. It's you and me. Do you know that actors tend to remember only the performances where something went wrong, and we triumphed over it? It's sort of like the old Tolstoy thing. All happy families are alike. All unhappy families. Well, you will remember. "Remember the night the understudy went on and ... ." Fill in the blank.
>
> L: It sounds like a real relationship onstage, where you're really bonded with that person.
>
> K: Yes ... you're not in this alone ... it's *us*. And there is a safety in numbers. The ensemble is truly, all bullshit aside, terribly important. 'Cause if I know you will bail me out, then I can relax. If I know, for example, you're really funny ... your adlibs will be hilarious should I screw up. So, there is that, in a good production, that love onstage. It's us against them.
>
> L: When you said that word, "love," your eyes got a little misty.
>
> K: Yeah.

Kathryn's stage fright is also triggered when she is working with people she cannot trust professionally, for example those who do not remember their lines or those who engage in other unprofessional behavior. If another actor is incompetent, she feels she can't relax and must be on guard for potential mistakes they may make. Her fear intensifies the desire for trust.

> Recently I was onstage with a man who was intoxicated, and it was ... It was a nightmare. Everybody had to bail him out with his lines.

Furthermore, her stage fright is triggered when she does not feel the protective forces of being part of a trusted ensemble. For example, being a new person in an established cast means that the expected bonds that develop over the rehearsal process may have not been developed with her.

By not knowing other actors well, the defensive components of trust leave her open and vulnerable to fear. This manifests in feeling alone in front of strangers and feeling pressure that she will not measure up to other actors' expectations.

Inherence. Kathryn feels that her acting talents were inherent, as they are for most actors. She notes that the ability to act ran in her family and her talents emerged at a young age. She also notes that there is a mystery connected to the personal origins of her ability.

> K: I have a very distinct memory of being in the third grade in Santa Barbara, California, and I wanted to go home, so I told the teacher I felt sick and she sent me to the nurse, and I made the blood leave my face. Said, "I've got to be pale. I've got to be pale. I've gotta look sick." I made the blood leave my face and the nurse said, "Oh, you look terrible. I'm calling your mother." This was my first sense of I could have power over adults. I had felt powerless before. And it was a couple of years later that I got some stage training and started to sort of manipulate that.
>
> L: What do you think that will is about?
>
> K: Hmmm! Now you've got to talk to God. Don't you?

Difference. Kathryn believes that actors are different than non-actors because actors are more sensitive to stimuli and are more aware of their surroundings and of the people and events in their lives. This sensitivity has to do with an ability to communicate a passion and to make an audience feel it.

> Oh, an actor … a good actor is more aware. They hear, they see, they smell. I can do your smile, I can hear your accent, your voice. I'm a mimic. I'm more interested. OK, let's get down to that. How 'bout that? An interested person, who is really watching and really listening, and sadly I think the vast majority of people are not really curious, don't allow themselves to be constantly delighted and surprised. If I say some people are more alive, that would be it. That would be it.

Kathryn also believes that actors are "more alive," that they often possess a certain charisma, and that others believe actors are more interesting. She believes that these factors set actors up for negative feelings from others. These negative feelings include feeling "smaller" and feeling "somewhat like a failure."

> If an actor shows aliveness, others get suspicious. They smell that you are more alive … and that makes them shrink up and feel smaller. It makes

them feel somewhat like a failure. Isn't that why we must set up our celebrities and rip them down? It's almost like a Greek myth!

Actors will often tell you it's as if you announce to the world you want to be an artist and immediately, they roll boulders down the hill at you.

It's human sacrifice. You feel a little bit like a human sacrifice. I'm up here doing all of this for both of us, and you're just sitting there on your ass. Maybe that's why drama has always been more sacred.

Service. Kathryn feels that the purpose of acting is to help the audience to rehearse and remember important life events. Actors help audiences to feel deeply.

Well I'm very clear about that. It is helping the audience to rehearse and to remember. We help the audience to rehearse for the big moments that are coming: love, death, fear.

But at the same time, we are helping them to remember things they have already experienced: love, death, fear, joy. So, we are allowing the audience to feel through us, sometimes things that they don't allow themselves to feel.

And definitely in terms of good writing, whether it's film or theater, saying things well that they have felt, but could not articulate … the actor, in serving the playwright we are articulating these things … that the mass of people have vague, general feelings about, but cannot put it into words.

And the playwright, with the help of the actor, gives it a name and a place, and a clever phrase or a memorable phrase. And that, I feel, releases the audience to say, "Yes! That's what I wanted to say!"

Kathryn feels that what actors give cannot be bought in a society in which so many things—elections, relationships, status—have a price. However, the truth that is delivered onstage cannot be bought. This makes the actor's service priceless.

Oh, you know it's like a drug that you can't buy on the street … what drugs can you not buy? Genuine laughter from strangers cannot be purchased. You can purchase fake laughter, but it doesn't sound the same. Genuine, spontaneous, and thrilled applause. You can hire people to put their hands together, but it's a different thing.

When Kathryn is acting onstage, she experiences a feeling of doing something of spiritual importance.

I really feel connected to the holy origins of theater … particularly if you're in a good play, a play that makes the audience weep, a play that makes them laugh at bad people *(laughs)*. Uh, for example, it's great to be in *[name of play]* because they are so ready for the transformation. That moment of transformation is *holy* or *[name of play]*. Grown men sobbing into their wives' shoulders, and you made that happen … when you're doing something important, and particularly onstage, with the audience, I'm—I'm Cardinal Mahoney, goddammit!

The color red. Kathryn was asked to remember the feeling of stage fright in her body and to notice whether the feeling had a color associated with it. She stated, "It is red." When describing the feeling and the color, Kathryn moved her arms and hands in a hyperactive manner.

Almost like the blood is pulsing. Because the blood is definitely pumping in your body and pulsing behind your eyes. And a positive word would be *exhilaration*.

Motivation. The experiences above reveal that for Kathryn, acting is a positive experience. They contribute to a feeling, before performing, that Kathryn calls "stage fright"; it is an affirming and "exhilarating" energy that motivates her to perform. For Kathryn, stage fright can be a voice that says, "Get out there!" that prompts her to make her entrance.

I'm not nervous. I'm excited. The analogy I would use, the metaphor would be the horse in the gate before the race … they are quivering all over their bodies as if they were in danger, but it's not danger. It's anticipation of when the bell goes off, the gate opens, now I'm going to run … I want to get out there and do it.

Yes. It's exciting. It's gonna be good. Gonna knock 'em dead.

Physical attack. Kathryn's description of her positive associations to this red, exhilarating energy quickly changed to a description of a negative form of stage fright, which manifests physically. Her heart beats rapidly, she loses moisture in her mouth, her tongue seems to swell, and her mind races. She feels anxiety, fear and feels that she needs to escape. She needs to pace and move around to dispel her energy. She also needs to connect to other actors. When stage fright hits her onstage, other actors have told her that she closes her eyes and she blushes. Kathryn feels that these physical manifestations involve shame as well as fear.

But when something actually goes wrong onstage, then you literally go into physiologically "flee or fight."

Feeling alone. Her stage fright is triggered in a few situations: when she feels defenseless and alone. The stage fright in turn creates more intense feelings of loneliness. For example, the presence of a critic might trigger negative stage fright. Kathryn feels that she is not in a position to defend her work against their potential negative commentary. She feels that there is no escape from, or defense against the critic's negative words and that she has no recourse. Kathryn states that she often forgets positive reviews, but always remembers negative ones. It is not so much the content of the review; knowing that she cannot answer back and must endure the criticism causes her great distress.

Fear of failure. Kathryn experiences another negative form of stage fright, which is different from the positive, anticipatory form of stage fright. A central component is fear of making a mistake onstage. She feels that she will do something wrong publicly. She also fears that she will make some sort of mistake and let down her fellow actors. When she imagines failing, she states that it feels like committing a crime.

> Again, it's fear … of failure … the subconscious still goes, "Oh my God! Oh my God! I'm going to fail! In front of strangers."

Shame. Her fear that she will make a mistake or the occurrence of an actual mistake results in a feeling of deep shame in Kathryn. "That's true shame and humiliation," she stated.

> The thing that people are frightened of. The thing that non-pros, the people who are not in performing, dread. "Oh, I could never do that. I could never memorize all those lines. I could never get up in front of people."

Fraudulence. Another aspect of stage fright for Kathryn is the fear of being found to be a fraud.

> Fear that you'll be found out. I've heard a lot of actors say this. "They're gonna find out that I really don't know what I'm doing. Somebody's gonna call me on this. I'm getting away with something here."

> I'm doing something magical here and if I show my weakness, if I fail, if I blow it, you will see that the *Wizard of Oz* is the man behind the curtain.

Loss of love. Kathryn's fear of public failure in the audience's eyes is a central theme. However, Kathryn feels that the audience can be a positive and affirming source of validation and support.

> "The audience can lift you on their shoulders and carry you out of the room." It comes up at you in waves, the love, again. The love is coming up, and it's a palpable thing. And a good curtain call. That's—that's what makes it addictive.

The discussion contrasted Kathryn's experience of stage fright against what she feels is positive about her acting experiences and her sense of purpose is as an actor. For Kathryn, the meaning of stage fright is the loss of love and admiration from the audience and the feeling of communion that comes with their connection.

> Again, I'm afraid it has to be love. I want them to love me. I don't want them to just like me. I want them to feel my pain. I want them to be with me. I want them … they must love me. And if they don't love me … if I fail, they will stop loving me. I'm sorry, that's just … that's it.

> That's my accumulated wisdom of all the actors I've ever talked to and worked with.

Death. The fear of doing something wrong and the dread that makes it feel like a certainty is like "impending death." She states, "This is stage panic! This is disaster mode." When negative stage fright occurs, she experiences it as "the reverse of my life flashing before my eyes."

> Appearing before a live audience is like appearing before a firing squad. They can kill you!

Duality. Kathryn notes that this terror exists alongside the exciting and motivating force of stage fright. The excitement and horror are intertwined.

> When it's good, it's ecstasy. But that's why the opposite is true. When it's bad, it's nightmare. It's horror.

> The fear is part of the excitement, which is part of the draw. "I can do this. Watch this. I could do this. Watch me." The other voice is saying, "Oh my God, oh my God, oh my God!"

Dreams. In his play *The Actor's Nightmare*, Christopher Durang (1984) creates the character of George Spelvin. (This name is traditionally employed in the theater by an actor when he or she wishes to use a pseudonym.) In the play, George is alone onstage, with no idea who he is portraying, what his lines are, or in what play he is appearing. He is filled with horror and embarrassment as he explains his predicament to the audience. This "actor's nightmare" is a common experience for actors. Kathryn describes her stage fright manifesting in this kind of dream. She has the same "stage fright dream" before every production.

> K: It's the same dream. I'm onstage. I'm wearing the wrong costume. I don't know the lines. I didn't learn the lines well enough. I'm going to have to fake it. And so sometimes, I fake it in the dream. I'm speaking complete gibberish. And usually there's someone in the audience, someone specific, a famous producer, my dead sister, my parents. They're seeing me fail.

L: What's that like?

K: Just horrible. It's a nightmare! You wake up in a sweat. It's like being chased by serial killers with a knife. Wake up just feeling sick. And then it takes a few seconds before you go, "Oh, geez, it was just a dream."

Permanence. Kathryn feels that her stage fright is permanent. Although its nature has changed over the course of her career, she feels it is a permanent aspect of performing.

It's the fright. Because you're—you're having all of this happen very fast. "Oh my God, I just blew that line. Oh my God, now what am I going to say? Oh, thank you, how you bailed me out. Now I have to keep going and acting like nothing ever happened."

She feels that stage fright is part of experiencing the positives of acting.

It is like a deal with the Devil … to get the one I have to face the other.

Changes. Kathryn describes how the manifestation of stage fright has changed over the course of her career. When she was younger, her fear was about not being liked by the audience and not gaining their approval. Furthermore, she felt less able to tolerate it earlier in her career. "When you're 26 it can stop you in your tracks," she stated. However, she felt she could cope with it more easily then because she was stronger emotionally.

On the other hand, sadly, I have seen it more often happen to elderly actors than young ones. 'Cause young ones have a confidence that they can sort of bullshit their way out of it. They have maybe more ego. Fresher ego. What I've noticed increasingly as I get older and I'm working with people even older than I am, they really become a little frozen, and you have … you, whoever's younger is gonna have to do the talking.

Now, she is not concerned about the audience liking her. She is concerned about her lines and being able to experience the opportunity to be "swept along" in the story.

And that's the difference between being a young performer, which is, "Do you love me? Do you love me? Look at me! Look at me!" and I'd say immature performers go on needing that, "Love me! Love me!" thing.

But mature performers—now, I'm talking about decades and decades of this—I just want to be swept along. It's why I never had to be the lead. I wasn't obsessed with playing the lead. I'm happy to be character support, because it's the same journey, not as hard *(laughs)*.

Responsibility. Kathryn feels a responsibility to the performance. When fear strikes, she must recover and go on. "There is no choice in live theater," she states.

Coping. Kathryn describes precurtain activities that help her with negative stage fright: preparing her role, going over her lines, dressing, checking her hair, moving her body, doing a warm-up, checking the audience, and talking to other actors. When onstage, Kathryn copes with stage fright by focusing on "being in the moment" and being in the fantasy of the play. By focusing on the story and the characters and not on her internal state, her stage fright can be eliminated or avoided. She is more able to cope in a drama, as the "fourth wall" is protective; in a comedy, the laughter from the audience reminds her she is onstage and makes being "in the moment" more difficult. Kathryn also uses self-talk to combat the negative aspects of stage fright.

> And you can say to yourself, "You got these lines down. They wanted to see you. You can do this in your sleep. It's a stupid part. "Here are all of the things you buy yourself off with. "It's OK, K. You don't really want to be in this show anyway. "I will say my mantras to myself. Uh, if you allow me to use bad language, "Fuck them. What do they know anyway?"

Kathryn copes with stage fright by finding places where she can control the audience by making them laugh.

> If you can make them laugh the first time, they will keep laughing, like obedient children.

Kathryn tries to deal with stage fright by checking the audience to "find out who they are." When she gets a sense of the audience, she feels more confident and regains a sense of control.

> Are they laughers? Are they quiet? Are they slow? How do 400 people decide so quickly, as a group, how they're going to respond? It's a miracle. Four hundred, probably strangers. Two hundred, at least, strange couples are suddenly going, "Oh, this isn't very good." They're not gonna laugh as much. Or, "This is a laugh riot! I'm gonna fall out of my chair and roll down the aisle."

> It's a slow audience tonight. Actors will come off-stage and say, "They're slow. Take an extra beat." Right?

Another important coping mechanism that Kathryn uses is forgiveness. In her experience, if she forgives herself and other actors for making mistakes and incorporates any mishaps into the performance, the audience will be forgiving as well.

> If we forgive ourselves and make it look like part of the plan the audience will forgive us and love us.

Essential description of stage fright: Kathryn

Stage fright is a potential for loss. The potential feels so real, the loss so possible, that enduring it is horrible. What is the loss? It is the loss of being who I was meant to be. It is the loss of doing what I was meant to do. As an actor, I believe my mandate is to serve the human cause. It requires that I feel and live the lives of characters onstage so that I may assist audiences in living their lives and dealing with all things human: their loss, their love, their pain, their joy. When I accomplish these things well—and it is not always easy—I feel transcendent. When the audience, other actors, and I connect and experience great life truths onstage, we have been through something together that is priceless. We are transformed. We have generated and felt love.

Stage fright is red. It moves quickly. At first, it invites me to these things. But then it tries to prevent me from experiencing and possessing these things. It stops me by attacking my body: my heart beats wildly, my breathing increases, my extremities tremble. My mind races and my tongue swells. I no longer have control of my body. It attacks my sense of competence. I feel out of control in my mind. I feel defenseless and alone. I will disappoint the audience. I will disappoint and shame my fellow actors. I fear I will fail as an actor. It attacks my honor and dignity. I feel ashamed and humiliated. It attacks my reason for living! I fear I will fail in my duties to others and to whatever force has made me what I am. It attacks my belief in the purpose of what I do. I fear I will be thought of as a fraud. It makes me hate the audience. It turns this potential loving friend into a despised, despised enemy. All of these attacks feel as if I were in a battle. Perhaps I will fail. Perhaps I am a fraud? This fear is so intense, that I experience it exactly as one might experience impending death.

But there is no escape. I must continue. If I can find some way to connect to the audience, if they can forgive my flaws, perhaps there will be a respite. If I can muster the strength to remember my purpose onstage, I can overcome it. At times, I triumph over it. I fulfill my purpose. And they will love me. Maybe not me, but the truth I speak. And I won't be alone. But only until the next show, where it will repeat its attack again, as it has in various forms throughout my life. Or in my dreams. In order to feel the joy, the love, and the transcendence of what I do, I must endure stage fright. It is the deal with the Devil.

Interview with Marty: introduction

> But I didn't tell anybody I wanted to be an actor, because in the Bronx you don't screw around with no drama, all that crap, you know?

Marty is an 88-year-old actor. His love for acting began when he was an adolescent. In his neighborhood, a "settlement house" was opened for the adolescents in the area. It was here that he took his first drama classes and acted in his first plays. He did not begin acting professionally until after earning a college degree and serving in World War II. Upon returning from the service, Marty tried many occupations until he decided to pursue what he enjoyed, which was acting. He studied Method Acting in New York and worked as an actor in New York in the theater and in film. Marty also has worked in regional theater in the United States and abroad. He also has had regular award-winning roles in various TV series. He calls himself a "character actor." Marty recently completed the successful run of a play, and still considers himself a "working actor." As a beginning actor, he did not experience stage fright. However, negative experiences with acting teachers and actor training caused him to develop stage fright when performing. By noting how these experiences affected his acting process, Marty was eventually able to recover his confidence. He described talking about the experience as "interesting" and hoped to contribute information that might be helpful in understanding the actor.

The thematic aspects of Marty's experience are listed below. An essential description of stage fright from his perspective follows the presentation of themes:

- expression
- communication
- expansion
- excitement
- difference
- service
- the color black
- physical attack
- fear of failure
- self-absorption
- shame
- confusion
- inhibition
- doubt
- mystery
- responsibility
- coping

Interview with Marty: themes

Expression. Marty remembers being drawn to acting. In his earliest experiences, he felt acting was a way to express himself.

> I was only 16, I think, at the time of my first character part. And my experience onstage was kind of interesting, which is sort of the whole thing, really. I was very shy as a young man. As a teenager, particularly. And, um, very unverbal. Then all of a sudden, I'm onstage and I'm expressing myself beautifully, and I'm getting angry and I'm getting loving and I'm getting

puzzled or I'm getting … all these things I do in life but have to account for or have to answer to. And they just do 'em, and there's no … nobody's gonna hurt you for it, you know? So, I liked that aspect of it. I liked being … doing all these things I couldn't do in life onstage.

Yeah, express myself like crazy, which is what I needed to do. Express myself right. It's a form of expression. And I really thought how important that was for me at that time.

And I seemed to do well onstage. I seemed to be very comfortable up there, you know? Even at 16 doing these parts, you know.

Marty feels that expression is still a central factor in his desire to act.

L: In this stage of your life, versus earlier in your life, is the feeling of being onstage the same? Do you still feel that sense of being able to express yourself and that the audience likes you?
M: Yes. Yes.
L: So, it still feels good.
M: Yes. Still feels that way it's … who I am and what I wanna do. And I know who I am, and I'm here. Yeah.

Communication. Marty felt that he could establish an important connection with the audience. He felt he could communicate with them.

And also, the audience reaction to me was kind of interesting. They … they liked me, usually. You know? And I sensed this when I walked out onstage and I … for the first time, I didn't know what the hell was gonna happen, you know? But the audience seemed to be with me.

I loved the quiet moments when the audience was just listening. There was just no sound at all. Just … and I know something was going on. Something important was going on with the audience, as well as me, at the time. And I remember that not happening in life quite the same way, you know. That's kind of interesting.

Marty expresses connection and caring toward the characters he plays.

I love to be able to do a really good part with a beginning, and middle, and an end. A part with a development that has a line and you could see … could see what was happening to the person that, would you … when you care about the person.

Expansion. Marty feels that his acting and stage experiences expanded his awareness of the world.

L: So, what happened onstage was different from what would happen in life.

M: Yes. Oh, very much so. Very much so. It's like a whole new world, you know, opened up to me. And I also realized, even at that early age, that I was pretty good. I could tell by my own senses, by the audience reaction, listening … I was good. I couldn't do very much. This is one thing that I could do pretty well, which is important for me.

Excitement. Marty experienced excitement appearing onstage.

When I did Summer Stock, I'd go out onstage, had a lot of energy onstage. I'd come out and *(explosion noise)* like a rocket, you know?

And the audience for some reason liked me. And I knew this, and I got good reaction, and so the fear of going out there never really entered into it at that time.

Difference. Marty remembers having apprehension about telling others he was interested in acting. He felt that the desire separated him from his peers.

But I didn't tell anybody because in the Bronx, you don't screw around with no drama, eh, you know, all that crap, you know? So, I didn't tell anybody I took the course.

Service. Marty states that he believes acting has purposes beyond entertainment. These include communication and enlightenment.

Well, you could say, to show man unto himself. To entertain. To enlighten, as the case may be. To communicate something that's difficult to communicate in life.

The color black. Marty associated his feelings of stage fright with the color black. More specifically, the image of a "black mark" against him indicating that he was "wrong."

I suppose it would be black … because it's a bad feeling … it's a wrong feeling. You are wrong … like having a black mark against you … a black mark on your record.

Physical attack. Marty's stage fright manifested in physical symptoms including shallow breathing and confusion.

Well, like most fears, I guess, your breathing gets shallow. Just the shallowness of breathing. The breathing changed considerably.

You become very concerned about what's happening and what's going to happen, you know. Instead of just being in the moment, you … your head's all over the place with all the possibilities of, uh …

Yeah, but fear can be overpowering too, as we all know, you know. Um … and at times, it was pretty strong. Fear of going out there and doing something.

Fear of failure. The primary feature of Marty's stage fright centered on feelings of failing. However, it was not always the case.

The only time I remember being frightened onstage is when I didn't know what I was doing, or … or something happened onstage that was not supposed to happen. You know, I got a little leery, a little wary of, how am I gonna handle that? But far as general stage fright, I don't remember that happening then.

Marty's stage fright began when he felt he failed in applying a favored acting technique.

It happened for me, it started for me, when I started studying acting … most teachers then were teaching the Method, or their idea of Stanislavski's Method. And I couldn't get it. I tried so hard to make it my own, to make it make sense to me, to make it … allow it to help me, and I couldn't do it. It just didn't work for me.

Marty's comparison of himself to others, feeling that others were making demands on him, and the resulting confusion contributed to his feelings of failure.

Hated the demands made on me. Wonder why I can't do this. All the other guys seemed to be doing it pretty well. So, all that stuff is going all at the same time. A big mish-mash of stuff.

Self-absorption. Marty stated that when he experienced stage fright, he was self-absorbed and not using his instincts. He was not "in the moment," was self-absorbed, and was concerned about the technique rather than the moment-to moment circumstances of the play.

M: It put me totally in my head. "Where have you been? What's the wea- ther like outside? What's your option? What's your adjustment? Uh, what are your obstacles? What are … ?" Jesus Christmas! It's all in my head, you know? And I'd try to use it, I'd walk out onstage and … I didn't know what the hell I was doing. And if my instinct dries up or gets sidetracked for any reason, I don't know what the hell to do. And I'd walk out onstage to do a part and I just couldn't be there. It would dominate my performance. The, uh, the Method.

L: Is that what made you feel anxious, or is that what gave you stage fright is being in your head?

M: Yes. Yes. Yes.

Shame. Marty felt feelings of shame when experiencing stage fright.

Well, I felt it was wrong. I felt it was bad. I didn't want it to happen, so I was trying to get around it, go through it, lose it.

Yeah. That this feeling was a bad feeling. A wrong feeling. You know. I didn't like it. I was very unhappy with it. But I still stayed with it.

Confusion. Marty's attempt to use preferred acting techniques contributed to his stage fright, which manifested in confusion.

I was really a mess up there. And I tried to use it onstage. I just couldn't function at all. I really couldn't, you know. I was tied up in knots. 'Cause I'm an instinctive actor. And this stuff from class, from the Method that I was taught, was, as I say, all intellectual stuff. Supposedly, you only use it as—as homework, and then throw it away when you get onstage and allow yourself to be there in the moment, but I find it very hard to do that.

If I started worrying about it, my actions and adjustments and relationships and needs and obstacles and … just totally going around and around and around in my head.

Inhibition. Marty feels that stage fright inhibits him from expressing himself.

Tying you in knots, preventing you from doing what you wanna do.

Doubt. Marty feels that stage fright manifests in self-doubt.

What happens is you begin to doubt yourself. You begin to feel you don't have talent. You begin to feel that you shouldn't be an actor. You begin to feel that you can't make it. That happened to me a lot when I started to use the Method. And the more I tried to use it, the worse the fear got. Wanted to sit down and cry sometimes because I was trying so hard. It's not good. Nothing's happening. Part of me began to feel untalented and … you're in the wrong profession and should be selling insurance like my father suggested.

For Marty, this self-doubt is central to his stage fright experience. Doubts about himself as an actor and a person are intertwined.

M: Your self-worth is at stake.

L: Your self-worth as an actor?

M: And as a person, too. They go hand-in-hand. For me they do. Yes. It's as important as that, that your self-worth is very much involved. And if you can't do it, get out.

Mystery. Marty felt that there is some psychological aspect of stage fright that he could not quite articulate. This remains a mystery to him.

There's something else here which I'm trying to get at, you know. I don't know. I kept thinking there was something else. Something else. Something else I haven't touched on, and I … I don't know if that's so, or what it might be if it is so.

Responsibility. Marty felt a responsibility to stay with and apply a favored acting approach even though it contributed to his stage fright.

See, if I was smart, or cagey, I would just say, "Well, screw it. I'll do something else. I'll do what I want to do." I was the kinda guy if I had a job to do, I stayed with it until I did it or failed doing it. And so, I stayed with it and tried to use it … it was difficult at times. Very difficult just to get past a certain point.

Coping. Marty has coped with his stage fright by trusting his instincts as an actor and by not using techniques that were uncomfortable for him.

Now I don't get nervous onstage. Now, I don't get nervous when I start a part.

I get a little trepidatious, if I use that word again, uh, a little nervous hoping I … about some lines that I'm not sure of and stuff like that, you know. But it's nothing like my self-worth involved, you know, and all that. Just, I don't wanna screw up that moment.

Essential description of stage fright: Marty

I've been acting since I was 16 years old. That's a long time. Even though I was just a kid, being onstage was great. I used to shoot onstage like a rocket. Bam! It allowed me to express myself, without having to answer to anyone. I could feel love, hate, joy, rage … all of the things that 'cha couldn't show in real life. Not in my neighborhood, anyway. When I was onstage, the audience was with me, you know? It opened a whole new world to me. And I felt that I was opening a whole world to the audience. And that was important to me. After the war, and after going to college, I tried a lotta things. I finally decided to be an actor because it is the only thing I really enjoyed.

I only got stage fright when I got involved with that Method Acting. It really messed things up. When I used it, all I could do was think about myself. Where are you going? What is the weather like? What is your adjustment?

Jesus Christmas! It got me into my head. It tied me up in knots! It got so bad that before I'd go onstage it was hard to breathe. And I got confused. I began to doubt myself. I didn't know what the hell I was doing! Am I any good? Am I going to blow it? I felt wrong. It was a bad, wrong feeling that I had. Like a black mark against you! And I tried so hard to do it right, 'cause I thought I was supposed to. But I just couldn't. And sometimes I would just put my head in my hands and cry. I felt so bad. What happened to that happy kid who shot onstage like a rocket? The kid that the audience liked?

I don't really get stage fright now. There may be more to it, but I think I learned my lesson. I put all that Method crap aside and focus on the character. On the story. And I let myself go. I trust myself. I trust my instincts out there. Sure, I may get a little trepidatious (sic), but that's normal for an actor. Who wouldn't get nervous in front of all those people? But I don't have that terrible fear anymore. No. I just focus on the character and react from my instincts. Do my work, ya know? I love playing a good part, where you see the character change. But I don't let anyone tell me what to do now, or how to act. I. Trust. My. Gut. And I'm still shootin' out there like a rocket! Bam!

Interview with Peter: introduction

> *It feels like you are stripped bare … that everyone can see your flaws … even flaws you don't know you have. It is feeling of wanting to curl up and disappear.*

Peter is a 48-year-old actor. When he was a small child, he recognized that he was drawn to "anything creative." When he was exposed to drama in elementary school, he recognized that he had the ability to perform. After acting in plays in elementary school, high school, and several performing groups, Peter desired formal training as an actor. He studied with various teachers and in workshops before he moved to London and completed conservatory training there in his 20s. After returning to the United States, Peter acted in film, TV, theater, and musicals. He currently supports himself in between acting jobs as an interior designer and as a host for parties and variety shows. He describes his stage fright as normal to "debilitating." On a few occasions, he has briefly fainted before appearing onstage. In the interview, revealed that he felt inadequate discussing his stage fright because he felt that he should understand it more deeply. Furthermore, he stated that despite his extensive acting experience, he has never discussed his stage fright. He relies on spirituality to face down his fear.

> But, boy, the truth is that, nobody talks about it. I mean, people say they have stage fright, but it's almost like everybody's agreed not to dive into what it means, or what it feels like, or what it is.

The thematic aspects of Peter's experience are listed below. An essential description of stage fright from Peter's perspective follows the presentation of themes:

- attention
- expression
- communication
- freedom
- trust
- safety
- courage
- inherence
- difference
- service
- the colors black and purple
- motivation
- physical attack
- feeling alone
- inhibition
- fear of failure
- shame
- death
- permanence
- change
- dreams
- responsibility
- coping

Interview with Peter: themes

Attention. Peter was initially drawn to acting as a way of getting attention.

> As a child it was a need to get love and attention … being onstage was a quick way to get attention and love.

Expression. Peter also felt that acting filled the need to express himself.

> I recognized that I needed to express myself creatively, and I had the gift, ability, and talent—even though at that early age, I didn't understand those things—but I knew that I had that thing, and I was desperate to express it.

Communication. Peter's initial need for attention and expression evolved into the need to communicate.

> As an adult I have evolved much more … I desire to connect deeply and intimately with the audience … to communicate with them and enrich their lives. Not so much needing attention anymore.

> I truly want to touch other lives, I have a chance to give a gift of revelation or insight and make someone else feel as deeply as I always do.

Now I want to reveal who I am ... even a character who only has parts of you as a person, you can use those parts to know yourself in a deeper way as our lives are so full of inner variety. And we share those deeper aspects ... they may never have been known by another, but they can be purged, shown, expressed through the variety of different characters that we play.

Freedom. Peter's early acting experiences allowed him to feel alive, complete, and free.

> Appearing onstage was the time where I felt the most alive and the most completely who I was. I felt completely free.

> It felt like I was fully the person that I was meant to be while I was onstage. And it gave me great joy.

> It was not about being someone else, it was about creating other people for the joy of participating in their life. It's not that I didn't want to be who I was. It is an adventure. Being another character is a great way to have an adventure.

At this point in his career, Peter experiences the same freedom, yet it is a deeper experience.

> Well now, I'm not getting that early childhood rush of pure, innocent joy. I'm a lot older, I've done a lot of stuff, I know what I'm doing, I know how to use my training and my techniques to enhance my performance. Therefore, as a creative artist, I feel much more satisfied.

> Being inside a work of art is so amazing. The sets, the costumes, the way the lights mix, and being with other talented people ... everything is thought out meaningfully ... the joy of being inside a creative place ... what I wish real life was ... real life is haphazard and messy and scary ... the intensity of being onstage is addictive! You can't get that experience anywhere else. You are in this constructed place, but you are also free. Isn't that interesting?

> It's a larger experience. It isn't as selfish as when I was a child. I share the excitement, the fun, and the joy of it with the people that I'm performing with and with the audience. It's deeper and richer.

Trust. Peter feels that trusting others onstage is necessary for successful performances. Experiencing this trust is a positive experience for him.

> When you are onstage with another person, and working closely with them, you are really there for each other ... so much more so than in real life ... in real life it could take years to develop the same kind of trust actors develop so quickly with each other ... and they are bonds that can last for life.

When trust is absent, his stage fright is triggered. If Peter feels that his onstage relationships are unsafe, his stage fright worsens.

> The realization that … I'm possibly unsafe in the performance arena. What I mean by that is, I … someone's either just said something to me that was negative or destructive or mean, or I've just realized or heard about someone or a group of people onstage that I'm gonna be working with, who are not in my sight.

> If I feel like I'm not in a safe team environment, that's the catalyst to that darker one. The times that I've experienced the dissociative episodes is when there's conflict within the people that I'm working with onstage, probably due to a violation … a potential violation of trusting onstage.

Safety. Peter feels a sense of safety onstage.

> There is a safety that happens onstage. In life there are no written lines, you can't script your day … you can't make it the best. There is a lot of uncertainty … being onstage meant that I could create certainty. I could create what it should be. Now I can recognize I felt so out of control in real life, onstage I could make what was happening onstage be wonderful.

When Peter felt unsafe, his stage fright worsened, creating a loop of fear that keeps escalating and making him feel worse.

> There is a horror of stage fright that makes me know how unsafe I feel. When I was unsafe, I felt more stage fright.

Courage. Peter feels that despite the positives of acting, it requires courage to step onstage and face the audience. His experience of courage is intertwined with his spiritual beliefs.

> It takes courage to walk out on that stage. Without knowing that God has my back, I can't drum up my own courage. Well I can, but it's … that courage has a lot more vulnerability to it than knowing God has your back (laughs).

Inherence. As a small child, Peter remembers a feeling of knowing that he was meant to act. He feels his abilities are inherent. He feels the ability to act is "a gift."

> I knew even as a child that I had something to do … and when I started acting, I knew that that this is what I was born to do.

> I think it's a gift given by God, and it's in me. It's a part of my DNA.

Difference. Peter feels that actors are different from other people.

> I think we have a separate and unique ability to observe other people that other people don't have. Perhaps other kinds of people have similar abilities. I think those abilities are far more limited.

> Actors usually are far more animated, and, I think part of the reason why we are special is that because we have a unique ability to bring joy to people.

Peter feels that he has been judged negatively for being an actor.

> I would often be on the defensive, with the classic, "I'm an actor." "What restaurant do you wait tables at?" And I would use that joke as a deflection because I felt humiliated. If I said to someone, I was an actor, but I couldn't back it up with something I was doing right then, or had recently done.

Service. Peter feels that for him, acting serves a higher purpose.

> We use storytelling as a continuum for our species, to learn who we are, to get, to grow, and have courage.

> I think there's a higher purpose in acting because, not only are you someone who is hearing the stories, you are the one participating in telling the stories. And we can teach, enhance other people's lives, we can touch people's hearts, we can change people, we can bring, uh, revelation to them.

> I think that, as an actor, we are communicators … there is a higher purpose in being a performer. We are creators. God is a creator. We are fulfilling a function that is a … uh, something that is purely from God. Being an actor absolutely *can* have a higher purpose. It doesn't necessarily have one, but I think that it can, and I believe that I am a part of that.

The colors black and purple. Peter associates the colors black and purple swirling together to describe two aspects of his stage fright: excitement and terror.

> Well, I think it would be a bipolar character. It would have two object-ives. Stage fright is so easy to describe color-wise. Deep purple and black, swirling around and never mixing. Constantly rolling. The purple is related to the intensity and the vibrancy of a performance. Darkness. Um, the loss of … probably … probably the classic, the loss of memory of lines, going up, having no idea … the awful void. Probably because it's one of the darkest, blackest fears for any performer … not the unknowable, but the unfathomable, the thing that cannot be touched … it's like from, um, *Harry*

Potter, don't mention his name, Voldemort, don't mention his name. It's so dark, it's so black, do not say the name. I think there's a similarity there. You can mention that you have stage fright, but we're not getting into it. It's too overwhelming. It's too powerful. It's Voldemort. Stage fright is Voldemort. That's a perfect metaphor.

Motivation. Peter describes a positive form of stage fright that enhances his performances by helping him to be more alert and present in performance.

I had normal stage fright for me, which is heightened adrenaline, nervousness, but not debilitating.

There's the vibrancy and intensity of a performance that often is directly linked, in my experience, to standard, manageable stage fright … that enhances a performance, because you're alert and sharp, and you can therefore be more present in the performance … and I know that being present and 'in the moment' in a performance is essential for a truthful performance. So, I use it to my advantage, if I can.

Peter describes a state of motivating fear as "tough love."

Tough love. Forces you into a better performance.

Physical attack. Peter's stage fright registers as concern about his body movements, which causes his self-consciousness to increase.

I get hyperconscious of the way my arms move, which I hate. I get hyperconscious of the way my—my mouth and lips form and move, which I hate, and it adds to the fear.

Peter also experiences light-headedness and loses focus.

What happens is, I get light-headed, I lose the ability to focus on what's around me, and it's as if clouds of darkness, like webs of darkness start spinning around in my head and in my eyes, and I lose the ability to function tangibly right then.

Peter physically registers the emotion of fear in his gut. As he described the feeling, he made a gesture with his hand to indicate the intensity of the feeling.

That sensation of dark webs flying around me happens the moment I realize I do not know what's about to happen. But it doesn't happen in my head, it happens in my gut. There's a terror that takes over in my gut right then.

Peter experiences shortness of breath and shaking in his hands.

Shortness of breath. I shake and my knees feel weak and unsteady. My hands shake and I must become careful what I do with them to mask the shaking … I feel like the blood in my veins has thinned out and I'm not getting enough oxygen. It's like a wave of fear that passes through me.

Feeling alone. A central feature of stage fright for Peter is an acute sense of feeling alone.

The fear of the unknown … . I feel like it's all crashing in on me and there is no "other side" to get to. Very apocalyptic actually. I also feel isolated and alone as if no one has the ability to help me out of the overwhelming nature of it.

Inhibition. Peter feels that stage fright contains a restrictive and inhibiting factor.

Stage fright has the potential to prevent a strong and wonderful perform- ance by dulling my abilities. It stifles freedom of emotional range. It limits what I want to … what I know I can do. It cuts off nuance.

It feels like … being choked or cut off. It must be destroyed *(laughs)*!

Fear of failure. Peter feels that a fear of failure is central to his stage fright experience.

Well, as an actor … there seems to be a sense of extremities. I'm either amazing, or I'm a failure.

I either get, uh, lauded and revered by the audience … or I was terrible in the performance, whatever.

So, so much of the stage fright really roots itself in the fear of failing in that moment.

Peter feels stage fright is the "catalyst" for failure. It causes hypervigilance and the need to try to control its emergence in order to ward off failure.

Yeah. If you're not on guard, stage fright will be the thing that will take you down and will be the catalyst to your failure onstage … If I allowed it to. If I allowed it to overwhelm my mind, yes. It would be the catalyst for failure.

Shame. Peter feels that if he fails as an actor, he will be publicly shamed.

Instead of being present for the performance, I'm present for a failure on a large scale, with people watching the failure. Which, of course, fills … is the

fear of the shame that would come. How can I survive after something …
a failure that large, in front of a lot of people?

Peter describes a feeling of potential or actual humiliation when he is experiencing stage fright.

It feels like you are stripped bare … that everyone can see your flaws …
even flaws you don't know you have. It is feeling of wanting to curl up and
disappear.

You are so exposed … if I could pinpoint exactly what it was, I could find
a solution, but it is as if I don't even know these flaws.

Death. Peter describes severe stage fright as feeling like a "death experience."

I feel like I'm on the edge of a precipice about to plunge to my demise, the
rug is being pulled out from under me, my world about to collapse.

There were two times in my life where I've fainted. It's almost like I'm
shutting down. So, it's kind of, sort of like a death experience. It feels like
the beginning of losing consciousness.

I started dissociating. I started feeling … I started having dissociative lapse
in time. The … um, which was very unusual. And I remembered that this
experience had happened to me other times as well.

Permanence. Peter has experienced stage fright all of his life. He feels it is
permanent.

P: I've always experienced stage fright.
L: Really? All your life?
P: Always. Yes.

Peter has managed the psychological aspects of stage fright through spiritual
practices. The physical manifestations are ongoing and, he believes, enduring.

However, the internal physical feeling is pretty consistent.

Changes. Peter feels that his relationship with stage fright has improved
throughout his career.

After I got with my technique of getting on my knees and surrendering it
to God, more and more, I feel confident in God having my back regardless
of the circumstances that I'm in. So, there is, I would say, an escalation in
my perception.

However, the physical manifestations of stage fright remain constant.

> There's always that adrenaline, there's always that knot in the stomach. But I don't think that the physical manifestation of it has as much power over me as the confidence that I get, knowing that I'm safe.

Dreams. Peter describes having the dream called "the actor's nightmare."

> To this day, I still have "the dream." The classic dream that I am onstage and it's not that I've forgotten my lines, it's that I come to from a dissociative episode and I am inside of a show that I've been doing, but I'm coming out, just like a blackout. And I don't know who these people are. I don't know what the set is. I don't know where I am. And I have no conception of what the show is, or how, or what character I am. It's the absolute extremity of lack of knowledge, the blackness, and the dark … the black thing.

Responsibility. Peter feels that despite the intense discomfort, he must make his stage appearances.

> Classic. The show must go on. It's like there is an agreement when I commit to a show that barring extreme circumstances, like a death, or a tragedy, I WILL go on. Stage fright is not an option for declining an entrance.

> Also, there is a need to give to the audience all that I am and all that I can do. To have the opportunity to "show my stuff" is very special and I WANT to make it happen. These needs are stronger than the stage fright. Usually.

Coping. Peter copes with stage fright onstage by finding a tangible solution.

> Then I come to, and I find a solution. Either saying something that is appropriate in the context, even if it's not right, or doing a bit of business, or allowing the other actor to know that I'm in trouble. So, it passes through me, but I immediately jump to some resolution.

Peter copes with stage fright on a larger scale using spiritual practices that are aligned with what he feels is his purpose as an actor.

> OK. This is what I do. Honestly. I find a time, usually it's in a bathroom or somewhere private, where no one's gonna walk in on me, and I get on my knees and I put my hands in the air and I say, "God, I can't do this. I have the talent and the gift, and I know my lines, but I can't do this. I don't have … It's too much for me. So, I give it to you." And that's what I do. I surrender the performance to God.

And, I also ask for favor from the audience. I ask God to give me favor from them, which is specifically designed to diffuse my fear of an audience not liking me.

By surrendering his fear, Peter feels a sense of relief.

I feel a sense of relief or a sense that … It doesn't purge the physical manifestation of the stage fright. But I choose to believe that God is gonna take care of me.

By surrendering, Peter paradoxically gains a sense of inner strength.

It reminds me that I have strength. I become very aware that I am wholly dependent on God and trusting him. When I can access His strength and fear does not rule me, I am not and will not be subject to it.

Peter's sense of confidence through surrender gives him satisfaction.

I get a great satisfaction from overcoming obstacles and this obstacle is so visceral that the pleasure of pushing past it is unique and fulfilling.

BUT this is where my trust in God comes in because He is the rescuer. He is the one who has the power over fear. Even if the emotional distress of it stays or lingers, I have the confidence and strength to go on.

Essential description of stage fright: Peter

When I was a child, I was drawn to anything creative. Stories. Colors. Music. Dance. Those things were the world to me. When I played my first part in school, I instantly knew that I was going to be an actor when I grew up. I felt so alive! So free! At first, I craved the attention—and the love—of being onstage. I guess I didn't feel much of it off-stage. But anyway, being inside of something creative: the lights, the costumes, the sets, all of it was constructed to be so much better than real life. To be more heightened than real life. To be more excellent. Real life could be so unpredictable. Onstage, I could have great adventures! Excellent adventures! Play different characters and feel deeply. Now I know that the Lord has given me the gifts to act and perform. He used my circumstances and my need for love and attention for His Purpose. For His Glory. When I get up onstage now, I know that God is using my performances to communicate truths to the audience. To touch them. To bring them joy!

Stage fright is Voldemort. It is one of the darkest and blackest fears of any performer. It is the unfathomable thing that cannot be touched. It's so dark, it's so black, do not say the name! I know when it is coming. My knees and hands begin to shake. I get hyperconscious about my arms and my lips. The blood in my veins thins out. I get light-headed. I can't focus! I suddenly feel restricted. It's as if clouds of darkness, webs of darkness, start spinning around in my head and in my eyes. Oh no! I have to get onstage! What if I blow it! What if I blow it in front of all of those people? The webs descend into my gut. The webs strip me bare. I am completely exposed. I feel like I'm on the edge of a precipice about to plunge to my demise, the rug is being pulled out from under me! My world about to collapse! I lose the ability to function. Oh no ... I am alone. No one can help me now. I am ... losing ... consciousness ... I ... a ... .

Stage fright wants to extinguish me. Extinguish my purpose.

BUT God is my WEAPON. God is my courage. I get on my knees and I put my hands in the air and I say, "God, I can't do this. I have the talent and the gift, and I know my lines, but I can't do this. It's too much for me. So, I give it to you." And that's what I do. I surrender the performance to God. I become very aware that I am wholly dependent on God and trusting him. I can access HIS strength and fear does NOT rule me. I am not and will not be subject to it. HE is the Rescuer. HE is the one who has the power over Fear. Even if the emotional distress of it stays or lingers, I don't care! I have the confidence and strength to go on. And I do! The webs disappear and I am filled with His Peace. His Safety. I lean on Him. And I go onstage for his Glory. And all is well.

7 Your stage fright experience

We are not alone: the essence of stage fright

In the previous section, our actors described what stage fright was like for them and the various features of it emerged. Our actors expressed several themes in common revealing the universal aspects of stage fright. Indeed, it is a common experience for actors, so we are not alone. Our actors have tried to extinguish its symptoms, have looked to its causes, and have feared—and expected—it return. Here, the revealed stage fright themes are presented in summary form in service to the illumination of its presence in fellow actors. This summary organizes the themes in three parts, as they were presented in the interview section. It begins with the themes related to (1) *the draw to acting and the acting experience*, continues with (2) *the stage fright experience*, and concludes with (3) *the nature of stage fright* in the actors' lives. The section concludes with the single *essential composite description* of stage fright in the actor amassed from the eight individual descriptions. Because the individual *essential descriptions* of stage fright in each actor culminate in a *composite description*, there was a possibility that some of the features of the individual actors might be lost. Therefore, in addition to the shared themes, the divergent (i.e., *nonessential*) themes are also presented below.

What do we do now: our own account

The fact that actors do not talk about their stage fright has been discussed, and this "culture of silence" is reflected in research (Nordin-Bates, 2012). Acknowledging its presence often brings shame, doubt, confusion, and in some cases, resignation or the decision to leave acting altogether. By admitting its presence we are speaking the truth. By taking the step of facing it—now—we are contributing to solving stage fright in the greater world and within ourselves. We are beginning to recover what stage fright has caused us to lose. One of the most powerful ways of doing this is to make the elusive realm of feelings, images, and thoughts concrete. Writing, drawing, painting, and so on are powerful means of expressing our internal worlds. Your willingness to express your internal world—stage fright—in these ways can change its constricting and destructive energies into something enlivening and transformative.

Join us: how to use the next sections

In the next sections, please review any or all of the aspects of stage fright that resonate with you. If you feel hesitancy about any particular one, this may be an invitation to look at that aspect within yourself more deeply. Notice how you feel about each one. Heard? Relieved? Excited? Acknowledged? Affronted? Critical? After reading a section, please answer the question that appears next to the bullet point. You can refer to your journal and, as before, write in any form you wish. The purpose here is to join our actors by delivering an account of your own unique stage fright. You are invited to reveal your own experience and to investigate and amplify each aspect of your stage fright. It is recommended that you respond as candidly as you can, in as much detail as possible. Answer each question until you *literally have no more to say or convey.* Allow memories, images, songs, and lines of dialog—whatever comes up for you—to emerge in your field of awareness to be seen, heard, and recorded. You will begin to give your stage fright a voice and to hear its meaning and message for you as you gain greater insight and understanding about its presence in your life.

Steps for reviewing each theme:

* find a comfortable space free from distractions
* take a few moments to relax
* enter a reflective frame of mind
* read each theme and the actor's description
* notice what thoughts come up about the theme
* notice what emotions come up about the theme
* notice any sensations in your body
* ask yourself how this theme resonates with you
* allow any associations, memories, thoughts, lines of dialog, and so on to emerge
* write them down in any form you wish until you have nothing more to say

The draw to acting and the acting experience

Childhood experience. All of the actors shared a *childhood experience* that was central to their draw to acting and their experience of acting. These early events often have a sense of magic, play, spontaneity, and appreciation. Childhood onstage appearances provided a sense of safety and refuge and supplied a venue for personal communication and expression. Being onstage was a setting where their heightened internal fantasies could be played out. Most of the actors recalled a particular experience that encouraged them to later embark on a career in acting. Some of the actors noted that there was a family history of acting that influenced their involvement in the theater. The literature shows that as children, actors have been found to be more sensitive than other children, have more vivid inner worlds than ordinary children do, and tend to imitate others as an outlet for these heightened impressions (Kaplan, 1969; Goldstein & Winner, 2009). The actors' descriptions of their childhood experiences related to acting confirmed this idea.

Alex remembered a pivotal event when she was nine years old, performing for the cast of a musical that her father was directing. Bill recalled being onstage in elementary school where he finally felt free from shyness and his inability to connect with others. Elizabeth recalled an important experience of performing at four years old during one of her father's orchestra shows and enjoying communication with the audience. Jake remembered, as a young child, performing with his family in community theater, and Jimmy remembered always having the desire to act, although his first acting experiences did not occur until he was older. Kathryn recollected being cast as the Wicked Witch at a young age. It was a performance that she feels set the course of her life's direction. Marty remembered the impact of appearing onstage at a settlement house in his neighborhood, and Peter recalled being deeply affected while appearing onstage at a very young age. In every instance, these experiences were meaningful events that contributed to the actors' inclinations toward acting.

- **To the actor: describe your childhood experience that drew you to acting.**
- **And/or what made you know you wanted to be an actor?**

Communication. All of the actors stated that *communication* was a major theme that emerged regarding their experience of acting. Although two actors disclosed that their initial impulse to act was "expression," which *Webster's* defines as "to show or reveal" (1989, p. 503), they related that this impulse evolved into a desire for a two-way communication, or an exchange, between the audience and them. Communication allows them to give hard-found information to audiences. When audiences receive, are affected by, and respond to this information, actors believe that along with the audience they are impacted emotionally, and that all expand, mature, and evolve as individuals. All were highly committed to their responsibility to communicate as actors. A common aspect of this theme was articulated by Marty who said that when onstage, he had the feeling that the audience was "with" him and that that there was something "important going on between us." All of the actors discussed using the playwright's words to communicate deeper truths to the audience through their roles. Katherine used the word "communion" to describe this delivery. *Webster's* (1989) defines *communion* as "the act of sharing or holding in common" (p. 298). It is noteworthy that this word holds the double meaning of "partaking of the Eucharist" (p. 298), during the sacrifice of the Catholic Mass. Katherine also noted "the holy origins of theater" related to communication and that at times it is like "human sacrifice" onstage.

Past research indicates that acting is rooted in exhibitionism (Fenichel, 1946; Bergler, 1949; Blum, 1976; Nagel, 2004). It is significant that one-way expression, defined as "to show or reveal," is more in line with the idea that actors are merely exhibitionistic. The actors' responses that they wish to communicate rather than express reveals that this is not necessarily the case. Furthermore, the literature states that the actor's personality possesses characteristics of vanity, the need for glory and applause, and the will for power (Fenichel, 1946) and attention (Gabbard, 1979). These aspects are more in line with those who wish to make exhibitionistic pronouncements than with those motivated to exchange truthful notions and emotions. The interviews reveal that actors ultimately wish to communicate human truths to audiences. Alex said, "It is not me up there, but the character delivering the playwright's words through me."

Alex detailed her progression from wanting to engage in a one-way *expression* of her internal experience to desiring a two-way *communication* with audiences as a "give and take" that became increasingly important to her as she grew into an adult. When she gives to audiences and receives their responses, she experiences this as a literal physical event, which she describes as "shattering," in which she feels she changes and evolves as a person. She aims to assist audiences in having this same experience. Elizabeth remembered looking out into the audience as a young girl and desiring "communication" with the audience, even before she knew the meaning of the word. She counted communication as a primary goal for her as an actor. Jake remembered being labeled "the clown" in his family. He knew he had a more serious side and appreciated politics, history, and philosophy. His draw to acting continues to involve a deep desire to communicate these more serious parts of himself and to have them acknowledged. Kathryn stated that this ability to communicate with the audience is deeply important, and is less about conveying her inner experience and more about communicating deeper "truths" to an audience by acting the playwright's text. When she prepares a role, lives the part, and communicates emotional, psychological and philosophical truth onstage she is in "communion" with the audience members who receive it. Marty also noted that when he is onstage, he values the connection between his character and the audience, especially in the silences, when the audience is listening. "Something important was going on with the audience, as well as with me." For Peter, communication has been an important theme. As a child, he longed for attention. At this point in this life, he wants to communicate meaningfully with audiences so that he can enrich their lives and they can enrich his life.

- **To the actor: describe your desire to communicate as an actor.**
- **To the actor: have you ever felt a sense of oneness or communion with the audience?**

Danger and courage. Alex, Bill, Jake, Jimmy, Kathryn, and Peter equated performing on the stage to danger, courage, or *danger* and *courage* combined.

They often feel exposure to risk and must bravely navigate being onstage moment by moment. Acting can be dangerous (Hays, 2017). The potential for accidents, mistakes, weaknesses or failures of their instrument (i.e., their bodies) and for public ridicule were concerns of the actors regarding appearing onstage (Brandfonbrener, 2000). The hesitations generated by the awareness of these dangers contradicted the historical and current view in the literature that actors are actively compelled to go onstage to display themselves or to show-off. The stage fright experience reveals that actors are aware of the dangers of performing beyond the potential lack of approval by an audience. *Courage is* defined by *Webster's* (1989) as "the quality of mind or spirit that enables one to face difficulty, danger, pain, with firmness and without fear" and "to act in accordance with one's convictions in spite of criticism" (p. 334). Although Kaplan (1969) notes that actors are brave (in that they dare to attempt to recapture the fantasies of childhood when appearing onstage), the literature does not highlight that the actor possesses courage when performing. However, all of the actors felt that courage is required to face the practical dangers of the stage. Furthermore, courage mitigates the common response to such dangers, which is to flee.

The actors' conception of courage makes room for the presence of fear. The fact that actors perform in the face of fear is known as a *counter-phobia*, as described in the *Psychodynamic Diagnostic Manual* (PDM Task Force, 2006). Counter-phobia occurs when a desired activity is pursued despite fear, as opposed to a *social phobia*, in which a desired activity is avoided due to fear (*DSM-V*, 2013). Stage fright is a universal condition experienced by anyone who places himself or herself in front of an audience (Gabbard, 1983), however our actors' responses indicate that their fear is not necessarily due to pathological factors or negative past experiences. The responses signify that it is a universal reaction to a situation that is literally dangerous. Actors face their dangers bravely and act in accordance with their convictions.

Bill noted the potential things that could go wrong onstage like failure and being disliked by the audience. Jake observed that "live theater involves danger." In addition to being exposed, he noted the numerous things that can go wrong during live performance including accidents, not being in control of his instrument (i.e., his body, mind, and artistry), and other performance failures. Kathryn also feels that the immediacy required by performing in live theater is dangerous. She noted "the danger, thrill, and vocal response" created by the audience. Five of the actors felt that acting required courage. Alex observed that because of her severe stage fright symptoms, the act of going onstage requires heroism on her part. She noted, "If everybody who has stage fright didn't go out onstage, nobody would be out onstage." Bill stated that courage is something that audiences cannot share with actors because audiences are "too afraid to do it." He feels that having bravery is necessary to perform. Jake feels that actors must possess more courage than those in other professions because of the public exposure required for acting. "It takes tremendous courage to do that night after night." For Jimmy, the experience of exposing himself emotionally, physically, and psychologically is a courageous act. "It's … a courageous thing to do." For Peter, "It takes courage to walk out on that stage."

- **To the actor: describe the feeling of danger you have when acting.**
- **To the actor: describe the feeling of courage, and how it felt to come against danger when acting.**

Difference. As a group, actors have been reported to feel that they are *different* from nonactors (Robb, Due, & Venning, 2016). According to the interviews, as compared to nonactors, actors feel that they "see the story in things"; are more interested in others and in the world; are more sensitive to stimuli and aspects of the world; are more animated; are more charismatic; are more able to communicate to others; and are more committed to communicating truths about the human condition to others. Peter feels that actors have "a separate and unique" ability to observe others that nonactors do not have. He feels that actors are generally more animated than others and have a distinctive ability to bring joy to others. These differences have been reported in the literature (Hammond & Edelman, 1991a; Marchant-Haycox & Wilson, 1992). Furthermore, actors respond to the world with more feelings and emotions (Blum, 1976; Goldstein & Winner, 2009). The responses in the interviews support this idea. The actors reported that they feel more capable of responding to the world with more emotion and sensitivity than nonactors do.

Many of the actors felt that others view them negatively, due to the assumption that actors want to be the center of attention. Past theorizing indicates that actors are self-involved, and that acting is thought to be rooted in deep voyeuristic and self-gratifying drives (Bergler, 1949). However, the interview responses indicate that there is a heightened interest in aspects of the world and of others for their own intrinsic value. In addition, actors possess an inherent motivation to incorporate these known aspects into their performances and to communicate their meanings to audiences. The actor's desire to connect with audiences for the purposes of connection contradicts the notion that acting is merely self-gratifying.

Another difference actors perceived about themselves is related to the actual expertise required. An overriding theme was the intense psychological, emotional, physical, and observational skills that actors must employ to do good work. The actors felt that most other jobs do not require these intense and varied skills. This has also been reported in the literature (Robb, Due, & Venning, 2016). Jimmy stated that actors have to be "superhuman in their humanness." Jake feels that actors have a more difficult time professionally than do others, due to the courage needed to perform in front of audiences. These statements exemplify the perceptions that actors hold about their work and how they compare their vocation to the qualifications needed in other professions. Although the standing analytic literature contends that acting is a manifestation of a form of regression and an unconscious desire to return to the play of early childhood (Bergler, 1949), actors in our interviews see the requirements of their work as acts of evolution, which require constant emotional, psychological, and artistic growth as actors mature in their craft.

Additionally, some actors had the experience of being judged negatively for being actors due to the perception that acting is not a valid occupation. This was found to be the case in a study of Australian actors (Robb, Due, & Venning, 2016). As Bill stated, "What we do is not seen as real work." Marty remembered having apprehension about telling his peers that he wanted to act. He felt that if his desire were known, he would be met with disapproval because acting was not considered a serious endeavor by his peers. Peter feels he has been viewed negatively by nonactors. He recalled instances of others questioning him about his employment, and because he could not consistently report that he was appearing in a role—due to the unstable nature of the profession—he was met with criticism.

The actors are aware that nonactors perceive them as being different. For example, actors are aware that as a group, they are seen as unstable. The literature also reports this notion (Weissman, 1961; Bates, 1991). Although the interviews did not attempt to address this question specifically, nothing in the interviews indicated the presence of overall emotional instability in the actors. Media attention certainly reveals instability of actors on a regular basis. However, several actors revealed that longevity in the theater requires dedication, professionalism, and persistence. Some actors relayed anecdotes of irresponsibility within the profession, noting that some actors were fired from productions because of an instability that negatively impacted a production or the performance of other actors. They reported that this is not tolerated in the professional theater, and actors with this personality characteristic usually have short careers because of their psychological, emotional, artistic, and professional inabilities.

The actors also discussed the preconception that actors act because they find themselves unacceptable, they wish to become someone else, and they have difficulties accepting who they are (Fenichel, 1946; Kaplan, 1969). The interviews do not support these ideas. Several actors clarified that their desire to act did not stem from a need to become someone else for the reason that they did not like themselves or wanted to run from themselves. On the contrary, one of the aspects that actors mentioned as a positive outcome of acting was the joy of acting for its own artistic sake, as well as for developing more self-awareness and growth.

According to the interviews, actors believe that attributes of their personalities cause negative reactions from others. The literature suggests that actors have a fear that the audience will feel jealousy and hostility toward them, and will retaliate against them (Freundlich, 1968; Gabbard, 1983). Katherine stated she has perceived jealousy from others, disclosing that "they smell that you are more alive, and that makes them shrink up and feel smaller. It makes them feel somewhat like a failure." Bill, Jake, Jimmy, and Peter noted the historical negative attitudes that viewed actors with suspicion because they were thought to be dishonest. Four actors stated that they have experienced this bias in their own lives. Three actors revealed that they felt others perceived that their desire to act was a way of getting attention from others. Although the early analytic literature states that actors are deceitful in their attempts to obtain narcissistic gratification and attempt to portray themselves as what they are not (Fenichel, 1946; Nagel, 2004), the responses show that actors have a strong and humble commitment to finding and revealing truth to others. Furthermore, the literature also reveals that negative stereotypes about actors exist in psychology and in the greater society (Reciniello, 1991; Nemiro, 1997; Novick, 1998). The responses reveal that actors experience this personally.

Actors feel that their differences make them a unique group. Bill feels that actors have been viewed negatively by society throughout history. He noted that although people want to be entertained by actors, "they don't want to hang with them." He feels that actors are viewed with suspicion by others. Bill went so far as to say that actors form their own distinct "culture." He also noted that actors have to "stick together" due to their differences and the perceptions that nonactors hold about them. *Culture* is defined by *Webster's* (1989) as "the sum total of ways of living built up by a group of human beings and transmitted from one generation to another" (p. 353). Noting the historical nature of acting, the traditions passed down from one generation to the next, and that actors perceive their uniqueness as group, this definition seems quite applicable here. It has been reported that actors feel they are part of a "tribe" possessing aspects of warmth, comfort, connection, and similar values (Hays, 2017) and that nonactors are considered "civilians" (Robb, Due, & Venning, 2016, p 10). In many fields, culture is generally respected and considered when theories and perspectives about attitudes and behaviors of a particular group are formed (Sue & Sue, 1991). The historical literature does not seem to address what makes actors unique but instead what makes them pathological (Reciniello, 1991). Although some studies attempt to correct this imbalance, the correction has not been fully attained.

- **To the actor: describe times when you have felt that as an actor, you were/are different from others.**
- **To the actor: describe times when others felt you were/are different.**

Inherence. The actors' responses revealed that their desire to act and their acting abilities are *inherent*, which *Webster's* (1989) defines as "existing in something as a permanent and inseparable element, quality, or attribute" (p. 732). More than "just a job," acting is what the actors' feel they were born to do. Bill articulated it directly when he said, "You are *born* an actor." Actors felt that their desire to act was something that they could not change. This has also been termed, "The calling" (Robb, Due, & Venning, 2016). Although they described having to endure uncertainties of the profession, the pitfalls of "the business" did not—or *could not*—change their identities as actors. Nonactors may change professions or occupations, and their identities may change along with them.

However, in support of earlier findings, the actors reported that they identified with the profession and the vocation despite their individual employment status (Phillips, 1991). Several actors described having to take other jobs or pursue secondary occupations outside of the acting profession during the slow times between productions in an effort to supplement their incomes. However, each participant never lost the belief that being an actor is a core aspect of his or her identity.

Many actors feel that they are "born to act" and that being an actor is an inherent part of their identity (Nordin-Bates, 2012). Alex noticed at a young age the presence of her talents. She indicated an intense need to perform the "people inside of me," which she remembers as a constant in early childhood. She feels that she was born to act. Bill noted that being an actor is not something you become, it is "something you *are*." Jake feels that his talents are innate and likely inherited from his father. He stated that acting is "in my blood." Because Jimmy came from a family in which the arts were discouraged, he did not acknowledge his desire to act until his 20s. However, looking back, he feels that his talents are intrinsic to his personality and have been present all of his life. Kathryn also feels that her talents are inherent and she believes that this is true for most actors. She notes that even as a young child she could transform her voice, her body, and her affect to take on other characters "and have power over adults." Peter feels that he was "born" to act. He feels that being an actor is "part of my DNA."

- **To the actor: describe the feeling of knowing that you *are* an actor.**
- **To the actor: describe the feeling of innately knowing how to act.**

Service. The actors felt that through acting, they are providing an important psychological, emotional, and societal *service* to others. This service spans from assisting individuals and audiences to serving society as a whole. In its simplest form, actors feel that they are providing entertainment, and that they are helping to distract viewers from personal troubles. Actors also note that getting others to laugh can lift their moods and make their life experiences more enjoyable, even if only for a few hours. Several of the actors believe that this is the "very least" that they do as actors. They also feel that the audience can, simply by viewing a performance, have the opportunity to deepen their imaginations, experience aspects of the human condition, and understand eras, places, and situations that they may not encounter in everyday life. Actors also believe that they facilitate emotional experiences in audiences. Furthermore, actors feel that at its core, acting delivers psychological, emotional, and human truth to audiences to help them manage life and come to deeper understandings of what it is to be human. Katherine articulated this when she said that actors help audiences to "rehearse and remember important life events."

Many of the actors feel that this service transcends everyday concerns and may even be spiritual in nature. This corresponds with a study connecting stage fright to joy (Simmonds & Southcott, 2012). The actors reported that they felt connected to the historical and ancient functions of acting, which include storytelling, ritual, holy sacrifice, and catharsis. Jake articulated his work as a "sacred journey" whereby the actor enters the world of the imagination and the irreal to assist audiences in tending to their souls. Most actors felt that acting was what they were "called to do." All of the actors felt that acting has the potential to reach and affect audiences in profound and meaningful ways. The psychological literature does not generally reflect how actors feel about acting as a service. Most of the theorists do not appear to be actors, nor do they appear to have experienced the draw to acting and the deep sense of service actors possess. Other theorists have found that actors have a truthful connection to and passion about acting (Phillips, 1991). Taken at face value, the interview responses indicate that instead of being self-serving, actors have a deep sense of service to others. Actors also have a deep need to find and reveal human realities. It seems that acting—an ancient and current vehicle for the expression of truth—has been at times misperceived as deception (Bates, 1987). Although the interviews did not attempt to reveal whether actors were motivated by deceit, this theme present in the literature was not revealed in any of the indicators of the actors' experience.

Alex believes that actors create a place where actors and audiences can come together to connect, to ignite their imaginations, and to "shatter," or to drop defenses and to expand emotionally and psychologically. Bill believes that actors assist audiences in feeling, educate audiences about life events, and provide entertainment. Elizabeth feels that by viewing actors' performances, audiences gain broader perspectives about the world, are educated, and are entertained. She feels that actors' performances can avert the audiences' attention from their own troubles. Jake feels that as an actor, he has inherited an ancient responsibility to entertain and educate audiences so that they have a better understanding of humanity in order to tend to their souls. He feels that this service is spiritual in nature. He calls it a "sacred journey" upon which actors have embarked for thousands of years. Jimmy feels that as well as providing entertainment, acting has a "high standing" and that it is a service that "can change people's lives" by revealing truth about relationships and the human condition. Kathryn feels that actors provide a "priceless" service in a society where so many things can be bought. She feels that actors help audiences to "rehearse and remember important life events." She feels similarly connected to the "holy origins of theater." She also believes that actors are providing a spiritual service when they reveal truths to an audience. Marty feels that actors perform a service by providing entertainment, by bringing enlightenment, and by trying to "communicate something that's difficult to communicate in life." Peter feels that actors participate in storytelling, which is vital for the continuity of the human species. He believes that actors teach, enhance the lives of others, touch people's hearts, and can facilitate change. For Peter, acting is a form of creativity that reflects the divine creativity that originates from God. As an actor, he feels he is part of a spiritual purpose.

- **To the actor: describe how you feel acting is a service to others, to the world, to the cosmos.**

Other facets

The actors presented themes unique to their individual experiences regarding their draw to acting. *Attention* emerged as a theme Elizabeth and Peter. The desire for attention and interest from others initially drew them to acting. As a child, Elizabeth felt that acting was the best way to get others to notice her as she held negative opinions about her appearance. Peter also felt as a child that acting was a way to get the attention and love he was not experiencing in his personal life. However, both stated that as they matured, their draw to acting evolved into the need to *communicate*, which was identified as an essential theme.

- **To the actor: describe the feeling of needing—or not needing— attention.**

Clarity emerged as a theme for Bill. He notes that he is able to transfer the intense concentration and reflection needed in his onstage life to his offstage life. He feels that his capability to discern life events with more clarity is due to the influence of acting.

- **To the actor: describe how acting clarifies your ability to understand life events.**

Excitement is a theme that emerged for Elizabeth and Marty. All of her life, Elizabeth has felt the pleasant anticipation of being onstage. "Yeah, when everything's cookin', it's … nothing like it in the world." For Marty, the excitement of making his entrances was a positive experience that continues to this day. "I'd come out *(explosion noise)* like a rocket, you know?"

- **To the actor: describe your feelings of excitement when acting.**

Expansion was a theme for Alex and Marty. Alex feels that an expanded awareness of self and others is the result of successful communication. She experiences this as a literal physical event where her "self" is developed through acting. Marty felt that his experiences onstage broadened his horizons and expanded his emotional, psychological, and imaginative awareness of the real world.

- **To the actor: describe how acting has expanded you as a person.**

Expression was a theme for Alex, Bill, Jimmy, Marty, and Peter; they described a desire to express themselves as an early primary factor in their draw to acting. Alex described feeling an internal psychological and emotional pressure due to a feeling that she possessed many internal characters, whom she describes as "all of the people inside of me." She felt a strong need to convey them, and doing so onstage provided much relief. As a child, Bill found it difficult to convey personal feelings and aspects of himself. As a teenager, he found acting was an effective means of expression. Now, when he acts he can reveal parts of himself that he "would not" reveal in his personal life. Jimmy noted that he was a sensitive child and felt things deeply. He wanted to express his emotions through acting. He feels that if he did not and does not express himself, he will regret it in later life. Marty felt that he could not safely express himself in his neighborhood, where there was peer pressure to behave in a prescribed way. Acting was a way to "express myself like mad" and convey strong emotions. Peter's early memories include a desire to express himself creatively. He found that acting was the most complete vehicle for expression, as he was able to do so "inside" a creative endeavor, such as a theatrical production.

- **To the actor: describe your need or desire to express when acting.**

Freedom emerged as a theme for Alex, Bill, and Peter. Alex experiences being onstage as freeing, but for her, it also has a quality of "release." She feels she has much "content" in the form of many internal characters, perspectives, and emotions. Discharging them in performance provides this sense of release. Bill described the "freeing" experience of being onstage and living out scenarios that he would not live out in his personal life. As a child, Peter felt free to be completely himself onstage. Now, as an adult, he finds that this freedom extends to having adventures onstage.

- **To the actor: describe how acting makes you feel free.**

Safety was a theme related to the draw to acting for Bill, Elizabeth, Kathryn, and Peter. Bill revealed that as a child and as a pre-teen he was inhibited and shy. He had difficulty speaking with and connecting to others. His first stage experiences gave him a sense of safety. He found that he was good at performing, and being onstage provided a sense of security he had not experienced before. For Elizabeth, being onstage offered a sense of safety, but it was a much more visceral experience. She vividly described being under the warm pastel lights as "the safest place in the world" and like "being in mother's womb again." This sense of safety occurred in her earliest acting experiences and continues to this day. For Kathryn, being onstage and playing other characters provided a refuge from disliked aspects of herself and from the outside world. She was teased by her older sister and her parents were distant. Accessing other characters onstage felt like a safe harbor. She could experience being other people and therefore not a target for attack. For Peter, life was unpredictable and chaotic. The scripted, rehearsed, and beautifully designed world of the stage brought him the peace and safety that he was not experiencing in his offstage life.

- **To the actor: describe how being onstage make you feel safe.**

Transcendence, which is the feeling of existing above and apart from oneself and the material world, appeared as a theme for Kathryn and Jake. Kathryn stated that when she is delivering emotional, psychological, and philosophical truths to the audience, "I have transcended my own self." The power of the words she speaks allows her to rise above her own frailties. She noted that this is a common experience for actors who have matured into their craft. She yearns for this feeling and she calls pursuing it "following your bliss." Jake described the transcendent aspect of acting as "your soul awakening." He is in "the now of now," the present moment where he has gone beyond himself. He states, "I've really felt that I have soared, that I have flown above the ground, free, connected to myself, but disconnected and almost free from the earth."

- **To the actor: describe any expansive, soulful, transcendent feelings or experiences you have had related to acting.**

Transformation was a theme for Kathryn. She feels that as a person, she changed onstage and became another person who possessed different experiences and abilities. In an important childhood performance, she "suddenly had a power I hadn't felt before in my life. I was the character and not myself."

- **To the actor: describe when and how you felt transformed as an actor.**

Trust emerged as a theme for Jake, Kathryn, and Peter. For Kathryn, shared stage experiences with other actors form deep attachment bonds, which generate personal and professional trust—and even love—onstage. The presence of this trust enriches her performances and protects her from stage fright. Jake feels he acts for the love of the work and the love felt for and from the audience. Peter noted that the trust among actors that is required for successful performances creates deep and potentially life-long bonds that would take much longer to develop outside the rehearsal and performance process. Peter also feels that the presence of trust with other actors helps to prevent his stage fright.

- **To the actor: do you relate to any of these themes?**
- **If so, which ones?**
- **Describe any other aspects of your draw to acting and the acting experience to complete as clear a description as possible.**

The stage fright experience

Colors, associations, and stage fright personified. In addition to the physical and psychological manifestations of stage fright, actors related stage fright to a *color* and drew *associations* that symbolized their less rational meanings of the stage fright experience. In several cases this allowed deeper unconscious aspects of the stage fright experience to emerge. Colors associated with stage fright were *red* for chaos and horror, *white* for frozen immobilizing fear, *maroon* for dead and lifeless blood, and *black* for shame, the unspeakable horror that is stage fright. Other colors were *orange* for excitement and *purple* for the vibrancy of performance. Metaphors for stage fright included "a black mark on my record" for failure and shame, and red "Hell" for the experience of eternal punishment. Stage fright appeared as a "Relaxed Fellow" who whispered doubts to the actor to keep him offstage. Stage fright was personified by several actors as "the Devil." In the actors' experiences, the Devil chases an actor frozen with fear, so there is no escape. The Devil chokes the actor, strangling the life force. The Devil drains the life-blood from the actor, so they slowly lose consciousness. The Devil also offers excitement and motivation. However, to attain these positives, actors must "strike a deal with the Devil." The joys of performance must be paid for with the price of stage fright.

Actors *personified* stage fright and were able to view the condition from the perspective of a character with an objective. For Alex, the feeling was "red horror." She noted that the color was associated with the Devil's red face. She connected the agitated feeling she experiences in her body with an image of the Devil chasing her onstage. Bill associated the color "orange" to his stage fright who is a "Relaxed Fellow" who urges him to stay backstage with him where it is safe. Elizabeth stated that her stage fright felt like "frozen white." She associated this color with a memory of a literal intruder who threatened her life. The danger imposed by this person caused her to feel frozen with fear, "like icicles." This felt identical to the fear she experiences when stage fright is present. Furthermore, she stated that she felt as if stage fright were literally choking her. Jake described the feeling as the color "maroon." He associated this to the lifeless blood of a placenta, blood that has no more vitality, and that smells of death. For Jake, stage fright is a "demon" who slowly taps his life force through strangulation.

Jimmy said that stage fright felt like "red chaos" in his stomach, which he described as "Hell." Kathryn described the feeling as "red exhilaration," like a horse about to run a race. She also associated it with the character of "the Devil" with whom she strikes a deal so she can feel the joys of performance. Marty associated the feeling of stage fright with the color "black." He stated that it felt like "a black mark on my record," signifying that he had done something wrong. Peter described the color of stage fright as "purple and black swirling," as he envisioned it as a "bipolar character." The purple is related to the vibrancy of performance. The black represents a feeling like "being choked or cut off." It is related to "the darkest blackest fears of any performer … the unfathomable thing that cannot be touched … do not say the name." Peter stated, "Stage Fright is Voldemort."

Often it is within the realm of fantasy that our fears and hopes are most vividly articulated. Fantasy is rooted in the word *phantom*, which means a "mental process, a sensuous perception, a faculty of the imagination" (Onions, 1996, p. 344). The appearance of the Devil, who wants to destroy the actor's process, intentions, and wishes, brings into focus the core function of stage fright: to destroy what is creative, to stop communication, and to eliminate service. Although the literature discusses the debilitative aspects of stage fright, when compared to what actors revealed was the nature of their vocation (i.e., the creative, educative, cathartic, and restorative aspects), these destructive fantasies seem to imply that stage fright possesses facets of the metaphoric battle between the life-instinct and the death-instinct (i.e., Eros and Thanatos; Freud, 1962, p. 30) or between the forces of creation and annihilation. In this realm, stage fright is a destroyer.

- **To the actor: as you recall your stage fright, notice if or what color comes to mind.**
- **To the actor: draw or paint what your stage fright looks like.**
- **To the actor: if stage fright were a character, what would its objective be?**
- **To the actor: if stage fright was a character, in what circumstance, setting, and time period would it live?**
- **To the actor: create a dialog with your stage fright.**
- **To the actor: what does stage fright want from you?**

Death. An essential theme of the stage fright experience revealed in the interviews was that stage fright contained features that are sometimes metaphorically—but often literally—analogous to the experience of anticipated *death*. The literature has also described stage fright as a feeling that is similar to or worse than the fear of death (Berry & Edelstein, 2009). Bill felt that he was about to be "eaten alive by a monster." Elizabeth described an actual event during which her life was literally threatened by an intruder. Her stage fright felt as if she were actually being choked to death. Jake also revealed that stage fright felt as if he were being strangled. "Something's about to strangle you ... or you're being strangled." He said that it feels as if all of the blood were draining from his body, which creates a "slow but unstoppable progression to nothingness." Marty and Bill said stage fright is like "impending death," or like "going before a live firing squad." Jimmy stated emphatically that his experience is comparable to facing destruction and death. "It felt like I was going to the guillotine." For Kathryn, it can also feel like "impending death." She experiences "the reverse of my life flashing before my eyes," and feels that the audience will kill her. She compared appearing before an audience to "appearing before a live firing squad." Peter's stage fright can feel like a "death experience. I'm on the edge of the precipice about to plunge to my demise ... my world is about to collapse." To stop and consider these feelings is a sobering exercise in understanding. Not only does stage fright hurt, according to the literature and the interview responses, it feels like the worst experience of being human: experiencing death (Kohut, 1984; Marshall, 1994).

- **To the actor: recall if your stage fright has aspects of death.**
- **To the actor: describe how stage fright threatens your onstage life.**

Fear of failure. The interviews revealed that a *fear of failure* was central to the experience of stage fright in the actors. This fear manifested in negative anticipatory thoughts about their general competence. It also manifested in negative thoughts that they would make a specific mistake. This confirms the idea that stage fright is characterized by inner critical voices that generate a fear response to their directives (Lloyd-Elliott, 1991). Actors also feared that they would not be able to find a solution to their mistakes in order to maintain the illusion of the play. Actors also feared that other actors would make mistakes. Individual fear was generalized to fear that the actor would disappoint his fellow actors and the audience. The interviews also revealed that actors feared that they would not live up to their higher goals of enlightening and enriching the lives of others.

Several actors noted that when they were younger, their fear of failure centered on being approved of by the audience. A recurring theme was that as the actors matured in their craft, they were less concerned about the audience liking them and were more concerned about reaching their internal standards of artistry. Several actors articulated that actors who survive in the profession do not maintain this early concern about audiences. Maturation in the technique of acting includes forgetting about audience approval and looking to inner approval for a job well done. The literature indicates that stage fright is primarily a fear of not receiving narcissistic gratification from audiences (Novick, 1998). The interviews revealed that this may be the case in immature performers, but the actors interviewed have matured in their craft have left this particular concern behind. Although the interviews did not attempt to address this question of development, the interview responses suggest that actors may go through developmental milestones which may include mastery of this fear.

For Bill, the experience of the fear of failure involved worries that he would "screw up" before going onstage. He also characterized stage fright as a negative voice that tried to convince him that he would make a mistake. Elizabeth's fear of failing onstage centered on not fulfilling her professional responsibilities and disappointing the audience and her fellow actors. Jake feared that he would fail in his attempts to perform as an accomplished artist and to fulfill his inherited task of enlightening audiences. Jimmy's fear of failure concerned being at fault or making an error, especially one related to his ability to remember his lines. This fear was fueled by negative thoughts, which in turn reinforce and amplify the fear. Kathryn feared making a mistake in public, letting down her onstage peers, and setting them up for making potential mistakes. She experienced the fear of failure as if she had committed a crime. Marty's fear of failing concerned feeling pressure to use favored acting techniques that did not work for him. The more he tried to apply them, the more he failed, which created a negative cycle. Peter's fear of failure revolved around the anticipated moment of making a mistake onstage in full view of the audience.

- **To the actor: describe your fear of failure.**

Inhibition. Acting is a physically, psychologically, and emotionally communicative act. Alex, Elizabeth, Jake, Jimmy, Marty, and Peter revealed that stage fright *inhibits* these forms of communication in several ways. First, actors described episodes of physical inhibition and even immobility when stage fright attacks. There is a physical sense of being "frozen," "trapped," and "tied up in knots." Actors described being unable to move at all or being unable to move certain body parts. Stage fright also causes a form of mental inhibition and immobility. Actors described the mind as being "frozen" and "blank," with an inability to think or plan ahead. These forms of inhibition feed into the fear of failure because they inhibit the actors from making entrances, remembering their lines, and solving problems. These components confirm that a central element of stage fright is *blocking*, which is the sensation of losing control of one's expressive powers, including speech and movement (Kaplan, 1969). This sense of inhibition also negatively affects the actor's artistry. When inhibition strikes, actors feel that they are not able to be childlike and spontaneous, that they are not able to experience and express a full range of emotion, and they are not able to access the full scope of their creativity. The presence of inhibition means that the joy of performance is lost. The interviews confirm the idea that stage fright is a creative problem which the actor confronts by defying his or her fear in pursuit of creative expression (Kaplan, 1969).

Alex experienced a form of physical and mental immobility called "a pause." She was unable to move or speak. Her mind was in a state of "literal blankness." Elizabeth experienced physical inhibition to the point of being unable to move. She experienced this as being "frozen." This immobility extended to a form of mental inhibition which she calls "brain freezes," during which her mind went blank. Jake experienced a feeling of artistic restriction that prevented him from doing his best. It obstructed mental, emotional, and artistic access to his "inner child," which brought freedom to his work. "Your instrument is being constricted, so that you are not your best and you're not your fullest." Jimmy feels that positive aspects of his personality are restricted from emerging when he is dealing with stage fright, especially before he goes onstage. Marty feels that stage fright inhibits him from expressing himself, "tying you in knots, and preventing you from doing what you wanna do." Peter feels that stage fright restricts and inhibits potentially strong performances by dulling his abilities, cutting off nuance, and stifling his emotional range.

- **To the actor: describe how stage fright inhibits you and your acting.**

Physical attack. All actors experienced *physical* responses related to stage fright that felt as if they were under *attack*. The physical manifestations range from mild to severe symptoms which include cold sweats, difficulty breathing, dry mouth, mild to severe gastro-intestinal difficulties, heart palpitations, lightheadedness, physical and mental immobilization, reactivity to stimuli, shaking, self-consciousness, a swollen tongue, vocal problems, watery eyes, and weakness in the limbs. One participant reported dissociative events and fainting spells. These and other physical symptoms have been well documented in the literature (Marshall, 1994). However, a qualitative understanding of the physiological experience highlights the reality that stage fright hurts. The subjective accounts presented by these actors deliver a more immediate reminder that it is painful. One participant described physical effects so debilitating that he had to isolate himself the day before performance. Another participant said that the physical experience was so intense that on two occasions he fainted. When another participant was describing his experience, he said he just wanted to put his head down and cry. Some of the literature describes stage fright as a symptom of regression, of shame, as a fear of envy of the audience, and even a universal condition (Gabbard, 1979, 1983). Stage fright can be intellectualized and analyzed, but ultimately, it is a painful physical and emotional state.

Alex's symptoms included difficulty breathing, a racing heart, the sensation of running, and the impulse to not speak. She later developed stomach pain and extreme physical reactivity to stimuli. Bill experiences dry mouth, watery eyes, lightheadedness, and an upset stomach. Elizabeth becomes physically immobile, loses the ability to speak, and experiences stomach pain. Jake experiences shallow breathing, cold sweats, and he loses vocal control. Jimmy experiences extreme symptoms including gastro-intestinal difficulties and stomach pain that require him to isolate for hours at a time. Kathryn experiences rapid heartbeat, dry mouth, and a swollen tongue. She feels compelled to move quickly. When onstage she closes her eyes and she blushes. Marty experienced shallow breathing and confusion. Peter becomes self-conscious about the movements of his lips and arms. He experiences pain in his stomach, shortness of breath, weakness in his knees, and shaking hands. He experiences lightheadedness and the inability to focus. At times, he dissociates. He recounted incidents of being so frightened that he fainted.

- **To the actor: describe your physical responses that occur when you are experiencing stage fright.**

Shame. Alex, Elizabeth, Jimmy, Kathryn, Marty, and Peter experienced feelings of *shame* as central to their experience of stage fright. *Webster's* (1989) defines *shame* as "the painful feeling arising from the consciousness of something dishonorable, improper, ridiculous, etc., done by oneself ... disgrace, dishonor, or regret" (p. 1310). Although fears of failure were centered on doing something wrong or making a mistake, shame is the feeling of *being* wrong or *being* a mistake. This deep sense of being defective is coupled with a profound sense of potential embarrassment. This state of unworthiness, disgrace, and dishonor is perhaps one of the more difficult aspects of the experience of stage fright. Another actor's sense of shame included rapid and repetitive negative thoughts about his intrinsic worth. Whereas the fear of failure seemed to involve the potential for mistakes, shame seems to involve a core sense of disgrace in front of others. The psychoanalytic literature states that stage fright is caused by the unconscious fear of castration and shame, or "the specific fright of the exhibitionist" (Fenichel, 1946, p. 361). In accordance with Gabbard (1983), the interviews confirm that shame is a central component of the stage fright experience. However, the interviews do not confirm that an actor's sense of shame is rooted in exhibitionism.

Alex stated that she feared "being found out for *me.*" Elizabeth described shame as the feeling of "running down the street naked" and being "inadequate." Jimmy's sense of shame involves internal self-questioning about potential embarrassment. Kathryn experiences feelings of "true shame and humiliation" as an outcome of making a mistake onstage. She noted that "non-pros" dread this, and are too afraid to appear on a stage. During his stage fright episodes, Marty experienced shame as if he was doing something wrong. He articulated, "It was a wrong feeling." Peter's sense of shame revolves around failing onstage and the resulting disgrace he might experience. "How can I survive after something … a failure that large, in front of so many people?"

- **To the actor: if you have them, describe your feelings of shame.**

Other facets

Another of the more difficult aspects of the stage fright experience for our actors is the feeling of being entirely *alone.* For Bill, stage fright is like falling in the air, grasping at nothing with nothing to hold on to. For Jake, stage fright feels like being in an intermediate place between being connected to the life force which sustains him, and being autonomous, where he can rely on his own powers and instincts to survive. This place of transition feels as if there is no umbilical cord of safety, yet the first independent breath has not been taken. "You're on your own now, aren't you? You're out in the world, by yourself. Good Luck!" For Kathryn, her stage fright is triggered when she feels defenseless and deserted. When she does not have the opportunity to shield herself against a negative critic and cannot voice her response, she feels alone. Aloneness triggers her stage fright, which intensifies the feeling of being alone. Peter's experience of aloneness is characterized by the feeling that "it's all crashing in on me and there is no other side to get to." Peter feels that no one is able to help him out of "the overwhelming nature of it."

- **To the actor: describe your fear feelings of being alone when stage fright strikes.**

Conflict emerged as a theme for two actors, Jake and Jimmy. Jake experiences stage fright as a battle between a "demon" and his "actor-self." The demon wants him to fail, and he wants to conquer the demon in combat on the "proving stage." For Jimmy, internal conflict is characterized by one part of himself that is hyper-critical of his efforts and another part that tries to encourage him to say the lines that he is certain he knows. These two parts of himself engage in a rapid internal dialog that feels like a vicious battle.

- **To the actor: describe your fear feelings of conflict and struggle between different parts of yourself when stage fright strikes.**

Confusion, a sense of bewilderment, and a lack of clarity emerged as a theme for Marty. When experiencing stage fright, he had thoughts that went "round and round" and about his work at such a moment, he stated, "I didn't know what the Hell I was doing."

- **To the actor: remember feeling confused. Draw a picture of what it felt like.**

Control emerged as a theme for Elizabeth. She feels that stage fright is an unknown part of her that is controlling her and trying to get her to do what it wants rather than what she wants.

- **To the actor: describe the feeling that stage fright has control over you. Create a dialog with stage fight, like an improved scene, and ask it what it wants.**

Doubt and the feeling of uncertainty about one's talent or the uncertainties of the world emerged as a theme for four actors, Bill, Jake, Jimmy, and Marty. Bill experiences doubt as an internal voice that questions his abilities and tells him that he is not able to perform. Jake experiences doubt as a "self-doubt demon" that tells him, "You're not good enough to do this." This voice deepens his reservations about meeting the requirements of performance or the expectations of the audience. Jimmy questions his own adequacy when he doubts his ability. He asks himself, "What if I'm not good enough?" Marty's doubt began with questioning whether he could effectively act in a prescribed way. This doubt then spread to his questioning his talent and whether he had chosen the right profession.

- **To the actor: describe how stage fright causes you to doubt your talent and ability.**

Familiarity emerged as a theme for two actors, Alex and Jimmy. Alex stated that her stage fright feels familiar to her now, and its presence is part of her "ritual" in preparing to go onstage. Jimmy feels that although his stage fright is debilitating, there are known and comforting aspects of it due to its longstanding presence in his life. At this point, despite the severe discomfort, he connects to and is comforted by the fact that stage fright is a familiar and recurring experience

- **To the actor: describe how stage fright feels familiar.**

Fraudulence, the feeling that presenting one's talents is an act of deceit emerged as themes for two actors, Alex and Kathryn. For Alex, the feeling of fraudulence is centered on her perception that the audience has the power to define her. She feels they will see her as misrepresenting herself. "These people are gonna find out I'm a fake, that all of my stuff is smoke and mirrors," she stated. For Kathryn, the feeling is that the audience will find out that she does not know what she is doing. She also feels as if she is "getting away with something" onstage. "If I fail, if I blow it, you will see that the *Wizard of Oz* is the man behind the curtain."

- **To the actor: describe how stage fright causes you to feel like a fraud.**

Loss of love emerged as a theme for Kathryn. She described the palpable waves of love that come up from the audience. For Kathryn, stage fright is the fear of the loss of this love. "They will stop loving me … That's my accumulated wisdom of all the actors I've ever talked to and worked with."

- **To the actor: describe how stage fright makes you feel a loss of love.**

Motivation concerning the experience of stage fright emerged as a theme for four actors, Bill, Jake, Kathryn, and Peter. Bill experiences a sense of energy that acts as a "springboard" and a "helper" that prompts him onstage. He also looks forward to the positive experiences that happen there. This anticipation adds to his feelings of motivation to perform. Jake's experience of motivation involves a feeling of "daring." For Jake, the dare and the challenge of rising above his stage fright and appearing onstage contribute to his motivation to get onstage. Kathryn experiences an "exhilarating" energy that propels her and motivates her to perform. She compares it to a "horse anticipating the bell that will begin a race. It's gonna be good. Gonna knock 'em dead." Peter relates to the vibrancy and intensity of performance that encourages him to get onstage. He also experiences motivation as an internal sense of "tough love" that forces him onstage and into a better performance.

- **To the actor: describe how stage fright can be motivating.**

Stage fright as a *necessity* emerged as a theme for two actors, Alex and Bill. Alex feels that her stage fright has become a routine part of her pattern of performing. She stated, "It feels ritualistic now." She does not feel she could go onstage without it. It has become a necessary feature of her performance experience. For Bill, stage fright is necessary because it allows him to perceive danger. He compared this to the fear a hunter must have to protect himself from the threat of being attacked by a bear. Stage fright feels necessary to prepare for going onstage.

- **To the actor: describe how stage fright can feel like a necessary part of acting.**

Protection emerged as a theme for two actors, Bill and Jimmy. For Bill, stage fright protects him from the perceived dangers of the audience and functions as a kind of self-preservation. The desire to remain backstage where it is safe helps him to re-focus so he can actually go out onstage. Jimmy feels that stage fright protects him from having to face up to the true nature of his talents, which he suspects may not be as good as he hopes. Stage fright protects him from facing feared inadequacy. "Maybe if it wasn't there, I'd really find out if I were up to snuff or not."

- **To the actor: describe how stage fright protects you and keeps you safe.**

Self-absorption emerged as a theme for two actors, Jake and Marty. Jake's focus becomes averted from the reality of the character and shifts to concerns about himself. This concern takes him "out of the moment." He watches himself and becomes self-conscious. He is no longer in the play but in his "head." Marty also stated that self-absorption related to stage fright took him "out of the moment" and into his "head." He became concerned about correctly applying certain acting techniques and did not trust his instincts. He became focused on his own chaotic thoughts and his attention turned inward rather than to the moment-to-moment circumstances of the play.

- **To the actor: describe how stage fright makes you self-absorbed.**
- **To the actor: do you relate to any of these themes?**
- **Describe any other aspects of your stage fright experience to complete as clear a description as possible.**

The nature of stage fright

Changes. Although the actors' responses show that stage fright is permanent, the actors revealed that stage fright changes over time. Some actors stated that they have gained mastery over the physical aspects, but negative thoughts still arise. Others revealed that they have gained control of their thoughts, yet they still experience physical symptoms. However, the results indicate that actors feel that stage fright is always a possibility, and its manifestations remain uncertain.

Early in the actor's development, stage fright centers around love and approval from an audience. Later, actors' stage fright is more concerned with the desire to reach personal and artistic excellence and with not disappointing others, such as the audience or their fellow actors. As the actor matures, concerns center on meeting internal standards of artistry and reaching that state of "transcendence" onstage. This may parallel changes in fears thorough the lifespan as experienced by the wider population. For example, when we are children, we fear the dark, ghosts, and strangers. As we mature, we may have fears about life choices, taking care of responsibilities and real life events. As we grow old, our fears may focus on mortality, what we will leave behind, and questions about an afterlife. Although the interviews did not attempt to track changes in stage fright, the responses reveal that stage fright might change in concert with an actor's maturation in the craft, which may parallel predictable milestones in human development.

Furthermore, the literature revealed that stage fright is generally associated with a fear of the loss of love and approval from the audience, which is narcissistically driven (Blum, 1976; Nagel, 2004). Although one participant stated that stage fright felt like fear of the loss of love, it was characterized as a feeling that was experienced early in her career. Furthermore, this characteristic did not emerge as an essential theme. Several of the actors said that the more primitive form of stage fright, including fear that the audience will withdraw approval, may exist in immature actors, but it cannot remain if one is to survive and artistically thrive. Artistic evolution precludes this beginner's preoccupation and seems to generate changes in how stage fright may manifest over an actor's career.

Bill, Elizabeth, Jake, Jimmy, Kathryn, and Peter felt that the nature of their stage fright has *changed*. Bill feels his stage fright has from fear to excitement. Elizabeth's stage fright has lessened in its physical manifestation, that is, her inability to move. However, the mental aspects, such as the inability to remember or to think, remain unchanged. Jake's stage fright has changed from the fear of not being liked and judged by the audience to concerns about fulfilling the professional and artistic aspects of performing. Jake feels that stage fright changes as actors mature in their craft. Jimmy's stage fright has changed in that it is now of shorter duration than in the past, but the feeling and intensity have not altered. When Kathryn was younger, it was fear of not being liked by the audience. Now she is more concerned about forgetting her lines, and she does not want the fear to inhibit her from being swept along in the journey of performance. Peter feels that although the physical manifestations of stage fright are still present, the psychological aspects have lessened.

- **To the actor: has your stage fright changed? If so, when and how?**

Coping. All of the actors reported ways of *coping* with stage fright. Some have tried various psychological interventions, including psychotherapy and hypnosis. Some have tried medical interventions, including tranquilizers and acupuncture. Some have tried spiritual interventions. Before appearing onstage, actors engage in techniques to control the physical aspects of stage fright, including stretching, deep breathing, voice and speech exercises, and other physical preparations. Mental techniques to address psychological concerns include positive self-talk, rationalization, acceptance of stage fright, minimizing the perceived dangers, and giving up a sense of control over the uncontrollable. Several actors revealed that ultimately spiritual techniques are the most helpful interventions. Dedicating the performance to others; meditation; connecting to the holy origins of theater; forgiving the self and others for feared or actual mistakes; and praying to God for courage, comfort, and excellence in performance are ways that actors spiritually cope with this intense fear.

Alex has tried "everything," including medical, psychological, and spiritual interventions to cope with her fear. Nothing has worked. Now she accepts its presence and focuses on her sense of responsibility to the audience and to the ensemble. Immediately before an entrance, Alex "counts down," and "launches" herself onstage. Bill has coped with stage fright by controlling his breathing, by concentrating on his performance tasks, by connecting with other actors, and by acknowledging what he can and cannot control. He ultimately deals with stage fright by accepting its presence in his life, by not fighting it, and by seeing its positive aspects. Elizabeth always checks the audience before performances. She copes mentally by seeing it as a part of her that tempers feelings of self-importance. She copes spiritually by following a meditation practice in which she internally focuses and asks for strength from a higher power. Jake uses positive self-talk and trusts himself. He also dedicates performances to individuals. Giving over a performance to their honor reduces his fear. Jimmy addresses practical matters such as training, preparing, and rehearsing his lines. He receives emotional support by calling his wife before he makes an entrance. Jimmy also copes by rationalizing the purpose of his stage fright. He feels that it provides him with an excuse when performances do not go as well as he has hoped. He feels that ultimately he should address the psychological process related to stage fright, but he does not feel ready to do that. He does not feel at this time that he can face the outcome. Kathryn engages in pre-curtain activities, by focusing once she is onstage, by engaging in positive self-talk, and by checking the audience. She also copes mentally by forgiving herself for making mistakes. Marty coped with stage fright by being true to himself, trusting his "gut," and returning to acting techniques that felt comfortable to him. All of these actions eliminated his stage fright. Peter copes with stage fright by finding solutions to immediate onstage problems. He also practices prayer before each performance. Ultimately, Peter turns his fear over to God. "I surrender the performance to God … He is the one who has power over fear."

- **To the actor: how do you cope with stage fright?**

Permanence. Alex, Bill, Elizabeth, Jimmy, Kathryn, and Peter stated that their stage fright is *permanent.* They have tried psychological, medical, and alternative healing practices to cure stage fright, have accepted its presence, and have reframed it as a familiar and motivating aspect of performance. Some continue to battle with it, often at the expense of their health. Although some theorists consider it pathological, others contend that is a universal aspect of performance (Gabbard, 1983; Naistadt, 2004). Several of the actors revealed that they were embarrassed to discuss their stage fright. One participant said, "I should be over this by now." The literature attempts to explain stage fright from psychological and physical viewpoints. Other than palliative interventions there has not yet seemed to be a "cure" for this condition, which speaks to its enduring quality. It also speaks to the fact that there is little to no research on stage fright in actors, and perhaps curative interventions will be found. The sense of stage fright that has emerged involves the feeling that there is something defective about the sufferer, and that the feeling of fear signals danger. Perhaps the acceptance of the permanent and universal aspects of stage fright may help to mitigate the embarrassment and shame that sufferers feel, not only in their experience of it, but in the very fact that they suffer it at all.

For Alex, stage fright has persisted since childhood. She continues to experience it every time she performs, regardless of the venue or the size of the audience. She has tried medical, psychological, and spiritual practices to cure it. None have helped. She feels that it is incurable and permanent. Bill stated that his stage fright is permanent. "I experience it every time I go out onstage." Although the nature of her stage fright has changed, Elizabeth feels that its presence in her acting life is permanent. Jimmy also feels his stage fright is permanent. It has persisted from his childhood to the present. His physician recommended he consider stopping acting due to the negative effects of the stress on his body, specifically his heart. He is resigned to the idea that he will never be cured. Kathryn also noted that the nature of her stage fright has changed. However, she sees it as a permanent feature of her performing life that she must endure in order to experience the positives of acting. She calls it, "The deal with the Devil." Peter has experienced stage fright all of his life. Although spiritual practices have lightened some of the psychological aspects, the physical manifestations have remained the same. Peter feels they are permanent.

- **To the actor: do you feel your stage fright is permanent?**

Responsibility. All of the actors felt a sense of *responsibility* toward acting as a profession that was the primary factor in their performing despite the fear. They have an overriding sense of responsibility to themselves, to their fellow actors, to their part in creating a world onstage, and to audiences. This sense of responsibility and duty compels them to perform, and echoes the famous phrase, "The show must go on!" All of the actors said that they have always performed in the face of their discomfort because there is "no other choice" than to make their entrances on time and on cue. The actors revealed that this sense of responsibility and duty to others, to the profession, and to the vocation take priority over their own needs and were the primary motivators for appearing onstage.

Alex feels she has a duty to the audience, to her fellow performers, and to the imaginal world that they are creating together. "No matter how frightened I am ... I have to go out there." Bill stated that he knows he will always make his entrances, due to the felt presence of a "wall" that prevents him from leaving the theater. He also feels a responsibility to the other actors onstage who are depending on him. He feels he has "no choice" other than to make his entrance when the time comes. He believes, "You can't leave." A sense of responsibility to her fellow actors also compels Elizabeth to perform despite her discomfort. Jake feels a responsibility toward the profession. This keeps him performing despite the negative aspects of stage fright. Jimmy feels a responsibility to the audience. "There's no way you can walk away." Kathryn feels she must recover from stage fright and go on. "There is no choice in live theater." For Marty, a sense of responsibility to a favored acting technique worsened his stage fright. Without this responsibility, he feels he would have trusted his gut and experienced less stage fright. However, he feels strongly attached to his feelings of responsibility in carrying out his professional role. For Peter, despite stage fright, "The show must go on."

- **To the actor: describe your sense of responsibility when it comes to acting.**

Other facets

Dreams emerged for two actors, Kathryn and Peter, regarding the nature of stage fright. The "actor's nightmare" is a classic experience for actors, in which they dream they are onstage in an unknown play in an unknown part, with no memory of their lines or their circumstance. They discover themselves, center stage, in front of an audience, and are filled with terror and dread. Peter and Kathryn stated that the presence of this "actor's dream" heralds the actual stage fright experience. Kathryn continues to have this "stage fright dream" in the weeks before opening night. It is the same each time. In her dream, she is onstage speaking gibberish. There is usually an important loved one who is watching her fail onstage. She awakens in a sweat, feeling sick and as if she was being "chased by serial killers." Peter still experiences the dream "to this day." He characterizes the "classic" experience of being center stage and not knowing what is happening. The central feeling of the dream is "the absolute extremity of lack of knowledge ... the darkness ... the black thing."

- **To the actor: have you had the *actor's nightmare*? Describe it in detail.**

Duality emerged as a theme for three actors, Alex, Kathryn, and Peter, who viewed the experience of stage fright as two conditions merged with each other. For Alex, the experience of stage fright is the awareness that something awful will happen in concert with the knowledge that something wonderful will also occur.

Kathryn notes that terror exists alongside excitement when she experiences stage fright. "When it's good, it's ecstasy. When it's bad, it's a nightmare. It's horror. It's the fright. It's like a deal with the Devil … to get the one I have to face the other." For Peter, stage fright is a "bipolar character" that possesses qualities of vibrancy and motivation along with horror and unspeakable terror.

- **To the actor: have you had the experience of having two conflicting feelings at once? Describe it in detail.**

Mystery emerged as a theme for Marty. He stated there was some psychological aspect to stage fright that he could not articulate. He felt it was obscure and indescribable. "It's something I can't get at … There's something else I haven't touched on … or what it might be if it were so." For Marty, stage fright remained a mystery.

- **To the actor: does your stage fright have a sense of mystery to it? Can you describe it?**

The unexpected was a theme for three actors, Alex, Elizabeth, and Jake, who feel that their stage fright experiences are unexpected. For Alex, a stage fright episode is always a surprise and a shock, even though conversely, she knows it will always occur before their entrances. For Elizabeth, stage fright experiences cannot be anticipated. They occur unexpectedly, at different times during a run of a show, and under different circumstances. She cannot pinpoint a trigger or a pattern. Jake's stage fright can also occur unexpectedly. It can happen even when he is secure in a role and is well-rehearsed. He does not know when stage fright will strike.

- **To the actor: does your stage fright have an aspect of the unexpected? Can you describe it?**

And what is your experience?

Now that you have reviewed each component of stage fright and considered your experience of each one, take a moment to reflect on and accept the experience. Is your encounter similar to our actors, or are there any differences? What aspects were the most powerful for you? What aspects were surprises? Actors rarely discuss their stage fright openly. Going through this process has opened the door for more acceptance and discussion about its presence. Remember that almost all actors experience stage fright. The fact that you feel fear puts you in good company. It is natural and easy to assume that stage fright is a signal that you are not talented, are defective somehow, and that other actors are somehow more equipped than you. This is not the case. Begin to believe that your fear is not reflective of your creativity, your talent, or your worth. Acknowledge that you have faced your fear, and that you have demonstrated courage.

To review, the first part of the presentation of interviews included each actor's perspective of his or her experience of stage fright. In order to understand the lived experience of stage fright in context, the investigation was framed by the participant's views on (a) the draw to acting and the acting experience and (b) nature of stage fright. The *essential* themes, presented by six or more of the actors regarding the draw to acting and the acting experience are: (a) childhood experience, (b) communication, (c) danger and courage, (d) difference, (e) inherence, and (f) service. The nonessential themes, shared by five or fewer actors, included *attention, clarity, excitement, expansion, expression, freedom, safety, transcendence, transformation,* and *trust.* The essential themes, shared by six or more of the actors regarding the experience of stage fright are: (a) colors, associations, and stage fright personified, (b) death, (c) fear of failure, (d) inhibition, (e) physical attack, and (f) shame. The nonessential themes, shared by five or less actors, included feeling *alone, conflict, confusion, control, doubt, familiarity, fraudulence, loss of love, motivation, necessity, protection,* and *self-absorption.* The essential themes, shared by six or more of the actors regarding the nature of stage fright are: (a) changes, (b) coping, (c) permanence, and (d) responsibility. The nonessential themes, shared by five or fewer actors, include *dreams, duality, mystery,* and *the unexpected.* In the following section, the reader will find an *essential aggregate description* of the essential themes that emerged from all eight actors. The description is intended to provide a general presentation of the personal responses, to offer a composite representation of the experience, and to stay close to the actors' narratives. Furthermore, because the interviews are attempting to reveal the lived experience of stage fright from the actor's perspective, it will be written in the first-person monologue style.

Essential composite description: the draw to acting and the acting experience

I remember so vividly that *childhood experience* of my draw to acting. When I was very young, I remember noticing the details of the world around me, and this ignited my imagination. I noticed others: how they spoke, how they moved, how they behaved. It all fascinated me. When I first appeared onstage, I felt I was in a place where all I observed about the world finally mattered. I felt free to live out the images and emotions that were within me. Being onstage gave me the feeling of being safe, at home, and in my element. I felt free, vibrant, and alive. At times, I felt transformed. At times, I transcended my own self. I could soar! I could fly! These childhood experiences set the course for my life's path: I am an actor.

I act for a deep desire to *communicate.* With audiences, with other actors, and with myself. I am not talking about a one-way expression, where I tell audiences—you—how it is. I am talking about a two-way exchange of ideas, emotions, and truths where we both are affected. When a playwright gives me words to interpret and to deliver, I discover and feel and live an aspect of the truth of what it means to be alive. Through portraying other characters, I encounter and feel joy, rage, hatred, sorrow, love, fear, you name it. Then I deliver these human qualities to you, onstage, in real time, where we meet together in a theater. Your response, your understanding, and your acknowledgement of this work is signaled by your feeling, your laughter, your applause, your tears, your listening, and your silence. There is something important happening between us. I feel you with me. You feel me with you. We are connected, you and I. We are in communion. This is my essential task as an actor.

Acting is *dangerous*. Because acting in the theater is live, something can always go wrong. There is no safety net. There are sets moving, lights going on and off, and people moving in the dark. There are props and instruments that have to be used as if you have been using them all of your life. Other people may make mistakes. Missed lines, missed entrances, and accidents may occur, but we must recover and move forward, which increases the feeling of danger. Something may be affecting my instrument—me—where my body, voice, heart, and mind are weakened, which affects my performance and can create risk. I have to remember my lines, make sure I am in the "now of now," and make sure that I am emotionally connected to the moment-to-moment realities of the character and the play. I must also be aware of all of the things that can go wrong so I can protect myself. And of course, there is the presence of the audience. They can be friendly and loving, but they can turn on you. It feels as if they are a firing squad. It feels as if they can eat you alive when you are at your most vulnerable and exposed physically and emotionally. So it takes *courage* to walk out on that stage. When the time comes for any line, action, or bit of stage business, it must occur as predetermined by the play, so there must be no hesitation. You have to have a sense of courage to "just do it" and follow through. And, with so many eyes on you, and with so much that can go wrong, we need bravery to go out on that stage night after night. Dare I say it? Going out onstage is an act of heroism?

I believe that my acting abilities are *inherent*. Fish swim, birds fly, and I act. My abilities to observe, to internalize, and to communicate human truths through my body, voice, and heart are innate. They are in my blood. Acting is what I was born to do. It is not something I chose to do. It is something that I am. I *am* an actor. Even when I am not onstage, I am observing, feeling, wondering, and expanding. This facility is part of my DNA. Why? Well, you'll have to talk to God about that one. It's as simple as that.

Actors are *different* from others. We are different in how we see the world. We get at the story of things. We have to be more sensitive to and more aware of life events in order to physically, psychologically, and emotionally portray the human condition onstage. Every day, I hear, I smell, and I see. We have to be superhuman in our humanness. In particular, people fascinate me. I see your smile and I feel it form on my face. I can hear your accent and your voice, and your speech begins to register in my mouth, and your voice wells up within me. I see how you move your hand, tilt your head, and arch your brow, and I feel these movements stir in my own body. I register your essence and I feel it want to emanate from me. This brings me closer to you. I know you more. Do other people have this experience? I allow myself to be constantly delighted and surprised. We are more alive than nonactors. Sometimes others smell that we are more alive, and that makes them shrink up and feel smaller. It makes them feel somewhat like a failure. At times, they hate us for this. Isn't that why we must set up our celebrities only to rip them down? It's almost like a Greek myth! We are more alive. Now I know you are not supposed to say this, but there. I've said it.

We have a long history of this that has been passed down through the centuries. We have been seen as the charlatans, as the bohemians, as the hedonists of the world. What we do is not seen as real work. Even though people went to the theater to see actors, they did not want to associate with us, and this continues today. Actors are not respected unless they are movie stars and the public know who they are. All of this may be due to the assumption that actors want to be the center of attention. But that's not why we do it. We know our value. Because others view us differently, we have had to stick together. Is it too presumptuous to say that we are our own culture?

Acting is a *service* that tends to the audience and society in several ways. Central to our craft is storytelling, which has gone on for thousands of years. We come together to be changed by this work of art. This is essential for human existence. We also entertain you! We make you genuinely laugh! We show you the humor in things and distract you from your own life's troubles for a few hours or so. We also educate you about various scenarios of life. We show you how others live and broaden your knowledge of the world. You may incorporate this new knowledge, and it may have an effect on how you perceive and live your own life. We also help you to feel. By feeling ourselves and communicating with you, we help you to broaden your capacity for emotion within yourself and within your own life. Sometimes you feel through us the things that you don't allow yourselves to feel. By listening to us speak the playwright's words, we release you to say, "Yes! That's what I wanted to say!" We also seek to tell the truth about life onstage. We hold a mirror up to your face and say, "Is this you?" In a world where so many things can be bought, isn't gaining insight into the truth priceless? By showing you the truth, we help you to rehearse, to prepare for, and to reflect on the great moments of life that we have in common: birth, love, betrayal, and death. All the world's a stage, right?

Many of us believe that our service is sacred. Many of us believe that entertainment, education, and self-understanding tend to the soul. The actor's "sacred journey" is an ancient journey, and we feel called to this ancient vocation. Actors bring universal truths to society, and they have been doing so for thousands of years. We act out the dreams and fantasies of society. Some of us feel that our service is spiritual in nature. Some of us believe that acting is a gift of creativity that reflects the nature of God.

Essential composite description: the stage fright experience

Stage fright is a direct attack on my purpose, my vocation, and my very being. It registers as a literal *physical attack*. These assaults against my body may happen all at once, or a few at a time. I never really know. If you knew the plans of an intruder, you could defend yourself, right? When stage fright strikes, I have difficulty breathing. I cannot inhale deeply, and my breaths get shorter and shorter. Sometimes I get cold sweats and I get light headed. My heart races. At times, it feels like it is pounding out of my chest! Sometimes I feel as if I were running, even though I am standing still, trying to hold it together. Sometimes it is like butterflies creating a mild flutter. Sometimes it is a piercing stabbing pain in my core. Sometimes it is unbearable churning where I have to relieve myself over and over, hours before curtain. I become hyper-reactive and any sound, movement, or comment can make me jump. Or scream! Stage fright attacks my primary means of communication, my voice and my body. I get dry mouth, watery eyes, and a swollen tongue. I lose control of my voice! Sometimes I can't speak! My hands shake. My knees weaken. I become self-conscious about the movement of my lips and arms. Sometimes I can't move! Stage fright feels like it is literally choking me. I become confused and lose my focus. Webs of darkness invade my mind. I sometimes I dissociate. As it grips me, I feel my life force leave me. Sometimes it is too much and my body gives out. I lose consciousness. I have been known to faint.

Fear of failure is central to the stage fright experience. You can rehearse and rehearse, feel the support and camaraderie—and even love—of your fellow actors, and be as prepared as possible, but when stage fright strikes, I still feel like I am going to fail. The fear can be specific. I fear that I will lose my lines, miss a cue, or make a mistake in my blocking—you name it. Then I will spoil the performance for the audience. They came all this way, took time out of their day and paid good money to see this show, and I fear I will ruin it for them. I also fear that if I make a mistake, I will ruin the performance for my fellow actors. What if I don't handle that bit of stage business correctly? What if I skip a scene and throw everyone off? We have worked so hard for this night. What if I spoil it for them? My fears can be more diffuse. What if I fail and I am not the artist that I think I am? Or as capable? What if I do something awful? What a blow to my character as a person and as an actor! What if I fail and this is not what I am supposed to do? Maybe my father was right! Maybe! Maybe! What if? What if? These questions become ingrained in my thinking, and the fear of failure becomes a raging negative voice in my head that interrogates me and inflames the fear, making it even worse. Before I even begin, I feel like I have committed the most terrible crime in the world. And it will happen in front of everyone. Oh God!

Stage fright has a sense of *inhibition* that manifests in a few ways. Sometimes, when I am about to go onstage, or when I am on the stage, my physical sense of freedom feels constricted. Other times, when it is severe, my body feels restrained and I am unable to move at all. One time I had to be literally kicked onto the stage! Sometimes my mind is a blank. I can't think! I can't fathom what is supposed to happen next! I feel as if my mind is literally frozen. Sometimes stage fright restricts my artistry. When I am in "the now of now," connected to my childlike sense of wonder and freedom, and having transformed my own self, I am in the peak experience of acting. It is a transcendent feeling. I have hit the heights of my craft artistically, emotionally, and spiritually. Stage fright restricts this. It robs me of these aspects. I feel dull, limited, tight, and trapped. I feel like I am tied up in knots. I am not free as an artist, as a feeling being, or as a communicator. I am robotically going through the motions. I am not able to do my best work. I cannot fly. I am trapped in a cage.

When the physical attack, fear of failure, and inhibition happen, at my core I feel like I am wrong, like I am defective. Failures onstage or the fantasies of failure generate feelings of *shame*. It feels like I am—or will be—stripped naked in front of thousands of people, and they will see all of my imperfections. I will be scrutinized and all that is inherently wrong with me will be illuminated for all to see. I am defenseless. The audience has the power to know me more than I know myself. It is different from the feeling of failure where I will *do* something wrong, this is the feeling that I *am* wrong. Like I never should have been born. This is the worst feeling in the world.

Stage fright can feel like impending *death*. It feels as if the audience can eat me alive. It feels as if I am walking to the guillotine. Or a live firing squad. I am filled with horror and terror. Separate from this feeling of anticipation of death, stage fright can feel like I actually am dying in that moment. It is dreadful. It is huge! It wants to annihilate me! It feels like it is destroying me! I feel like I am falling with nothing to hold on to. I am in the intermediate place between life and death. It feels as if my blood is draining from my body. I feel the reverse of my life flashing before my eyes! The life force is leaving me. My world about to collapse. Oh God, no!

Stage fright feels like an attack by a real entity. It announces itself in a flash of *color*: red for horror; black for shame; maroon for lifeless, dead blood; and white for cold-frozen fear. Sometimes—but rarely—orange for excitement and purple for vibrancy. Sometimes stage fright appears as red chaos, or as red, pure hell. Stage fright *is* hell. Sometimes I know it is there because I feel like I am wrong, like I have a black mark against me. These colors transform stage fright into a person. Stage fright is *personified*. Stage fright can appear in my mind as a demon. This demon strangles me and sucks the life force out of me. It renders me old, burnt, and useless. It desires my slow and meandering death. As this feeling intensifies, I become desperate to return to the life force and regain my strength. I wish to return to the womb, but the demon whispers doubts and damns me as it drains my blood drop by drop. Stage fright can appear as the Devil's face with a long moustache and evil eyes. Stage fright chases me, and chases me even when I am frozen and can't move. I cannot get away! Stage fright can also appear as a mysterious intruder who breaks in, unannounced and tries to strangle me! I'm crying now. He wants to take my life! I don't know why! I don't know why!

Stage fright is not so obvious in its attempts to keep me offstage. He can appear as a Relaxed Fellow. He whispers soft doubts into my ear and cajoles me to stay back stage where it is safe with him. Sometimes, he will even let me feel excited about my performance. Why? Because I need him? Stage fright may strike a bargain. He may give me motivation and anticipation. What I wouldn't give for some of that! But like all good liars, the good deeds do not come without a price. To get these, I have to endure the horror and the terror. I must make my deal with the Devil. Stage fright is horrible when he loses his patience. He may demand the vibrancy of performance, yet he can't manifest his full powers if I do perform well. He wants both from me, and it is a horrible battle. When Stage fright is at the height of his powers, it is the darkest, blackest fear of any performer. It is so dark, so horrible, and so powerful. Do not mention the name! Do not say the name!

Essential composite description: the nature of stage fright

Stage fright has been a *permanent* part of my life as an actor. It has been with me ever since I began acting, to some degree or another. Its potential presence is always there. The venue or the size of the audience does not matter, as it can strike at any time. Sometimes the presence of a loved one or a colleague will trigger stage fright. Sometimes inexplicably, it will not occur. Why? I don't know why. I have tried every remedy. I have tried to cure it medically, psychologically, and spiritually. Nothing works. Nothing. It is an ongoing aspect of my life as an actor.

Despite its permanent presence in my life, I have noticed *changes* in how stage fright manifests. When I was younger, my stage fright mentally centered on concerns that the audience liked me, and it was at its worst. Now the thoughts that stage fright causes are concerned with my artistry and my professionalism. Now my thoughts are focused on doing my best artistically and less concerned about the audience. As actors mature as performers, our stage fright concerns move from the self to others, and it lessens. Will I meet the demands of the role? Will I be a giving and supportive cast mate? Will I be able to reach those transcendent heights? And share them? A focus on being liked or not good enough is for the younger actor. At times though, my mind still wrestles with negative thoughts of failure and shame. However, my physical and professional technique is stronger now than when I was younger. I can rely on it to help me focus on the task at hand. If I anticipate failure, I rely on my work ethic and years of experience to find creative solutions onstage. This has quieted my stage fright. Paradoxically though, I am more emotionally vulnerable than I once was. When I was younger I had less technique to rely on, but somehow I was stronger, tougher. Now that I have my experience to shield me, I am more in touch with my frailties. Stage fright is a bit quieter, but it still has the potential to take me down.

Most people run from danger. Why do I—we—persist in going on that stage? We do it for a deep sense of *responsibility*. You have heard it, "The show must go on!" This responsibility feels like a sacred duty. It feels like an unchangeable principle and unstoppable sense of commitment to the ethics of the profession. This ethic is not always tangible and it is not always easy to articulate. It feels like a wall that prevents me from escaping. No matter how frightened I am, I must go on that stage. There is no choice. I have always made my entrances and I always will.

Actors feel a responsibility to the audience. They have purchased tickets and have taken time out of their lives to come to the theater. They have come to be entertained, to learn, to feel, and to think. You can't tell them, "Go home!" I also have a responsibility to my fellow actors and the ensemble that we have created together. They are depending on me to do my part, as I am depending on them to do theirs. We support each other to get on that stage. I also have an obligation to the playwright to tell the story so that the message of the play can be delivered. I also remember my sense of duty to my vocation and to whatever higher forces are involved. All of these responsibilities can be articulated very simply: I do my job.

Acting is what I do. Stage fright has a permanent presence in my life. Stage fright cannot be avoided because I must go out onstage. And I cannot ignore it. Therefore, I must *cope* with it. I do so in several ways, depending on the severity of the episode. First, I cope by seeking its purpose. Is it protecting me from knowing the true extent of my talent? Maybe it is an excuse to justify performances that I thought could have been better? Maybe it is protecting me from danger? It is difficult to know. But I accept that stage fright is there. I accept its presence. I give up trying to control what I cannot control. I make room for it. It has been such a part of my life it is almost familiar, its presence almost like a ritual.

Before performances, I get to the theater early. I am well-rehearsed. I do my relaxation exercises, voice and speech exercises, and go over the role in my mind as I prepare to go onstage. I attend to my hair and makeup, my costumes, and my props. As the curtain time approaches, I focus on controlling my breathing. I refute the negative doubts, accusations, and thoughts that stage fright asks me to entertain. As my entrance approaches, I remember my training, my experience, and my rehearsal. I tell myself that I am the expert. I pump myself up. I tell myself, "This is gonna be good! Gonna knock 'em dead!"

Then I just go out there.

If stage fright hits onstage, I focus on being in the moment and being in "the now." I check the audience. Do they seem slow? Fast? By checking their mood, I can gain some control of the situation and assess how to deliver my performance. If I can make them laugh, I know they will keep laughing, and that helps me to cope. Sometimes though, I have to put the audience out of my mind, and I remember the "fourth wall" which strengthens my feeling of being in the fantasy of the play. I may look into another actor's eyes, and connecting with them helps me to get through the fear. I can let them know I am in trouble, and they will help me. If I have made a mistake, like a missed line or a wrong piece of business, I look for a solution that makes sense within the story of the play. I improvise. I trust my instincts.

Sometimes I have to look beyond myself to manage stage fright. I cope with it by forgiveness. If I forgive my fellow actors and myself for making mistakes and we incorporate any mishaps into the performance, the audience will be forgiving as well. Sometimes I dedicate the performance to another person, living or dead. In their honor, I do my best. Sometimes I meditate. Sometimes I ask for guidance from a higher power. At times, I surrender. I get down on my hands and knees and say, "God, I can't do this. I have the talent and the gift, and I know my lines, but I can't do this. It's too much for me. So, I give it to you." I surrender the performance to God. I can access His strength and fear does not rule me. I am not and will not be subject to it. He gives me the confidence and strength to go on.

And I go out there like a shot! Bingo! Bam! And ... "Curtain."

Stage fright will return.

So will I.

To the actor: my turn

- **Now that you have reflected on the essential components of stage fright, have added those unique to your experience, and have read this essential composite description, write your own monologue about your stage fright experience:**
  - **Write it in the "first person"**
  - **You may divide it into three parts, using these questions as a guide:**
    - *The draw to acting and the acting experience*
      - What drew you to acting?
      - What kind of acting training/background do you have?
      - What is it like to appear in front of an audience?
      - What do you believe is the purpose of acting?
    - *The stage fright of experience*
      - What is stage fright like?
      - What does the fear feel like internally/emotionally?
      - Does the feeling have a shape/color/texture?
      - Is there an image associated with this?
      - What does this image represent?
      - What physical sensations go with it?
      - If stage fright were a character, what objective would it have?
    - *The nature of stage fright*
      - What circumstances trigger stage fright for you?
      - How did/do you cope with stage fright?
      - Do these methods work?
      - What do you tell yourself about it?
      - Is/was it transient? Persistent?
      - Did/does it alter your performance?
      - What is it like for you to discuss it?
      - What do you think is the meaning or essence of stage fright?

8   Putting it all together

The state of the art: managing stage fright

At least you're not in this alone.

—Katherine

We have broken the silence about stage fright. We have heard from our actors. In reviewing their stories and applying your own perspective to the themes that they shared, you have created an account of your own stage fright. Stage fright is a part of acting and part of life. It manifests in a multitude of physical, cognitive, and emotional symptoms that sometimes derails our acting and our competent self-concept. As actors, we have seen that there is a long and entrenched history which has contributed to how people see us and how we see ourselves. Our actors did not give up. They stayed the course and became stronger as they weathered their stage fright. They gave their accounts of their experiences, and later described how their attitudes about themselves grew more positive with each performance. Katherine says, "At least you are not in this alone." It may be difficult to feel that this is true, but trust that it is. By acknowledging, accepting and talking about the presence of stage fright you are taking your experience seriously, refining your artistry, and promoting your growth. We have looked at the components of stage fright and addressed how they emerge uniquely in each individual, and in you. We have already done a lot of the work in previous chapters. Now, let's put it all together. Start by sharing your stage fright story with at least two trusted individuals who will support you in managing your fears. Join our actors in speaking about it. As you talk about your experience, accepting that you are not alone will lessen your stage fright.

Bit by bit: sorting this out

Your self-worth as an actor and as a person is at stake. They go hand-in-hand. It's as important as that, that your self-worth is very much involved. Gotta build that up.

—Marty

As we address our symptoms, we will find that their reduction will provide some relief and peace in order to proceed with our artistry. However, it is also apparent that whether stage fright is viewed from a physical, cognitive, behavioral, or emotional perspective, the underlying factor during a stage fright attack is the belief that *I'm not good enough*. This belief is rooted in momentary, situational, or ongoing *low self-esteem*. Self-esteem is such an overly used word that it has almost lost its meaning, but we should not discount it. It is defined as a realistic and appreciative opinion of oneself (Schiraldi, 2001). It is also described as the experience of feeling competent to cope with the basic challenges of life and being worthy of happiness (Brandon, 1969). Low self-esteem is associated with not feeling competent and not feeling deserving of joy. It generates ranges of negativity toward the self that are always present in the stage fright experience (Clason, Johansson, & Mortberg, 2015). We were not born with low self-esteem, but somehow, some way, this point of view was instilled in the many actors who experience stage fright. Whether this occurred in the distant past or during a particular performance event, stage fright is associated with the fear that we are not competent to complete our acting tasks well. Each individual actor must search their own history to discover where these seeds may have been planted. Review your responses to the questions in the preceding chapters and focus on those that shed light on how you may have lost your confidence and belief that you can handle acting—and life—challenges. Focus especially on the occurrence of negative criticism from past relationships. Reframe the experience in a way that will move you toward the opposite, positive belief, *I'm good enough*. As we go through other aspects of putting this together, all discussion will be pointing us to the end goal of believing in our calling, feeling proud of our artistry, feeling able to express our talent, and having positive self-worth. Katherine reminds us that

> It's fear of failure. Fear that you'll be found out. I've heard a lot of actors say this. "They're gonna find out that I really don't know what I'm doing. Somebody's gonna call me on this. I'm getting away with something here."

Kathryn also reminds us of our unique powers. "Oh, a good actor is more aware. They hear, they see, they smell. I can do your smile. I can hear your accent, your voice. I'm more interested." As we embrace our unique qualities and dismantle the belief that *I'm not good enough*, stage fright will begin to lose its power over us.

Hold on: it will get better

> *I was a child who was easily intimidated. I cried easily and was bullied. So, I felt weak and ineffective. Stage fright brought back these feelings, this fear of being a failure. Fear that I really don't know what I'm doing. But when I was the character, I was powerful, and I felt invincible. But getting from one to the other took practice.*
>
> —Kathryn

Our actors tell us that over time, and with experience, their stage fright lessened. Elizabeth tells us, "In the early days, there was total immobility. Now, I've gotten past it. There are times when I do shows, and I have absolutely no stage fright whatsoever. I'm nervous, but no stage fright." Like anything new we try, we are bound to feel ranges of anxiety before we have developed that particular expertise. Almost everyone feels some degree of discomfort when approaching a new task. Being a new parent, a new teacher, a new person in a company and even an experienced actor joining a new cast will feel some degree of anxiety. Bill says, "It's so great that we are talking about this. As I think about my first professional job, I was so terrified. But as I look back on it, what was I worried about? I was pretty good!" Our actors direct us to *hold on*, as it will get better, but we must decide to hold on and not give up. If our low self-esteem is active, we will tend to not rely on the basic sense of confidence that we naturally would have developed in a secure and perfect world. We will tend to use the feeling of anxiety to verify the "truth" of our core belief, *I'm not good enough*. It is crucial that we hold on here and tolerate the uncomfortable feeling that what we believe to be true (i.e., *I'm not good enough*) is *not* true. If we can accept this, then we must embrace the feelings that accompany the alternative belief— *I am good enough*—to extinguish our stage fright. You may be surprised that these feelings may not be immediately positive. You may feel disbelief, anger, shame, disgust, more fear, etc. At this juncture, we must not rely on negative emotions to reinforce the suspicion that we are unworthy. We must tolerate that this is not the case. This can be uncomfortable. We are designed to heal, and you are designed to heal from the negative experiences that have lessened your self-worth and have contributed to your stage fright. Our actors remind us that the more you act the more proficient you will become over time. Start by setting acting goals that are reasonably attainable. Engage in low-stress situations like volunteering to read stories or present monologues to children at libraries and schools. Then take on activities where the stakes are higher, like attending a local theater audition. Continue to gradually challenge yourself by taking classes to build your poise and expertise. Know that over time and with experience your stage fright will lessen as you set and reach acting goals. *Hold on*. It will get better.

The picture of a person: actor's self-concept

It is important to me to keep studying and to keep learning. It feeds my soul.

—Peter

In Chapter 2, you answered questions about your *self-concept* as an actor. Some actors perceive themselves as strong, competent, and optimistic about their acting, while others have a weaker self-concept regarding their acting and their pursuit of an acting career. Many actors are fortunate to have support from friends and loved ones and have not had to endure negative attitudes from others regarding their choice to pursue acting. However, even one negative experience can influence how we feel about being an actor. In addition, limited opportunities to perform can influence the actor's self-concept. Whether your self-concept as an actor is positive, negative, or somewhere in between, you can reinforce it by feeding yourself with positive experiences. Remember the performance that inspired you to become an actor. Find a supportive acting teacher, mentor, coach, or fellow actor who supports you in your artistry and goals. Read plays that you love and read books to help fuel your passion for acting and your commitment to the craft. It is important to be with other actors. If you are not already in a class, a program, or a cast, join one. If you are not currently acting, see other actors perform. Attend readings and plays and watch films and TV shows. Generate your own work by having readings and attending any audition you can, because actors *act*. Don't wait for "permission" to act or to be an actor. Start where you are now, today. Be proud of being an actor, own your identity, and remember your history as you move into your future.

Children and art: the actor-child

> So much of an actor's life is getting in touch with that inner child and being a child again and being free to play in the sandbox. Stage fright puts up rules. Stage fright almost becomes the parent, the authority figure, saying, "You can't do this. You're not good enough to do this. You're a failure. Grow up and do something more worthwhile."
>
> —Jake

Research has shown that as children, actors were different than those who grew up and entered other professions. Actors, when they were children, tended to have an early propensity for play and imagination and were interested in the "inner world" and "other worlds." They were oriented toward fiction, were attuned to others, and were inventive, often creating stories and plays at an early age (Goldstein & Winner, 2009). Peter tells us,

> As a child, I was fascinated and obsessed with the creative arts. I made up stories and plays and characters. I loved movies. I loved television. I loved costumes. I loved lights. Anything that was creative, I was drawn to. And when I discovered that in elementary school we could do plays, I immediately became desperate to be a part of that.

When we lose our way due to stage fright, we forget who we are, and why we act. We become disconnected from that free, spontaneous, creative, and fearless *actor-child* part of ourselves. Here are some suggestions to reconnect with this part of yourself. First, use your acting skills. As actors, we often remember events in our past to help us to feel what the character may be feeling. Use this same skill to remember your childhood memories of play. Recall your memories that represent your imaginative and carefree actor-child-self. Remember experiences of putting on productions in the backyard, turning blankets into castles on rainy afternoons, speaking in other voices, and making up invisible characters. Perhaps there is only one memory, perhaps there are several. Start by making a list of each memory, from the strongest to the weakest. Now fill in as many details as you can remember for each item on the list. Describe the setting, who else may have been there, the props and costumes you invented and the stories you told. See where you played and for whom you performed. See and feel yourself as your *actor-child-self*, play-acting and believing in the reality of your imaginative world without fear. Do not leave your list until you have reviewed each memory as completely as you can. Reconnect with and reexperience the feelings of wonder, freedom, and possibility of this time. These memories and experiences are precious. They will reinforce the fact that that your actor-child-self has been here for years.

If I could turn back time: the call to acting

> At that moment, as I was standing onstage, I knew I had to do this for the rest of my life. For some unknown reason, I knew innately, that there were a whole bunch of people inside me, and if I didn't get them out, I would implode. Because it was the first time in my life that I felt free, and I felt lifted, and I felt light.
>
> —Alex

We know that actors feel *called* to act and that is a powerful desire (Robb, Due, & Venning, 2016). To some actors, it feels like a "summons," or even a "divine call." Actors call it "bitten by the bug." These descriptions signify that the call to acting often happens in a flash, yet it feels intrinsic and part of our very identity. This is one of the most important moments in an actor's life. It could have happened during a particularly powerful moment onstage, during a curtain call, or in a class or during a rehearsal. Jake tells us, "One of my earliest memories was seeing *Peter Pan*. I remember being struck in that moment. One of the reasons I became an actor was because I wanted to fly. I wanted to learn how to fly." Other actors like Jimmy have a more gradual sense of knowing that they were called to acting.

> I wanted to be a musician or a music producer. And then I realized I wanted to be onstage myself. I was drawn to expressing myself onstage. A friend said, "Well, what about acting?" It dawned on me right then that I always had wanted to be an actor.

Stage fright causes us to lose our way and we wonder if we "should" be acting at all. You can find your way back by using your acting skills. Notice that when we are preparing a role, we often must go back in time in our minds to an important moment in the play to inform the present moment and to drive the current objective in the script. In the same way, go back in time in your mind and recall your "Why I Wanted to Be an Actor" story. Recall the moment, event, or time you knew that you desired—needed—to be an actor. Remember the circumstances, the feelings, and as many details of the moment as you can. Write it down in as much detail as possible. Reconnect with the feelings of being called, of knowing, and of being certain that being an actor is what you want to do and what you are destined to do. Stay with these feelings and notice them in your body. Incorporate these feelings and this certainty to help lessen your stage fright and to help you stay on your actor's path.

It's too darn hot: types of symptoms

> But when you are going through it, ya know, it's rough. But 'cha gotta face it so you can deal with it.
>
> —Marty

In Chapter 3, you answered questions to help determine how your particular stage fright manifests in your life. We can look at the specific *symptoms* and begin to get a picture of how different types of stage fright may emerge. Individuals who experience anxiety most of the time may have *Generalized Anxiety Disorder* (GAD). GAD is widespread. Many of the aspects of stage fright occur in individuals with GAD, but the symptoms emerge in a variety of situations beyond acting. Individuals who have GAD feel slightly anxious much of the time, and the idea or reality of acting exacerbates the anxiety level to a stage fright episode. If there is a family history of anxiety, there may be inherited or learned behaviors that contribute to GAD. If anxiety is only related to acting, an individual may have what is called a *Social Anxiety Disorder* (SAD) with a *performance only* aspect (*DSM*, American Psychiatric Association [APA], 2013). We know that public performance is a prominent fear of all individuals. The common appearance of stage fright may be tolerated and incorporated into the acting experience until it lessens as acting experience increases. However, it may be an aspect of an anxiety condition that will benefit from psychological intervention. Symptoms of stage fright can appear in certain *forms*. Symptoms that are comprised of mainly negative thoughts point to a primarily *cognitive* form. Stage fright symptoms that are comprised of mainly emotional reactions suggest a primarily *affective* form. Symptoms that are primarily physical signify a primarily *physiological* form. Symptoms that appear in counterproductive behaviors appear in a *behavioral* form. Stage fright almost always appears in a unique combination of these, yet one form may be prominent. If stage fright causes an individual to lose sense of time or space, they may be *dissociating*. If an individual's stage fright is very severe and they feel like they will die, then stage fright is complicated by *panic attacks*. Being able to articulate how stage fright shows up for you will be helpful in describing your symptoms should you decide that you need additional help to address your specific stage fright.

Back to before: reviewing your history

> It's important to talk about these things so we can get a handle on it. We research our characters pretty deeply, don't we?
>
> —Bill

In Chapter 4, you reflected on what possibly *causes* your stage fright. It is important to contemplate your responses. While stage fright may be activated by conditions like GAD or SAD, your stage fright may be rooted in your relational history. Ongoing difficulties in relationships can set the tone for feeling insecure and troubled due to recurring emotional stress. You may have experienced disapproval from a specific person like a parent, a teacher, or a friend. Negative evaluation by others—especially when we are actors—can influence how we feel about ourselves and go through life. Additionally, a traumatic past performance experience may have caused you some anxiety and fear that the event might repeat itself. Use your actor skills to see if you can analyze the cause of your stage fright in the same way you might try to understand a character you are playing who also has this fear. Actors often research and write a "character bio" to create a foundational narrative with which they might understand the character's back-story, objectives, conflicts, and emotions. Write *your own history* as if you were researching a character for a production. Start by making a timeline of your life. On the timeline, mark all of the significant events that have occurred in your life starting from birth and ending in the present. (You may wish to add familial events that occurred before you were born if they had an influence on you.) When it is complete, notice all of the events that you have experienced. See the arc of your life up to now, the way you would see the arc of your character's story before they enter the play. Now use the timeline as a starting point for writing your "bio." You may write about your life year by year, event by event, or you may divide your life into segments. Include as much detail as you can: where you were born, your family relationships, your likes and dislikes, your desires, your goals, and how meaningful events and experiences have influenced you. Allow the words to flow in a *stream of consciousness*. It is important to write *until you have no more to say*. Fifty pages are effective for using this exercise to self-reflect and uncover the causes of current issues (J. Bohannon, personal communication, July 7, 2018). If there are still events that contribute to low self-esteem or anxiety you will benefit greatly from resolving them. Often the act of writing illuminates and resolves past difficulties by giving us the place to organize our thoughts and feelings. Your own self-reflection may be enough, talking to another person about your experiences may be enough, or you may wish to seek out therapy or counseling to resolve any past events that still negatively influence you. Ask yourself what has caused your stage fright from the perspective of your history, your relationships, and your experiences. Remember that some anxiety is normal when performing. We are looking to see if you can identify any historical causes of your specific stage fright.

A light in the dark: therapies

> *As scary as stage fright is, there is nothing else in my life I would rather do more than what I do. Absolutely nothing.*
>
> —Bill

Acknowledging and discussing stage fright brings relief for many actors. But if your stage fright is persistent, you may wish to engage in psychotherapy to address it. The types of *therapies* available are varied and diverse. Each specialty is based on unique theories of human life that guide its approach to treatment. As you review the questions that steered you toward the potential causes of your stage fright, you can seek out psychotherapy based on the content of your responses. *Psychodynamic psychotherapies* are known as "talking cures" (Nagel, 2017). These therapies generally hold that psychological symptoms are caused by historical life events, unconscious conflicts, and difficulties rooted in relationships. In psychodynamic psychotherapy, past internal issues and events that have not been emotionally resolved are addressed. *Behavior therapies* contend that stage fright symptoms are learned behaviors. By addressing the external actions associated with stage fright, desired behaviors can be reinforced and undesired behaviors (i.e., avoidance, procrastination, fear of the performance setting, etc.) can be eliminated. These therapies focus on behaviors such breathing, appearing before audiences, and practicing (Jangir & Govinda, 2018). *Cognitive therapies* are based on the theory that thoughts and beliefs cause symptoms (Clason, Johansson, & Mortberg, 2015). Cognitive therapies focus on changing negative thoughts and beliefs associated with the stage fright experience to eliminate its symptoms. *Cognitive behavioral therapies* (CBT) combine behavioral and cognitive approaches. In CBT therapies, counterproductive thoughts and behaviors are identified and changed, eliminating the symptoms (Brugues, 2011). These therapies combine positive self-talk and relaxation techniques. *Integrative therapies* combine several approaches. EMDR (*Eye Movement Desensitization Reprocessing*) is effective in resolving past trauma by identifying disturbing issues and negative beliefs, and then processing emotions and thoughts connected to them to eliminate distress (Shapiro & Forrest, 1997). *Somatic Experiencing* applies body-based methods to help the mind and body heal (Levine, 2010). Other *alternative therapies* like hypnosis, biofeedback, and mindfulness training intervene at a variety of levels to bring relief to anxiety and improve functioning (Helding, 2016). Anxiety may also be relieved *medically* with anti-anxiety medication, anti-depressants, or beta-blockers (Kenny, 2011). Because stage fright often emerges in several forms, whether you intervene at a psychodynamic, behavioral, cognitive, integrative or alternative level, relief can occur. Anyone who wishes to evolve from wherever they are can benefit from self-discovery. When we as actors get to know ourselves, our acting deepens, and our sense of self expands and becomes more anchored.

Somebody loves me: self-care

> *Trusting that the instrument that I've trained and care for will somehow be able to take over and be released. Rather than the performer full of fear and self-doubt, the performer full of expertise and confidence.*
>
> —Jake

Attending to our whole body is a needed focus for performers (Hays, 2017). As actors, our entire being comprises our instrument: our physical, emotional, psychological, imaginal and spiritual selves. As musicians care for their instruments, we must care for ours. Committing to being more fearless includes committing to self-care habits that will support our acting goals. Our *physical* bodies need proper nutrition, hydration, exercise, and rest to function optimally. Performance stress can manifest itself in our bodies, causing difficulties with eating, drinking, and sleeping. While it seems that this is self-evident, we must recognize how anxiety compromises our self-care habits and we must make sure that we are attending to our basic needs properly. When our self-care is severely compromised, we are at risk of developing eating disorders, abuse of alcohol or drugs, and/or insufficient rest, which can directly impair our functioning and our instrument. Performance stress many also manifest in less than optimal posture and less than optimal breathing, resulting in physical difficulties that extend into our acting. Some actors use alternative therapies like the *Alexander Technique*, yoga, meditation, and other relaxation techniques to intervene from a physical perspective. We also must care for own *emotional* well-being. Some strategies for this have already been discussed like being kind to yourself and eliminating negative and destructive thoughts. Seeking out supportive family and friends, finding things we enjoy, having close artistic relationships where we feel supported, and having a mentor, coach, or therapist who can be a source of emotional guidance can all strengthen our emotional well-being. Close observation and study of our emotions and strengthening our command of them can augment our acting skills as well as our emotional life. Training in *The Alba Method, drama therapy,* and continued exploration of our emotional world through diverse acting methods, self-help, and psychotherapy can help us manage stage fright and create effective emotional regulation along with depth of expression (Blatner & Blatner, 1988; Dal Vera, 2001). We must also attend to our *imaginal* selves. We must care for and nurture our imaginations, our creativity, and our sense of play, wonder, and spontaneity. It may be difficult in our busy lives, but we must take the time to journal, to draw, to paint, and to day dream. We should strive to care for our imagination as fervently as we care for our physical bodies. We must also for care for our *spiritual* selves. Practices like prayer, mediation, connecting with nature, or reconnecting to a childhood belief is an important aspect of our self-care. We may benefit from surrendering our stage fright to a higher power, to God, to the magic of theater, or to the universe. As actors we are unique from other performers as our entire being is our entire instrument. We must treat it with care.

Happy talk: using positive messages

> *The subconscious still goes, "Oh my God! Oh my God! I'm going to fail! In front of strangers." But you can say to yourself, "You got these lines down. You can do this in your sleep." I will say my mantras to myself, "Yes I can! Yes, I can!" I scold the nasty voice, as if it were a child. And I get out there and do my job!*
>
> —Katherine

In Chapter 5, we looked at types of *defenses* against fears and negative thoughts and core beliefs that often accompany stage fright. As actors, we can be our own worst critics. Notice how you may defend against stage fright, how you may behave due to stage fright, and how you talk to yourself based on your core beliefs. Of these cognitive aspects, *catastrophizing* (i.e., believing that something is worse than it is or anticipating what might go wrong in the future) and negative beliefs about our *personal efficacy* are the most implicated in stage fright (Nordin-Bates, 2012). Negative thoughts often emerge from a negative emotional state, as our brains are designed to think thoughts that are in concert with how we feel. If we feel afraid, our brains will generate thoughts to justify the emotion (Dana, 2018). Then the negative thoughts will activate negative feelings and now a vicious cycle is at play. When we are in this cycle, it is essential that we intervene where we can. The most available way is to stop the negative message and replace it with a *positive message*. The positive thought will likely not feel true, so naturally we will fall back to the default negative thought, and the cycle continues. We must get past this cycle. Alex says, "So how do we get past it? I think that we need to congratulate ourselves. So, when we make it out onstage, it's 'Nice work. That was good. Good job!'" To reframe the negative mind-set that stage fright brings, here are some steps to take to intervene: (1) *accept* that negative pressure from yourself will worsen your stage fright; (2) *commit* to having a more positive mind-set toward yourself; (3) *notice* your negative thoughts and beliefs about your worth and competence as an actor; (4) *write* them down; (5) *replace* these thoughts with alternative positive thoughts about your worth and competence as an actor; (6) *write* these down; (7) *repeat* the positive thoughts to yourself aloud; (8) *feel* how your body responds as you say affirming things to yourself; (9) *repeat* this exercise daily even if it feels wrong or counterintuitive; (10) *refuse* to say things to yourself that make you feel bad or wrong; (11) *critique* your work constructively; and (12) *feel* your sense of worth and competence as an actor getting stronger every day.

That I can do: improv skills for stage fright

> *It's never your best performance when you're afraid. Because, you're self-conscious, you're not in the moment. You are the farthest thing from being in the now of now. You are not in the world of the character. You are not at that audition. You are not on that stage. You are somewhere else.*
> —Jake

We can look to our own art form to help us with stage fright. Studying *improv* is an invaluable way to address performance fears. Improv builds confidence and courage and expands creativity. Polsky (1998) gives a concise and practical approach to improv. There are several types of improv with specific directives, but generally improv exercises or performances have no scripts and the dialogue is invented spontaneously without any preparation. Actors may choose or be provided with given situations, relationships and tasks to orient their starting point. By acting on the spot, invaluable skills can be learned and strengthened to help to eliminate stage fright. Improv builds the ability to "think on your feet." This skill can help with *self-trust* that any mishaps onstage can be handled. Improv requires that actors be in the moment, in the "now," and living and being in the present. Stage fright is always accompanied by worry about what went wrong or what will go wrong. The requirement of having to be "in the moment" helps us to reign in this cognitive tendency. Improv acting demands active and careful *listening* to scene partners and honest responses without judgment. Without the constraints of a script, we are left with expression in the moment and having to come up with new ideas and choices to drive the scene. This careful "talking and listening" redirects the focus from the self onto the other actors. This can reduce the negative self-thoughts and preoccupation present in every stage fright experience. Improv requires a *positive mindset*. Improv actors must focus on what is possible and moving forward in the scene no matter what happens. Mistakes during improv can be fashioned into opportunities, and there is an automatic sense of forgiveness if something seems silly, out of the reality of the scene, or some other mishap occurs that would be seen as an error in a memorized and rehearsed scene. Actors must let go of "doing it right" as it is a given that anything can happen. In improv, actors must quickly *problem solve*. Overcoming obstacles repeatedly builds confidence and courage and strengthens the sense of self-assurance that mishaps can be handled productively. Improv involves being exposed, taking risks, and connecting to vulnerability. Through improv, the fear of failing at these aspects lessens considerably, and the ability to tolerate them is increased.

Words, words, words: memorization

I still get on a high when I get a role, I can't wait to sit down and start memorizing the lines. Lines used to scare me, but now it's part of the job.

—Elizabeth

Stage fright is often associated with the fear of forgetting lines (Nordin-Bates, 2012). The cognitive components of stage fright limit our focus and impair our memory. When we are anxious, this fear is amplified. *Memorization* is a crucial task as well as skill for actors. In addition, the actor needs to internalize the memorized material to the degree that it becomes transformed from remembered words into dramatic expression (Hays, 2017). Unless you are doing a staged reading, a voice over, using cue cards, or performing an improvisational scene, you must be able to memorize lines. However, even in these situations some memorization is needed, as actors rarely "just read" lines. This is something that improves with practice. If you have difficulty memorizing lines, here are some strategies to help you:

- **Highlight your lines in your script.** Highlight the lines in your text. See the pages of the entire text and get a *sense* of how many lines you have and when they occur. Look at the highlighted text over and over. It will feel like looking at a destination on a map before you start your journey.

- **Write out your lines**. Using a notebook, paper, or index cards, write out each line ten times, then on to the next line. Concentrate on the words as you write them. Notice which words come next. Writing in a colored ink may help you remember your lines. This is especially useful for *visual* learners. This helps our brains to *see* the lines and internalize them.

- **Understand your lines completely.** This crosses over into acting: understand the meaning, subtext, and objectives associated with your lines. Look up any unfamiliar words and absorb the sense of your lines. Not understanding the meaning of your lines can impair memorization.

- **Paraphrase your lines.** As you prepare the role, say the lines in your own words, then write down the meaning of each line, in the same order that they occur in the script. Get a sense of the meaning of the entire role in your own words. Knowing the lines in your own words will help with memorization of the author's text. It will also build confidence knowing that if you forget a line, you can use the paraphrase to get back on track.

- **Think of the lines as physical movements.** Like blocking or chore- ography that begins to feel automatic, say the lines over and over, aloud and by *rote*. You want to build to the feeling that the lines are automatic. Two lines in a typical script can be said on average in about five seconds. Repeating by rote takes much less time than you may think. Your muscles will remember the movements (i.e., *muscle memory*) of the articulators, and when your *body* has memorized the lines, it will feel automatic, much like how it feels when you sing *Happy Birthday* or ride a bike. This is especially useful for *kinesthetic* learners.

- **Listen to your lines.** Speak and record your lines one by one and listen to them over and over. When you can anticipate the next line, say it aloud in synchrony with the recording. This will feel like how it feels when you are singing along with a song. This is especially useful for *auditory* learners.

- **Make mental pictures of your lines.** Envision a cartoon or a mural that has symbols or mental pictures of words or images in each line. Write or draw them. Consider the lines: "I have loved you all the days of my life. I will till the end of time." You may mentally picture an eye, a heart, a calendar, an image for "life" and a clock. Drawing your mental picture or drawing a cartoon with *mental images/pictures/symbols* of the lines and sounds (i.e., repeating consonants, etc.) will help you associate one idea/ image with the next and the next.

We can do it: performance

Before, my stage fright was about the audience liking me, and it was at its worst. Now I enjoy my artistry and my professionalism. I love what I do.

—Elizabeth

Feeling unprepared for a *performance* may be a factor in stage fright. When you approach a role or an audition, ask yourself which elements you will need to address in order to allow you to feel as ready and as prepared as possible to portray your role. Various performance strategies like positive self-talk, focusing, and managing heightened stress are used by a variety of performers across diverse domains (Hays, 2017). To manage stage fright, it is important to create a plan for your preperformance activities.

- First, make sure your *preparation for the role* is complete. This includes deliberate line and blocking memorization, incorporation of direction, applied acting tasks, and adequate rehearsal. You can note vulnerable areas of performance (i.e., a line you can't remember) and devise an alternative plan (i.e., an alternative phrase) to compensate for it. Prepare more than you think is necessary.
- Second, have a *professional mind-set*. This includes focusing on your work, avoiding perfectionism, deciding that you are competing only with yourself, and seeing yourself as a competent and ready professional. Accept anxiety and frame it as *excitement*, say positive comments to yourself, and refute negative beliefs. Focus on the pleasure and satisfaction you feel from being an actor. Remember why you want to be an actor, trust the work, and think long term: any mishap is likely to be minor from the standpoint of your career and greater artistry.
- Third, address your *preperformance activities*. Make sure you arrive early and have adequate rest, food, and water. While you are preparing to go onstage, you can walk through the performance in your mind, review your lines, do a full physical and vocal warm-up, and do speech exercises and drills. You should monitor your energy levels, so you feel ready. Use *calming techniques* if you feel too much energy (i.e., breathing, listening to soothing music, using guided imagery techniques, etc.). Use *activating techniques* if you feel too relaxed (i.e., walking, jumping, listening to activating music, etc.). You may "contain" your anxiety by creating positive personal rituals like having a lucky charm, drinking a favorite tea, listening to specific music, etc. Find something personal to help you be anchored, calm, and focused.
- Fourth, address your *preperformance mind-set*. Encourage yourself. Tell yourself that you are capable and that you can rely on your preparation, your talent, and your instincts to perform well. Tell yourself to *stop* any negative future-oriented worries. Remind yourself that the audience is filled with individuals who want you to do well. Focus on this performance, moment-by-moment.
- Fifth, review your *performance mind-set*. The moment just before going onstage or the first moments onstage seem to be the most difficult for actors. Turn your focus inward and direct your thoughts and actions as if they are coming from your character. Focusing on expressing rather than impressing will help to reduce your stage fright. When onstage, remember to breathe. Remember you actor objectives. Stay connected to what you

are saying, doing, and feeling, "moment-by-moment." Be in each moment and avoid fast forwarding to future worries or rewinding to past mistakes. Resolve to move on from past mistakes or dropped lines. Stay focused on the story and as Katherine says, "Ride the wave." Jake tells us, "Trust your primal instincts to be on your own and make it." You can do it.

And I felt nothing: the role of criticism

> You cannot respond to a bad review. You're not allowed to write in and say, "Yeah, but I don't see it that way." It's a one-sided conversation. And because once you've read a bad review of yourself, those words remain burned in your consciousness for your entire life.
>
> —Kathryn

We know that negative evaluation by others is one of the greatest *fear aspects* of stage fright (Hays, 2017). *Criticism* is painful. It can derail acting progress, impair performances, and stall careers. We fear that negative criticism can damage our reputation, can cause us to lose respect from our peers, and can determine our worth. Actors are sensitive people. While this trait is desired and even refined in our training, our sensitivity—and fear of criticism—contributes to stage fright. Actors know that criticism can so damage our ability to perform that it is an unwritten rule in the theater that any reviews of a performance must not be discussed at the theater. However, the very nature of acting—and life—requires us to deal with responses from others. Criticism comes at us every day. It can come from *actual* sources like peers, teachers, directors, audiences, and critics. It can come from *imagined* sources when we wonder what people think of our performances, our efforts in class, or when we imagine that a criticism may happen in the future. It often emerges as an *inner critic* where we find fault with ourselves (Southcott & Simmonds, 2008). However, some criticism may contain a necessary perspective that we may need to apply to our skill set and move toward excellence. We can benefit from criticism, so we must decide how we will handle it to our best ends. We must first determine if the criticism is *toxic*. Toxic criticism hurts us badly. It may be directed at aspects of ourselves that are not related to our acting like our physical attributes or personal qualities that don't meet others' expectations. If we cannot pull anything constructive from the criticism and if there is nothing we can learn from it, we must discard it in order to preserve our emotional world. If the criticism is *constructive*, we can learn from it to improve various skills and to augment our acting ability. We must hear the content of the criticism as *dispassionately* as possible. In whatever form the criticism comes, take a moment, take a breath, and be as calm as possible. We can *manage* the criticism by setting limits on it, accepting it gracefully, keeping it in perspective, and possibly reframing it to something useful. However, constructive criticism can still be painful. When hearing any form of criticism, it is natural to *defend* against it using the various defenses we have reviewed. We may respond *emotionally* by feeling hurt or angry. We may *convert* the anger by acting it out on others or turning the anger inward toward ourselves. We may also wish to *protect* ourselves by not auditioning, not participating in class, or by limiting our performances. However, if we can learn to not fear criticism but to accept and even appreciate it, we can build resilience, shed light on areas where we may improve, and even conquer our stage fright.

Just breathe

> *Breathing.*
>
> —Jake

Research has shown that deep *breathing* is effective in managing stage fright (Studer, Gomez, & Hildebrandt, 2011). A few minutes of controlled breathing can activate our parasympathetic nervous system (PSNS) and quiet our sympathetic nervous system (SNS) when we are in a fear state (Wehrenberg & Prinz, 2007). As actors we know that breathing is the foundation of all physical and emotional expression. If we visualize our torso, we can see that the lungs take up a great deal of vertical space, housed by the rib cage. The lungs are separated from the lower abdominal area by a membrane called the *diaphragm*. When we inhale, the diaphragm descends as the lungs fill with air. As we exhale, the diaphragm ascends inside the rib cage like a parachute floating up the shaft of the rib cage (Calais-Germain, 2005). When our breathing is optimal our diaphragm moves efficiently, and we have full control of our voice and our emotions. Efficient breathing also regulates the timing and phrasing of our lines. When we are in a fear state, the upper chest raises, and the diaphragm does not make its full ascent on the exhale, causing our breathing to become shallow, the way it might be when attack is imminent. If we can consciously override this and reestablish our rhythmic and deep breathing, we can reorganize the anxious state. To calm yourself down with your breath, inhale deeply thorough the nose, hold the breath, then exhale through the mouth, and pause. As you inhale, visualize your diaphragm descending and feel your abdominal area expanding. As you exhale, visualize your diaphragm ascending and your abdominal area contracting. Repeat this cycle a few times, and then begin to mentally count a set of numbers on the inhale and the exhale. The numbers you choose should feel comfortable and not forced. Finding your comfort level is crucial as you should avoid under breathing or over breathing. The exhale should be longer than the inhale. For example, you may breathe in on a count of four, hold for a count of two, and exhale on a count of six, etc. The extended exhale is associated with calming the nervous system. Most individuals will feel immediately relaxed when deep breathing. If you become lightheaded or dizzy, please stop. If you are anxious, you may find that *sighing* is helpful as well. Studies have also shown that *laughing*, *singing*, and *humming* can also initiate a calm state by activating a vagal response in the ANS (Zimmerman, 2019). A quick and deep oral inhale, followed by short, stepped oral exhales simulates the breathing pattern of laughter, which can augment our mood (Barton & Dal Vera, 2017). When you are in a stage fright episode, conscious and deep breathing is the first thing you should apply. During preparation and even performance, remind yourself to breathe. When we are anxious, sometimes we forget to breathe, which initiates the anxiety cycle.

Make believe you're brave: the role of courage

No matter how frightened I am, no matter what's going on with me, I have to go out there. Even though nobody knows, when I get out there, I think that was pretty heroic.

—Alex

Stage fright is painful and our physiological and psychological systems generate various symptoms to avoid threat and pain. We have identified the types of fear that threaten us during a stage fright episode. It is easy to think that other actors are "naturally brave" and that fear is either something they do not experience or something that they can handle with little or no effort. This is rarely the case. Although the ethic "the show must go on" forced our actors onstage when they would rather have run in the opposite direction, they all agreed that the necessary element to step out onstage is: *courage.* Courage is not the absence of fear. Courage is not a state we reach where everything becomes effortless. Courage is *acting* while fear still is present. Facing fear *is* courage. Courage feels close to the feeling of fear mixed with excitement, but is empowered with support from ourselves, others, and the conviction that we can go after and reach our goals. Having courage is not easy. It comes from being *encouraged.* Sometimes we hope for encouragement from people who fail to give us that fortification. Sometimes those who encourage us go too far and become overprotective, harsh, or drive us to unrealistic ends. Sometimes that person is us. The encouragement that builds courage is direct, realistic and supportive, with a strong sense of assurance that you can meet your goals if you face your obstacles. We can all face our stage fright fears with courage, but this involves taking *risks.* Jake reminds us, "Theater involves taking risks. Actors take that risk night after night after night. You are in charge of your own instrument and how your instrument is going to respond to the other actors." We must first ask ourselves how willing and able we are to take risks and potentially fail. We must then take those risks and dare to appear foolish, or possibly feel shame if our efforts fall short. If our self-esteem is intact, we can tolerate making mistakes, risk being evaluated by others, and can proceed with expressing our artistry to its full effect. As actors we already possess the skills to act courageously. We act in scenes and monologues and portray characters who have objectives, face obstacles, and take actions to overcome them. If we can accept that our craft inherently requires acts of courage, then we can rest assured in the fact that we already know how to be brave. So be courageous! Our actors have had decades of experience between them, and the consensus is that courage born of self-acceptance and self-esteem is the key to finding joy and satisfaction in acting.

Let it go: forgiveness

So, if you stop and say, "Oh my God, I'm onstage. Oh my God, I just screwed up," you will fall to the floor. But if you make it about the story, the ensemble, I'm here for you, we're here together in this, it works. Forgive yourself and the audience will forgive you, too.

—Katherine

Much of stage fright centers on the fear of making a mistake and being negatively judged for it (Hayes, 2017). Our actors have said repeatedly that this fear is a constant in the acting experience. Paradoxically, the stress and tension this fear causes only increases the probability that an error might occur. As actors, we strive for excellence—but it is human nature to sometimes make mistakes. Human nature provides a remedy for the proper handling of errors, and that is *forgiveness*. The audience will forgive mishaps if the actor does their job, continues on with the story, and connects to the character so the audience can follow the story and can be moved. Audiences want actors to do well. They are not there to harm us. If a mistake happens during performance and you move on, it is highly unlikely that the audience will notice what went wrong. If it is apparent, like a missed cue, a dropped line, or some other mishap, they will also overlook it if they see the actor moving forward. If we focus on errors that happened or that could potentially happen, we are not doing our job. We are directing our emotional energy onto ourselves instead of allowing the audience to see the character we are supposed to be portraying. We are showing them a preoccupied actor instead. Therefore, we must aim our focus back to the character and off ourselves. We can use our acting skills to remind us to be in character, seek our character objectives, and be in the moment of the play. If a mistake happens, let it go. It happened. Forgive yourself. Move forward. If it is something you can learn from and correct on reflection, notice that, but only after the performance is complete. Katherine feels very strongly about this:

All of it happens very fast. "Oh God, I just forgot that line. Now I have to keep going and act like nothing ever happened." But it is a truism: if you forgive yourself and go on, the audience forgives you and goes on. They forget that it happened. But only if you forgive yourself and go on.

Forgive yourself if you make a mistake and move on. Forgive yourself and move on.

Embraceable you: making peace with fear

I think now it's not so much fear as excitement. Before, I didn't understand it. I didn't understand my own personal fear or where it came from. And now I understand it. My stage fright wants to keep me safe. But I can take care of myself. Nothing bad is gonna happen.

—Bill

In Chapter 7, you compared your responses to the presented themes of our actors' interviews and authored an *account* of your own stage fright. You gave words to your "enemy." Each actor's individual stage fright will be unique to them. When it emerges, we wish to avoid it. We may even hate our stage fright. Paradoxically, the more we resist stage fright, the worse it becomes. If we can accept and even embrace and make *peace* with the *function* and the *feeling* of stage fright, we are engaging in a key strategy to manage it. This is not an easy task. Our survival system activates in a way that causes us to avoid uncomfortable feelings. We must resist this tendency. If we can train ourselves to tolerate and *accept* the presence of stage fright, we can lessen the symptoms, avoid a negative downward spiral into more fear, and build *resilience*. Review your account and see if you can determine stage fright's *function* in your life. You may wish to use your acting skills and view stage fright as a theatrical character and determine its *objective*. Bill noted that his stage fright's objective was to keep him *safe*. Like Bill, your stage fright may want to keep you safe. Stage fright may wish you to be perfect, may wish to put you in your place, or may wish to keep you from trying. Whatever stage fright wants from you, like Bill, respond with your own *competence*. If stage fright wants you to be perfect, challenge this function. If stage fright wants you to fail, challenge this function. Stage fright may be a "part" of the self that needs healing and acceptance. Write a scene which contains a dialogue between you and stage fright. Your objective in this scene should focus on attaining acceptance and peace with this angry and frightened part. Another strategy to make peace with stage fright is to begin to accept and tolerate the *feeling* of fear. When feelings like anticipation, worry, or fear emerge, feel them and let them wash over you. As you feel the feeling, breathe, notice how you experience it in your body, and say things to yourself that will create a sense of *safety* and *worthiness*. All of our actors found a way to embrace their stage fright on the road to mastering it. As you go through this process, your *fear* can be transformed into *excitement*.

- **Safety thoughts:**
  - Accept that I have this feeling
  - I know that this is just a feeling like any other feeling
  - I can tolerate this feeling
  - I can handle this feeling
  - I am riding the wave of this feeling
  - I am embracing this feeling

- **Worthiness thoughts:**
  - I have value
  - I have something to say
  - I am prepared
  - I am capable
  - I am talented
  - I deserve to be here

Imagine that: your ideal performance

*Whatever stage fright I have fought has to do with telling myself, "I can do this," of wanting
to succeed, of seeing that I could succeed, imagining that I could succeed.*

—Jake

The imagination is one of the most powerful tools the actor possesses. In
portraying characters, we imagine that we are living the life of our character to
the degree that is seems very real in most aspects. By thinking our character's
thoughts, experiencing our character's emotions, feeling the sensations our
character would feel, seeing the world through our character's eyes and living
in the world of the play as if it is our real world, we imagine the character into
being. We can also use this acting technique to help us with stage fright. You
have looked back at your *actor-child-self* and have remembered the innocence
and creativity of your child's play—as well the moment you knew you wanted
to become an actor. Then you reviewed the events of your life to see where
your stage fright possibly began. Now, use your imagination to look forward
into the future. First, imagine who you would be without stage fright. Imagine
yourself without this fear. Imagine what it would feel like and what it would
look like. Spend some time developing the vision of what you would be like
in rehearsal, in auditions, in class, or in performance with the exhilaration of
excitement rather than the burden of fear. Now imagine that you are going to
give *your ideal performance*. Imagine yourself in your ultimate *performance space*. It
could be the Greek amphitheater, a Victorian London stage, a Broadway stage,
or another theater where you have been. Place yourself there. See the stage, the
audience area, and the wings. Now place yourself *center stage* and allow all of
your senses to feel as if you are actually there. As you stand center stage, breathe
in and out evenly, standing tall, with your eyes out, looking at the *audience
area*. Breathe in and out deeply. See yourself confident, competent, and ready
to express your talent. Next, notice that the audience area begins to fill with
people. Now see that the audience section is filled to capacity. See the audience.
Now notice that the lights on them dim to darkness, as blue, pink, and amber
light begins to shine on you from above. Now notice a *spotlight* on you. Feel
the audience watching you. You stand there, center stage, very tall, very ready,
and very competent. And take a breath. Now begin your ideal performance. See
yourself speaking a monologue from the beginning, through the middle, and to
the end. See yourself taking the physical, vocal, emotional, and creative journey
of your ideal performance. See yourself expressing your truth, your passion, and
your*self* with the full range of human emotion to the audience. As you complete
your monologue, look out at them. See them. There is a moment of silence, a
moment of *communion* between you. Feel this moment in your body. Take in
this moment between you. Then, notice that as you look out into the darkness,
where the audience sits, you see hundreds of pinpricks of white light. Take a
breath. Look. You notice that the pinpricks of light are tears. You have moved
the audience to tears! They see you, and you see them. Now take a breath. Now

notice that they stand up and *applaud* in appreciation for you, the actor, for baring your soul so that they may feel your emotion. Bravo! This is the feeling of a job well done. Take in the appreciation and take in the applause. Now in return, take your bow in *gratitude*—to the audience—for being a witness to your truth, and to your work. As you stand again, see the audience, and *share* in the exchange of appreciation. And take a breath. Notice how you feel. This is the feeling of your ideal performance. Remember this feeling. It will nourish you. Go on this journey often. You have gone back to the moment when you knew you wanted to be an actor. Allow your personal ideal performance to be your *anchor* for the *future*.

Being alive: meaning in life

> *If we dare use the word "transcendent." I have transcended my own self. As Hamlet says, "I am myself indifferent honest; but yet I could accuse me of such things it were better my mother had not borne me." My own frailties, my own inadequacies have been transcended through the power of those words in front of that audience.*
>
> —Katherine

All of our actors felt that acting served an important social and artistic service to society. They revealed that acting is a way for them to find and share *meaning* in their lives. Our actors described the heightened moments they experienced while acting in a play and when they felt "in the now," "in character," and "in the world of the play." These experiences can be described as being "in a flow state." *Flow* is an optimal peak experience where we feel immersed in, focused on, and feel complete enjoyment while performing an activity (Csikszentmihalyi, 1990). When acting, flow is associated with the notion of *presence* where we feel completely absorbed, in character, and engaged with the work (Nordin-Bates, 2012). It is in this experience is that our actors draw rewards from acting. Our actors even speak of a spiritual meaning and that there are moments onstage that are "transcendent." Spirituality may be that "mystery" that Marty described. Elizabeth calls acting her "soul's purpose." When Kathryn is acting, she experiences a feeling of doing something of spiritual importance. She said,

> I really feel connected to the holy origins of theater … particularly if you're in a good play, a play that makes the audience weep, a play that makes them laugh at bad people … they are so ready for the transformation. That moment of transformation is *holy*.

Recall the Greek actors. It was believed that a *sprit* entered the actor and *inspired* the character. Like them, we breathe life into the words on the page and create real characters. Acting is a highly creative and even spiritual act. This reminds us that acting is a *vocation*—a calling—as well as a profession. However, in our current incarnation, success as an artist is often equated with fame and monetary success. Actors, in many cases are reduced to products. The meaning of the ancient vocation of acting is often eclipsed by current monetary and practical concerns, which are also important. However, if we can remind ourselves that acting is a vocation and the origin of our calling is ancient and spiritual, we can rise above stage fright and learn from what it has taught us. Take some time to review all you have covered here. You, along with our actors, have learned about your fear and have looked at ways to manage it. We have reconnected to our child–actor–self and have imagined ourselves forward to our ideal performance. We have faced the *demon in the wings*. As we consider our lives as actors, we can expand our scope to embrace the notion that acting exists as part of our purpose and our calling. This is where we can derive meaning from stage fright and in life. By connecting to our purpose, we may see the big-picture of why we act, and delight in the role we have been gifted to play on the world's stage.

Hey, kid! Screw it! You're gonna be OK!

—Marty

I used to care considerably whether I'd be liked or not. Being a professional means not caring whether they like you. The focus has to be on the work. That's key. And it takes some courage, you know?

—Jake

It's not about you. It's about the role, it's about the character, it's about the play. It's about the performance.

—Katherine

Stage fright doesn't scare me as much as it used to. It's excitement. I turn my performance over to God and I know I will be safe. I enjoy the performance.

—Peter

Part of it is not letting anyone down. The other part is courage. Is it OK to say that?

—Bill

Now I feel like when I exhale, the audience exhales. When I get up onstage a release happens, and I exhale. I can give to and receive from the audience. And we share an experience.

—Alex

I think your first stage experiences are very powerful. Because if you have a great experience you will feed off of that or the fear that you will fail will keep coming back. So, keep trying—it's not medical school. Nobody dies from bad acting.

—Katherine

I still get nervous sometimes, but the more you do it the stronger you get. And when it's a good show, there's nothing that makes you as happy, or me as happy, as that.

—Elizabeth

I pump myself up. I'm my own cheerleader. I remind myself to be confident of what I do know. I remind myself that the demon's not gonna win. Having control over that fear.

—Jake

I name it excitement. "I'm not nervous. I'm excited." And a positive word would be "exhilaration." As we gain experience, we get back to that childlike freedom that got us here in the first place

—Katherine

I just concentrate. It's a philosophy I have, and I think if you don't believe it might not work. But I call for a power and strength to let me fulfill what I have to do, and know it's going to be OK and I'll be fine. And I go out and bingo!

—Elizabeth

Stage fright can hamper, it's a helper as well. It's the springboard that gets you out there.
—Bill

You have to find your own strength. I think fighting whatever stage fright I have fought in the past may have to do with some issue of that, of "I can do this."
—Jake

It's transcendence, ecstasy, and pure joy. But it's a deal with the devil. Talk about the devil. To get the one, I have to face the other.
—Katherine

Acting … it's a good life. It's good.
—Marty

References

Aaron, S. (1986). *Stage fright: Its role in acting*. Chicago: University of Chicago Press.

Actors Equity. (2017). *2016–2017 Theatrical season report. An analysis of employment, earnings, membership, and finance* (S. DiPaola, Ed.). New York. Retrieved September 29, 2018, from Actor's Equity website: www.actorsequity.org/aboutequity/annual study/2016-2017-annual-study.pdf.

Actors Fund. (2019). *History of the actors fund*. Retrieved July 8, 2019, from the Actors Fund website: www.actorsfund.org/about-us/history.

Adler, A. (2000). *The art of acting*. New York: Applause Books.

American Psychiatric Association. (2000). *Diagnostic and statistical manual of mental disorders* (4th ed., text rev.). Washington, DC: Author.

American Psychiatric Association. (2013). *Diagnostic and statistical manual of mental disorders* (5th ed.). Washington, DC: Author.

Anderson, L. (2011). Myself or someone like me: A review of the literature on the psychological well being of child actors. *Medical Problems of Performing Artists, 26*(3): 146–149.

Arial, M., Danuser, B., Gomez, P., Hildebrandt, H., & Studer, R. (2011). Stage fright: Its experience as a problem and coping with it. *International Archives of Occupational and Environmental Health, 84*: 761–771. doi:10.8202702.

Ayres, J. (1986). Perceptions of speaking ability: An explanation for stage fright. *Communication Education, 35*(3): 275–287. doi:10.1080/03634528609388350.

Barton, R. (1993). *Acting: Onstage and off* (2nd ed.). New York: Holt, Reinhart, & Winston.

Barton, R., & Dal Vera, R. (2017). *Voice: Onstage and off*. London: Taylor & Francis Group.

Bates, B. (1987). *The way of the actor*. London: Century.

Bates, B. (1991). Performance and possession: Actors and our inner demons. In G.D. Wilson (Ed.), *Psychology and the performing arts* (pp. 11–18). Amsterdam: Swets & Zeitlinger.

Battaglini, C., & Martin, E. (2019). Health status of live theatre actors: A systematic literature review, *Medical Problems of Performing Artists, 34*(2): 108–117.

Beck, J. (1995). *Cognitive therapy: Basics and beyond*. New York: Guilford Press.

Becker, G. (2001). The association of creativity and psychopathology: Its cultural-historical origins. *Creativity Research Journal, 13*(1): 45–53. doi: 10.1207/S15326934CRJ1301_6.

Benedetti, J. (1998). *Stanislavski and the actor*. New York: Routledge.

Bergler, E. (1949). On acting and stage fright. *Psychiatric Quarterly Supplement, 23*(2): 313–319. Retrieved June 16, 2008, from www/jstor.org. doi:102307/1124854.

Berry, M., & Edelstein, M. (2009). *40 stars tell you how they beat America's #1 fear*. Tucson, AZ: See Sharp Press.

Blatner, A., & Blatner, A. (1988). *Foundations of psychodrama: History, theory, and practice*. New York: Springer.

Blum, R. (1976). A psychoanalytic profile of the actor: Perspectives on career development. *Western Speech Communication, 40*(3): 178–188. doi: 10.1080/10570317609373901.

Bohannon, J. (2018, July 7). Personal interview.

Branden, N. (1969). *The psychology of self esteem.* New York: Jossey-Bass.

Brandfonbrener, A. (1992). The forgotten patients. *Medical Problems of Performing Artists, 7*(4): 101–102.

Brandfonbrener, A. (2000). All the world's a stage. *Medical Problems of Performing Artists, 15*(1+).

Braudy, L. (1997). *The frenzy of renown.* New York: Vintage.

Brestoff, R. (1995). *The great acting teachers and their methods.* Lyme, NH: Smith & Kraus.

Brockett, O. (1977). *The history of the theatre.* Boston, MA: Allyn & Bacon.

Brugues, A. (2011). Music performance anxiety—Part 2: A review of treatment options. *Medical Problems of Performing Artists, 26*(3): 164–171.

Bureau of Labor Statistics, U.S. Department of Labor (2019). *Occupational outlook handbook, 2018–2019 edition, actors.* Washington, DC: Author.

Cahn, D. (1983). Toward an understanding of the emotional nature of state communication apprehension (stage fright). *Communication, 12*(1): 91–103.

Calais-Germain, B. (2005). *Anatomy of breathing.* Seattle, WA: Eastland Press.

Clason, J., Johansson, F., & Mortberg, E. (2015). Individual cognitive therapy for professional actors with performance anxiety. *Annals of Depression and Anxiety, 2*(6): 1066.

Chessick, R.D. (2005). What grounds creativity? *Journal of the American Academy of Psychoanalysis, 33*(1): 7–28. doi:10.1521/jaap.33.1.3.65879.

Connors, M. (1994). Symptom formation: An integrative self psychological perspective. *Psychoanalytic Psychology, 11*(4): 509–523. doi:10.1037/h0079580.

Csikszentmihalyi, M. (1990). *Flow: The psychology of ultimate experience.* New York: Harper & Row.

Cullen, F., Hackman, F., & Mc Neilly, D. (2007). *Vaudeville, old and new: An encyclopedia of variety performers in America.* London: Routledge.

Dal Vera, R. (2001). Teaching violence. In R. Dal Vera (Ed.), *The voice and violence* (pp. 2–5). Cincinnati, OH: Voice and Speech Trainers Association.

Dana, D. (2018). *The poly vagal theory in therapy.* New York: W.W. Norton.

Dispenza, J. (2014). *You are the placebo.* New York and Carlsbad, CA: Hay House.

Duncan, A. (2000). *The hypocritical self: Actors, acting, and identity in Greek and Roman culture.* Philadelphia: University of Pennsylvania Press.

Durang, C. (1981). *The actor's nightmare.* New York: Dramatists Play Service.

Fehm, L., & Schmidt, K. (2006). Performance anxiety in gifted adolescent musicians. *Anxiety Disorders, 20*: 98–109. doi:10.1016/j.janxdis.2004.11.011.

Fenichel, O. (1946). On acting. *Psychoanalytic Quarterly, 15*: 144–161. Retrieved May 30, 2008, from www.jstor.org. doi:10.2307/1124853.

Fergusson, F. (1961). *The poetics of Aristotle.* New York: Hill & Wang.

French, D. (1998). The status of actresses in early Christian society. *Vigiliae Christianae, 52*(3): 293–318. doi:10.1163/157007298X00182.

Freud, S. (1952). Psychopathic characters on the stage. *Psychoanalytic Quarterly, 11*: 459–464. Retrieved May 30, 2008, from www.jstor.org. doi: 10.2307/1124852.

Freud, S. (1962). *The ego and the id.* New York: W.W. Norton.

Freundlich, D. (1968). Narcissism and exhibitionism in the performance of classical music. *Psychoanalytic Quarterly, 42*: 1–13. Retrieved May 30, 2008, from www.psaq.org.

Gabbard, G. (1979). Stage fright. *International Journal of Psychoanalysis, 60*: 383–393. Retrieved November 9, 2007, from www.wiley.com/bw/journal.

Gabbard, G. (1983). Further contributions to the understanding of stage fright: Narcissistic issues. *Journal of the American Psychoanalytic Association, 31*(2): 423–441. doi:10.1177/000306518303100203.

Garfield, D. (1984). *The actor's studio: A player's place.* New York: Macmillan.

Giorgi, A. (2009). *The descriptive phenomenological method in phenomenology: A modified Husserlian approach.* Pittsburgh, PA: Duquesne University Press.

Goldstein, T., & Winner, E. (2009). Living in alternative and inner worlds: Early signs of acting talent. *Creativity Research Journal, 21*(1): 117–124. doi.org./10.1080/10400410802633749.

Goodman, G., & Kaufman, J. (2014). Gremlins in my head: predicting stage fright in elite actors. *Empirical Studies of the Arts, 32*(2): 133–148. doi: 10:2190/EM.32.2b.

Grand, D. (2008). *A 'stage' in healing: Audition anxiety.* Bellmore, NY: Brainspotting Institute.

Hammond, J., & Edelman, R.J. (1991a). The act of being: Personality characteristics of professional actors, amateur actors, and non-actors. In G.D. Wilson (Ed.), *Psychology and the performing arts* (pp. 123–131). Amsterdam: Swets & Zeitlinger.

Hammond, J., & Edelman, R.J. (1991b). Double identity: The effect of the acting process on the self-perceptions of professional actors—two case illustrations. In G.D. Wilson (Ed.), *Psychology and the performing arts* (pp. 25–44). Amsterdam: Swets & Zeitlinger.

Hampton-Turner, C. (1982). *Maps of the mind.* New York: Macmillan.

Hays, K. (2008). *Performance psychology in action: A casebook for working with athletes, performing artists, business leaders, and professionals in high-risk occupations.* Washington, DC: American Psychological Association.

Hays, K. (2017). *Performance psychology with performing artists. Oxford Research Encyclopedia of Psychology.* New York: Oxford University Press. doi 10.10.93/acrefore/9780190236557.013.191.

Helding, L. (2016). Music performance anxiety. *Journal of Singing, 73*(1): 83–90.

Howe, E. (1992). *The first english actresses: Women and drama, 1660–1700.* Cambridge: Cambridge University Press.

Jackson, J., & Latane, B. (1981). All alone in front of all those people: Stage fright as a function of number and type of co-performers and audience. *Journal of Personality and Social Psychology, 40*(1): 73–85. doi:10.1037/0022-3514.40.1.73.

Jangir, S.K., & Govinda, R.B. (2018). Efficacy of behavior modification techniques to reduce stage fright: A study. *Indian Journal of Positive Psychology, 9*(11): 126–129. doi.org/10.15614/ijpp.v9i01.11756.

Johnson, L. (2009). Nobler in the mind: The emergence of early modern anxiety. *Journal of the Australasian Universities Language and Literature Association,* Special Issue, 141–156. Retrieved February 26, 2011, from http://aulla.com.au/.

Jung, C.G. (1989). *Memories, dreams, and reflections.* New York: Random House.

Kaplan, D. (1969). On stage fright. *The Drama Review: TDR, 14*(1): 60–83. Retrieved February 2, 2007, from www.jstor.org. doi:10:2307/1144506.

Kenny, D. (2005a). Performance anxiety: Multiple phenotypes, one genotype? Introduction to the Special Edition on Performance Anxiety. *International Journal of Stress Management, 12*(4): 307–311. doi:10.1037/1072-5245.12.4.307.

Kenny, D. (2005b). A systematic review of treatments for music performance anxiety. *Anxiety, Stress, and Coping, 18*(3): 183–208. doi:10.1080/10615800500167258.

Kenny, D. (2006). Music performance anxiety: Origins, phenomenology, assessment, and treatment. *A Journal of Music Research,* Special Issue: Renegotiating Musicology, *31*: 1–11. Retrieved June 4, 2019, from www.jmro.org.au/index.php?journal=mca2.

Kenny, D. (2011). The *psychology of music performance anxiety.* Oxford: Oxford University Press.

Kenny, D., & Ackerman, B. (2007). Anxiety in public performance, stress, and health issues for musicians. In S. Hallam, I. Cross, & M. Thaut (Eds.), *Oxford handbook of music psychology* (Ch. 36, 1–33). Oxford: Oxford University Press.

Kenny, D., Davis, P., & Oates, J. (2004). Music performance anxiety and occupational stress amongst opera chorus artists and their relationship with state and trait anxiety and perfectionism. *Journal of Anxiety Disorders, 18*(6): 757–777. doi:10.1016/j.janxdis.2003.09.004.

Kenny, D., & Holmes, D. (2015). Explorng the attachment narrative of a professional musician with severe performance anxiety: A case report. *Journal of Psychology and Psychotherapy, 5*(4): 1–6. doi: 10.4172/2161-0487.1000190.

Kielblock, A. (1891). *The stage fright: Or how to face an audience.* G. H. Ellis.

Kierkegaard, S. (1980). *The concept of anxiety.* Princeton, NJ: Princeton University Press.

Kogan, N. (2002). Careers in the performing arts: A psychological perspective. *Creativity Research Journal, 14*(1): 1–16. doi:10.1207/S15326934CRJ1401_1.

Koh, C. (2006). Reviewing the link between creativity and madness: A postmodern perspective. *Educational Research and Reviews, 1*(7): 213–221.

Kohut, H. (1966). Forms and transformations of narcissism. *Journal of the American Psychoanalytic Association, 14*(2): 243–272. doi:10.1177/000306516601400201.

Kohut, H. (1984). *How does analysis cure?* Chicago: Chicago University Press.

Kokotsaki, D., & Davidson, J. (2003). Investigating musical performance anxiety among music college singing students: A quantitative analysis. *Music Education Research, 5*(1): 45. doi:10.1080/14613800307103.

Konijn, E. (1991). What's on between the actor and his audience? Empirical analysis of emotion process in the theatre. In G.D. Wilson (Ed.), *Psychology and the performing arts* (pp. 59–73). Amsterdam: Swets & Zeitlinger.

Kvale, S., & Brinkmann, S. (2009). *InterViews: Learning the craft of qualitative research interviewing.* Los Angeles: Sage Books.

Lahr, J. (2006, August). Petrified: The horrors of stage fright. *The New Yorker, 82*(26): 38–42.

Langendörfer, F., Hodapp, V., Kreutz, G., & Bongard, S. (2006). Personality and performance anxiety among professional orchestra musicians. *Journal of Individual Differences, 27*(3): 162–171. doi:10.1027/1614-0001.27.3.162.

Lauronen, E., Veijola, J., Isohanni, I., Jones, P., Neiminen, P., & Isohanni, M. (2004). Links between creativity and mental disorder. *Psychiatry, 67*(1): 81–98. doi:10.1521/psyc.67.1.81.31245.

Lee, R., & Martin, J. (1991). *Psychotherapy after Kohut: A textbook of self psychology.* Hillsdale, NJ: Analytic Press.

Levine, P. (2010). *In an unspoken voice: How the body releases trauma and restores goodness.* Berkeley, CA: North Atlantic Books

Lloyd-Elliot, M. (1991). Witches, demons, and devils: The enemies of auditions and how performing artists make friends with these saboteurs. In G.D. Wilson (Ed.), *Psychology and the performing arts* (pp. 211–219). Amsterdam: Swets & Zeitlinger.

Lombroso, C. (1891). *The man of genius.* London: Walter Scott.

Marchant-Haycox, S., & Wilson, G. (1992). Personality stress in performing artists. *Personality and Individual Differences, 13*(10): 1061–1068. doi:10.1016/0191-8869(92)90021-G.

Marshall, J. (1994). *Social phobia: From shyness to stagefright.* New York: Basic Books.

Maxwell, I., Mark, S., & Szabo, M. (2015). The Australian actors' wellbeing study: A preliminary report. *About Performance, 13*: 69–112.

May, R. (1977). *The meaning of anxiety.* New York: W.W. Norton.

May, R. (1987). *History of the theatre.* Secaucus, NJ: Chartwell Books.

McGinnis, A., & Milling, L. (2005). Psychological treatment of musical performance anxiety: status and future directions. *Psychotherapy: Theory, Research, Practice, Training, 42*(3): 357–373.

McWilliams, N. (2011). *Psychoanalytic diagnosis, second ed: Understanding personality structure in the clinical process.* New York: Guilford Press.

Merino, L. (2011). *15 common defense mechanisms* [PowerPoint slides]. Retrieved September 2, 2019, from www.slideshare.net/mobile/Lucia_Merino/15-common-defense-mechanisms.

Meyer-Dinkgrafe, D., Nair, S., & Procter, D.C. (2012). Performance anxiety in actors: Symptoms, explanations, and an indian approach to treatment. *Canadian Journal of Practice Based-Research in Theatre, 4*(1): 28.

Mor, S., Day, H., Flett, G., & Hewitt, P. (1995). Perfectionism, control, and components of performance anxiety in professional artists. *Cognitive Therapy Research, 19*(2): 207–225. doi:10.1007/BF02229695.

Moss, R. (1991, December 29). Stage fright is the villain many actors must upstage. *New York Times.* Retrieved July 7, 2019, from www.nytimes.com/1991/12/29/theater/stage-fright-is-the-villain-many-actors-must-upstage.html?pagewanted=all&src=pm.

Nagel, J. (1993). Stage fright in musicians: A psychodynamic perspective. *Bulletin of the Menninger Clinic, 57*(4): 492–506.

Nagel, J. (2004). Performance anxiety theory and treatment: One size does not fit all. *Medical Problems of Performing Artists, 3*: 39–43.

Nagel, J. (2017). *Managing stage fright: A guide for musicians and music teachers.* New York: Oxford University Press.

Naistadt, I. (2004). *Speak without fear: Understanding the "why" behind your stage fright in public speaking situations.* New York: Harper Collins.

National Association of Schools of Theatre. (2019). *Accreditation.* Retrieved July 29, 2019, from http://nast.arts-accredit.org.

Nemiro, J. (1997). Interpretative artists: A qualitative exploration of the creative process of actors. *Creativity Research Journal, 10*(2–3): 229–239.

Nettle, D. (2005). Psychological profiles of professional actors. *Personality and Individual Differences, 40*: 375–383. doi:10.1016/j.paid.2005.07.008.

Neuringer, C. (1992). Freud and the theatre. *Journal of the American Academy of Psychoanalysis, 20*(1): 142–149.

Nordin-Bates, S.M. (2012) Performance psychology in the performing arts. In S. Murphy (Ed.), *The Oxford Handbook of Sport and Performance Psychology* (pp. 81–114). New York: Oxford University Press.

Novick, J. (1998). The actor's insecurity. *American Theatre, 15*(4): 20–22.

Onions, C. (Ed.). (1996). *Oxford dictionary of English etymology.* London: Oxford University Press.

Osborne, M., Kenny, D.T., & Holsomback, R. (2005). Assessment of music performance anxiety in late childhood: A validation study of the music performance anxiety inventory for adolescents (MPAI-A). *International Journal of Stress Management, 12*(4): 312–330. doi:10.1037/1072-5245.12.4.312.

Payne, T. (2006). *Fame: What the classics tell us about our cult of celebrity.* New York: Picador.

Percival, A. (October, 2019). Ex Eastenders star Katie Jarvis left hurt and "ashamed" after tabloid job shaming. *Huffington Post.* Retrieved October 29, 2019, from huffingtonpost.co.uk.

Phillips, E.M. (1991). Acting as an insecure occupation: The flip side of stardom. In G.D. Wilson (Ed.), *Psychology and the performing arts* (pp. 123–131). Amsterdam: Swets & Zeitlinger.

PDM Task Force. (2006). *Psychodynamic diagnostic manual*. Silver Spring, MD: Alliance of Psychoanalytic Organizations.

Polsky, M. (1998). *Let's improvise: Becoming creative, expressive, and spontaneous through drama*. New York: Applause Theatre Books.

Ponterotto, J. (2005). Qualitative research in counseling psychology: A primer on research and paradigms and philosophy of science. *Journal of Counseling Psychology, 52*(2): 126–136. doi:10.1037/0022-0167.52.2.126.

Powell, D. (2004). Treating individuals with debilitating performance anxiety: An introduction. *JCLP/In Session, 60*(8): 801–808. doi:10.1002/jclp.20038.

Prentky, R. (2001). Mental illness and the roots of genius. *Creativity Research Journal, 13*(1): 95–104. doi:10.1207/S15326934CRJ1301_11.

Reciniello, S. (1991). Toward an understanding of the performing artist. In G.D. Wilson (Ed.), *Psychology and the performing arts* (pp. 95–121). Amsterdam: Swets & Zeitlinger.

Reichenberg, L.W., & Seligman, L. (2016). *Selecting effective treatments: A comprehensive guide to treating mental disorders* (5th ed.). Hoboken, NJ: Wiley.

Robb, A., & Davies, M. (2015). Being inside the story: A phenomenology of onstage experience and the implications of flow. *About Performance, 15*: 45–57.

Robb, A., Due, C., & Venning, A. (2016). Exploring psychological wellbeing in a sample of australian actors. *Australian Psychologist, 53*(1): 77–86. doi:10.1111/ap.12221.

Robinson, M. (2019, July 7). 8 rules every theatre person must follow – Do you know all of them? *Playbill*.

Runes, D. (2010). (Ed.). *A dictionary of philosophy*. New York: Philosophical Books.

Salmon, P. (1990). A psychological perspective on musical performance anxiety: A review of the literature. *Medical Problems of Performing Artists, 5*(1): 2–11.

Sandgren, M. (2003). *The symptom of performance anxiety in relation to artistic development* (R. Kopiez, A. Lehmann, I. Wolther, & C. Wolf, Eds.). Proceedings of the 5th Triennial ESCOM Conference, September 8–13, Hanover, Germany, University of Music and Drama.

Schiraldi, G. (2001) *The self esteem workbook*. Oakland, CA: New Harbinger Publications.

Schore, A. (2011). *The science of the art of psychotherapy*. New York: W.W. Norton.

Schyberg, F., & Carlson, H. (1962). The art of acting: The actor as phenomenon. *The Tulane Drama Review, 6*(4): 66–93. doi:10.2307/1124733.

Scott, S. (2007). College hats or lecture trousers? Stage fright and performance anxiety in university teachers. *Ethnography and Education, 2*(2): 191–207. doi:10.1080./17457820701350582.

Seligman, L. (1998). *Selecting effective treatments: A comprehensive guide to treating mental disorders*. San Francisco: Wiley.

Seton, M. (2006). *"Post dramatic" stress: Negotiating vulnerability for performance*. Proceedings of the 2006 Conference of the Australian Association for Drama, Theatre, and Performance Studies. Retrieved August 20, 2018, from http:ses.library.usyd.edu.au/bitstream/2123/2518/1/ASDA/2006-Seton Pdf.

Shapiro, F., & Forrest, M. (1997). *EMDR: The breakthrough "eye movement" therapy for overcoming anxiety, stress, and trauma*. New York: Basic Books.

Simmonds, J., & Southcott, J. (2012). Stage fright and joy: Performers in relation to the troupe, audience, and beyond. *International Journal of Applied Psychoanalytic Studies, 9*(4): 318–329. doi:10.1002/aps. 327.

Southcott, J., & Simmonds, J. (2008). Performance anxiety and the inner critic: A case Study. *Australian Journal of Music Education, 1*: 32–47.

Sonnenmoser, M. (2006). Upstaging stagefright. *Scientific American Mind*, *17*(1): 84–85. doi:10.1038/scientificamericanmind0206-84.

Stanislavski, C. (1986). *An actor prepares* (E.R. Hapgood, Trans.). London: Metheun. (Original work published 1936.)

Steptoe, A., & Fidler, H. (1987). Stage fright in orchestral musicians: A study of cognitive and behavioral strategies in performance anxiety. *British Journal of Psychology*, *78*(2): 241–249.

Studer, R., Gomez, P., Hildebrandt, H., Arial, M., & Danuser, B. (2011). Stage fright: Its experience as a problem and coping with it. *International Archives of Occupational and Environmental Health*, *84*: 761–771. doi: 10.1007/s00420-010-0608-1.

Sue, D., & Sue, D. (1991). *Counseling the culturally different*. New York: Wiley.

Taborsky, C. (2007). Musical performance anxiety: A review of literature. *Update: Applications of Research in Music Education*, *26*(1): 15–25. doi:10.1177/87551233070260010103.

Tarnas, R. (1991). *The passion of the western world*. New York: Ballantine Books.

Tenny, F. (1931). The status of actors at Rome. *Classical Philology*, *26*(1): 11–20. doi:10.1086/361304.

Thomson, P., & Jaque, S., (2012). Holding a mirror up to nature: Psychological vulnerability in actors. *Psychology of Aesthetics, Creativity, and the Arts*, *6*(4): 361–369.

Truemen, M. (2012). Stephen Fry, stage fright and how to avoid it. *The Guardian*.

van Manen, M. (1990). *Researching lived experience: Human science for an action sensitive pedagogy*. London, ON: State University of New York Press.

Vasey, M., & Dadds, M. (Eds.) (2001). *The developmental psychopathology of anxiety*. New York: Oxford Press.

Webster's encyclopedic unabridged dictionary of the English language. (1989). New York: Portland House.

Wehrenberg, M., & Prinz, S. (2007). *The anxious brain: The neurobiological basis of anxiety disorders and how to effectively treat them*. New York: W.W. Norton.

Weissman, P. (1961). Development and creativity in the actor and playwright. *Psychoanalytic Quarterly*, *30*: 549–564.

Witt, P., Brown, K., Roberts, J., Weisel, J., Sawyer, C., & Behnke, R. (2006). Somatic anxiety patterns before, during, and after giving a public speech. *Southern Communication Journal*, *17*(1): 87–100.

Worthen, W. (1984). The idea of the actor: Drama and the ethics of performance. Princeton: Princeton University Press.

Zakaria, J.B., Musib, H.B., & Shariff, S. M. (2013). Overcoming performance anxiety among music undergraduates. *Social and Behavioral Sciences*, *90*: 226–234.

Zerbe, K. (1990). Through the storm: Psychoanalytic theory in the psychotherapy of the anxiety disorders. *Bulletin of the Menninger Clinic*, *54*(2): 171.

Zimmerman, E. (2019, May). I now suspect the vagus nerve is the key to well-being. *New York Magazine*. Retrieved July 29, 2019, from http://nymag.com.

Index